The Care of Men

The Care of Men

Christie Cozad Neuger and
James Newton Poling, editors

Abingdon Press
Nashville

THE CARE OF MEN

Copyright © 1997 by Abingdon Press

This book is printed on recycled, acid-free paper.

Library of Congress Cataloging-in-Publication Data

The care of men/Christie Cozad Neuger and James Newton Poling,
    editors.
        p.   cm.
    Includes bibliographical references.
    ISBN 0-687-01451-4 (alk. paper)
    1. Men (Christian theology)   2. Church work with men.   3. Men—
United States.   I. Neuger, Christie Cozad, 1952–   .   II. Poling,
James N. (James Newton), 1942–   .
    BT703.5.C37   1997
    259'.081—dc20   96-43401
                                                                                                      CIP

Unless otherwise noted, Scripture quotations are from the New Revised Standard Version Bible. Copyright 1989 by the Division of Christian Education of the National Council of the Churches of Christ in the USA. Used by permission.

05 06 — 10 9 8 7

MANUFACTURED IN THE UNITED STATES OF AMERICA

To Win Neuger — CCN
To Nancy Werking Poling — JNP

CONTENTS

Contents

ACKNOWLEDGMENTS

We wish to acknowledge our indebtedness to those who helped in the creation of this book.

United Theological Seminary who provided sabbatical time for Christie Neuger and who consistently offers intellectual and collegial support.

Our colleagues in the Society for Pastoral Theology who have engaged us in challenging and creative dialogue.

Former and present teachers, colleagues, students, clients, and supervisees who have guided our learning in these areas of care.

CCN and JNP

CONTRIBUTORS

Herbert Anderson, Professor of Pastoral Theology, Catholic Theological Union, Chicago, Illinois

Toinette M. Eugene, Associate Professor of Social Ethics and member of the Graduate Faculty of Northwestern University, Garrett-Evangelical Theological Seminary, Evanston, Illinois

Joretta L. Marshall, Assistant Professor of Pastoral Care and Counseling, Iliff School of Theology, Denver, Colorado

Donald H. Matthews, Post-doctoral fellow, African and African-American and Religious Studies programs, Washington University at St. Louis, Missouri

Randle Mixon, American Baptist pastor, pastoral counselor, adjunct faculty, Pacific School of Religion, Oakland, California

Christie Cozad Neuger, Associate Professor of Pastoral Counseling and Pastoral Theology, United Theological Seminary of the Twin Cities, New Brighton, Minnesota

Judith L. Orr, Academic Dean and Associate Professor of Pastoral Care, Saint Paul School of Theology, Kansas City, Missouri

James Newton Poling, Professor of Pastoral Theology, Care and Counseling, Garrett-Evangelical Theological Seminary, Evanston, Illinois

Edward P. Wimberly, Professor of Pastoral Theology, Interdenominational Theological Center, Atlanta, Georgia

INTRODUCTION

Christie Cozad Neuger and
James Newton Poling

This is a crucial time of transition for men in the Christian churches. Many men are no longer sure of their niche, their place in the church or in society. As womanist[1] and feminist movements redefine gender roles and challenge traditional masculine roles, men often don't know what to think or say about themselves.

I have tried to be sensitive to what women are saying. But every time I open my mouth, I feel put down. What do women want from men anyhow? (34-year-old African American businessman)

I have learned just to go on about my business. I don't have any male friends to talk to and sometimes it is better just to keep quiet. I just wish men and women could trust each other like they used to. (47-year-old European American male factory worker)

This is an exciting time for me. I grew up in the fifties and was never comfortable with the male stereotypes that were forced on me—to be athletic, tough, unfeeling. I find the new possibilities for being a man to be liberating, although I get scared sometimes. (55-year-old gay male pastor)

Men in the United States are struggling with changing expectations. Even men who have joined in solidarity with womanist and feminist visions sometimes feel displaced in their families, in their peer groups, in the job market, and without adequate psychic and spiritual resources for coping with these new stressors. Family life is increasingly complicated for men as traditional gender role complementarity makes way for more equitable role and task distribution.

13

Primary parenting, increased domestic labor, and shared economic responsibilities bring both benefits and tensions to family life for men. Many men need new foundations for self-esteem and identity and new support for an unknown future.

Changing gender expectations are aggravated by simultaneous changes in the economic system as under- and unemployment become more common in a time of global capitalism and decreasing workers' empowerment. As multinational corporations move capital to cheaper labor markets and free-trade agreements put workers from rich and poor countries in direct competition, job insecurity becomes a common fear and a widespread reality for many people.[2] Men who have based their identity on providing for their families and feeling financially self-sufficient face new losses at the turn of the century. What does it mean to be a man if he cannot aspire to a secure middle-class living for his children? How does a man develop a masculine identity if being middle-class is not even an option?

CONTEMPORARY MEN'S MOVEMENTS

The Million Man March held in the fall of 1995 dramatically illustrated the desire of many men to atone for past misdeeds and find new models of responsibility in marriage, parenting, church, work, and public life. The nonviolent march of hundreds of thousands of African American men created new hopes for a positive response to the negative stereotypes inflicted on many men in a racist society.[3]

Promise Keepers, a Christian evangelical men's movement, asks men to take a pledge of greater commitment and faithfulness to the family, to improved race relations, and to public leadership in church and society. Promise Keepers encourages men to go back to churches, marriages, and children and take greater responsibility for instilling honesty, temperance, tolerance, and old-fashioned family values. Hundreds of thousands of mostly European American men have filled football stadiums to take the pledge and have returned to implement their promises in their home communities.[4]

In addition to the Million Man March and Promise Keepers, three other forms of men's movements have emerged in response to the womanist and feminist challenges.[5] One form of organized men's

14

group seeks to maintain and increase the dominance that men have always had, for example, men's rights groups.[6] These groups take the position that God has ordained men to the headship of family, church, and society, and they actively oppose any changes which undercut male authority or privilege.

A second form seeks to develop an alternative masculinity that can empower men in their relationships with one another and with women, for example, the mythopoetic men's movement.[7] Robert Bly, Robert Moore, Sam Keen, and others have suggested that male strength and sensitivity can be combined in new ways to facilitate partnership with liberated women. Through retreats that include storytelling, grieving, and acting out ancient rituals and myths, men can heal their wounded self-esteem and mentor one another into a new masculinity for a future of egalitarian gender relationships.

A third form seeks to join in solidarity with and accountability to women's groups to change society; for example, men affiliated with The National Organization of Men Against Sexism (NOMAS).[8] Growing out of gay liberation activities and work in the domestic violence movement, these profeminist men believe that the radical womanist and feminist critique of gender inequality requires a new kind of partnership based on accountability of men to women. They reject the idea that an essential masculinity can be rediscovered through the Bible, men's rights, or ancient myths showing the way to the future. They call for men and women to work together to stop male violence and change the attitudes and behaviors of male privilege that create male dominance.[9]

In the African American community, the men's movement has taken a somewhat different course. As Edward Wimberly summarizes in chapter 6, African American men are critical of the white men's groups because of their ongoing racist assumptions and attitudes. Masculinity based on economic success, men's rights, and European mythology does not work well among African American men who struggle with economic survival and acceptance in the midst of discrimination, prejudice, and injustice. In its place, several unique approaches to understanding masculinity have developed including: (1) the Black Power/Civil Rights approach, which focuses on economic and political issues; (2) the evangelical biblical approach in churches, which focuses on the headship responsibility of men in families and in church leadership; (3) the full participation/integration model represented by Jawanza Kunjufu, for example, who focuses on helping black boys become men by taking their rightful place in an integrated society; and (4) the humanistic/rites of passage approach of Nathan and Julie Hare, which tries to recover the African heritage of myths and rituals to help men find a secure identity. Wimberly suggests a narrative approach as distinct from the other four. One can see in this literature how African American men have responded to the womanist and feminist critiques of masculinity with a culturally sensitive range of approaches. Toinette Eugene responds to the issues in Wimberly's chapter and the broader men's movements from a womanist perspective in chapter 7. She supports a change in men's consciousness that would lessen the oppression of women, but she vociferously reminds us that some of the forms of masculinity being asserted are actually much like the old men's movements that made women's lives more dangerous.[10]

Each of these types of men's movements has particular strategies for responding to the crises that men face at this time: reasserting male rights, recovering biblical or European mythology, or "refusing to be a man." But, especially in the European American churches, these approaches have had only limited acceptance.[11] In some ways it is fair to say that there is no organized men's movement within the Christian churches that responds to the womanist and feminist critiques of gender inequality. However, this does not mean that Christian men have not been dramatically affected by the womanist and feminist critiques of masculinity and male spirituality and by the secular men's movements.[12]

PASTORAL CARE AND COUNSELING WITH MEN

In a time of transition and crisis, some men turn to pastors and pastoral counselors for care. European American men are participating in couple and family counseling. Gay men are seeking pastoral care and psychotherapy in order to cope with the discrimination they experience. African American men are talking to pastors and chaplains about family and work problems. Men are meeting in various kinds of support groups to discuss their crises in work, health, sexuality, aging, and spirituality.[13]

Some men are looking to the church for help with their confusion. What does it mean to be a Christian and a man in Western culture? Given the crisis of men and masculinity, what is the church doing to prepare church leaders for the care of men? What kinds of materials are being produced by the church publishing houses to help men through this time of transition? What are seminaries doing to train new pastors about the changing needs of men in the church?

The Care of Men responds to these questions by focusing on the issues that men are bringing to the church: to its pastors, chaplains, pastoral care specialists, and peers. What are men saying they want from the church? What problems and concerns are they asking pastors about? In preparing this volume, we asked nine experienced pastors and pastoral counselors to reflect on their ministries with men. What are they hearing? What are men saying in the privacy of their pastoral relationships that they might not be comfortable saying in an open forum? What are their private hurts, their joys and concerns, their hopes for themselves and their families, their loves and hates? These nine authors searched their own practice of ministry and the available literature for the themes and trends regarding men today. The result is nine essays organized in nine different ways around issues that men are raising.

Each of the nine authors was asked to reflect on the following questions: What are the most important issues that men are bringing for pastoral care and counseling, and what are the issues they struggle with in private? How do these issues take shape, change, and develop over time? What are the theological themes and conflicts embedded in these issues? How do men's issues vary according to race, gender, and class? How does the race, gender, class, and sexual orientation of the pastor or pastoral counselor affect the care men receive? Where does the church provide the most and least help in working through these issues? What are the issues facing clergymen and male pastoral counselors as they attempt to provide pastoral care to men and their families? What should be addressed in the pastoral counseling literature that would be of most help in clinical work with men?

We invited the authors to be creative in thinking about these questions in the hope that we would include and go beyond some of the traditional issues like marriage, parenting, work, sexuality, and

17

so forth. The creativity in Maxine Glaz and Jeanne Moessner's book, *Women in Travail and Transition*,[14] served as a model for this volume.

Our two primary reasons for convening a mixed gender team of editors and authors were, first, that both male and female clergy offer pastoral care and counseling to men and have insights into the primary issues facing caregivers today; and second, that it is important to integrate insights from the women's movement and from womanist and feminist theology and philosophy into the contemporary care of men. A team of women and men working together in solidarity and accountability ensures that the issues raised by women oppressed under patriarchy will be addressed by both men and women.

The intention of this book is to help lay and professional church leaders, pastors, seminary students, professors, pastoral counselors, and chaplains respond to the pastoral care and counseling needs of men in the Christian churches.

REVIEW OF THE CHAPTERS

Contextual pastoral theology is the central method of the various approaches in *The Care of Men*. While the human needs for loving relationships and creative and sustaining work seem nearly universal among men, the way these needs are expressed and fulfilled varies widely depending on their social, economic, and religious context. Attending to men's particularity within diverse social and cultural contexts while maintaining dialogue with the broad range of Christian traditions undergirds the work of all the pastors writing in this volume. This shared understanding of pastoral theology provides a deeper unity to what may seem at another level to be irreducible diversity.

In the last twenty-five years the church has witnessed an epistemological revolution which has dramatically affected theological thinking about gender relationships. Largely ignored by mainstream theologians for centuries, social movements for gender equality have suddenly burst into the public consciousness. While some church leaders continue to say that womanist and feminist thought is a special interest, a passing fad, or a dangerous heresy, this volume invites the churches to face the radical implications of gender equality on the church's theology and practice. Our opening chapter reviews the debates about gender in society and in the church in order to provide a background and context for men's struggles with being male and Christian in today's world.

How has this revolution in thinking about gender affected the local church? This is one of the questions Christie Neuger brings to her research chapter about pastoral care of men in the church. Through a series of twenty face-to-face interviews with clergymen, Neuger explores what issues men are bringing to the church for care and how men go about seeking help from their pastors. The chapter also explores how clergymen look at men's issues and what impact their own gender training has on their ministries with men. The chapter closes by exploring the implications of this research for the kinds of training and support clergymen need in order to carry out their visions for ministry to and with men in the church.

Care of working-class men occurs at a time of rapid change in economic structures, gender equity, and racial equality. These changes affect a number of personal and relational problems, including survival and making a living, conflict in marriage, and fears about mortality and legacy. In response, working-class communities have developed particular forms of togetherness and resistance to oppression which must be understood and respected. "Hard masculinity" is a way of survival for some men with little economic and social power. Judy Orr suggests that the typical emphasis on individual and family counseling must be adapted to a model of "neighbor care," which she defines as "being there" during the daily events of men's lives. Thus, the pastor who, like a good neighbor, lives with the people and is available at times of transition and crisis is a model for the care of working-class men.

Given the effects of historical and institutional racism on the spirits and psyches of African American men, the church's care must be sensitive to the social and religious setting of their lives. Donald Matthews introduces the concept of "spiritual care" as an alternative to pastoral care because of the long history of spirituals and spirit-filled worship in the African American religious tradition. The crisis of African American men is aggravated by decreasing opportunities for adequate work and the effects of this on male-female relationships. Here, Matthews introduces the goals and methods of Malcolm X, whom he sees, despite his sexism, as a model of masculinity and of spiritual care.

After reviewing the reasons African American men have rejected the white men's movements and the alternative programs that have emerged in the black community, Edward Wimberly suggests a narrative pastoral approach, which involves exploring and editing the stories that African American men tell. Biblical stories are a major resource for this listening and revising process because of the historic influence of the black Christian churches. However, the negative influence of consumer, capitalistic United States culture has caused many African American men to become alienated from the church. Wimberly suggests that African American men will come back to the church if they are adequately understood and supported, and that they will benefit by seeing the world through the eyes of African American women who have preserved the egalitarian, an-drogynous, and spiritual resources from the African Christian past.

The Million Man March in Washington, D.C., in October 1995 occurred when we were writing this volume on the care of men. This historic occasion, which brought together in one place the largest number of African American men in history, has long-term implica-tions for the constructions of masculinity in United States society. Toinette Eugene asks those who attended the Million Man March, and by extension all men, how this men's movement will alleviate the suffering of African American women and promote partnerships between women and men to challenge the racism and sexism of this society.

Eugene's answer is complex. On the one hand, such partnerships between women and men are desperately needed for the sake of social justice and for the possibilities of intimacy between women and men. On the other hand, a historical perspective reminds women to be cautious about men's promises. Women must never forget the betrayals and oppressions of past men's movements. Eugene seeks to improve the care of men by reminding us of the resources in such biblical themes as creation, familyhood, and pastoral care, and in the heroic witnesses of saints such as Sojourner Truth.

Based on his ten years as a pastoral psychotherapist with men who have been victims and perpetrators of violence, James Poling explores the pastoral and therapeutic issues of working with men who have abused women and children. Touched by the struggles of some men with their trauma from the past, with their repentance for harming others, and with their determination to find new forms of masculinity, Poling explores the dynamics of pastoral care with men who want to stop violence and domineering control in their interpersonal relationships. After exploring the research and literature on male violence, Poling suggests guidelines for pastoral caregivers who deal with violent men. These guidelines first emphasize safety for women and children and then urge cooperative work with other community professionals and agencies with special expertise in issues of male violence. Finally he explores theological issues of salvation, confession and repentance, forgiveness, sexuality, sin and evil, and Jesus as a model of nonviolent authority.

Many gay men leave the church because of prejudice and discrimination; others hide their identities and needs and remain closeted. In either situation, adequate pastoral caregiving and spiritual nurture for gay men is unavailable. Randle Mixon appeals to pastoral caregivers to examine the prejudices of their own lives and traditions and to rethink how they offer care to gay men. Such a reexamination is a major undertaking given the historic and continuing distortions of gay life by Christian beliefs and practices. Mixon offers an overview of the particular issues gay men bring to open and affirming pastors and pastoral counselors.

Women and men have begun working side by side in new ways since the Civil Rights Act of 1965 prohibited sex discrimination in employment. At the same time, rules about how women and men relate to one another have shifted because of womanist and feminist critiques. These two changes have created conflict, confusion, and tension between men and women in the workplace. Joretta Marshall asks how theological values such as love, justice, and mutuality can be translated into the kind of collegiality that is honest about power differences but fosters alliances across gender lines and encourages working together for common goals. Men who feel compelled by the need for gender justice will seek to build collegial relationships even when these are difficult and full of potential conflicts. Marshall urges pastoral caregivers to provide care for men who experience the pain

21

and hurt of change, and also to actively work to change the systems that perpetuate gender injustices.

Herbert Anderson explores how the construction of masculinity contributes to the difficulty many men have addressing grief in the midst of profound loss. Whereas traditional images of manhood lead many men to hide their feelings and suppress their grief over multiple losses, Anderson suggests how pastoral caregivers can help men enhance their freedom to grieve. One way is to help men develop new ways of thinking about being human and being men. The biblical stories of King David and Job, the Lamentations of Jeremiah, and the example of Jesus can help critique and recon-struct masculine stereotypes that have been captured by a capitalist society. Men can learn to grieve and thus become more reliable partners with grieving women.

In our conclusion, we examine some of the common themes of the articles, and suggest guidelines for practice in the care of men. Focusing on the care of men can be a creative way to approach the church's theology and practice in a time of transition and crisis in gender relationships. We believe that the model of pastoral care and counseling presented in this volume can help church leaders move beyond fear and backlash to creative partnership and openness toward God's future. The end of gender stereotypes and their constraints on human behavior and spirituality is one of God's gifts to our generation. We invite you to embrace these new opportunities for challenge and growth as you build appropriate new models of ministry with men and women in the church.

CHAPTER ONE

GENDER AND THEOLOGY

Christie Cozad Neuger and
James Newton Poling

That we live in a time of significant transition is not a unique point of view. Since change is a given of life, all time periods exist in the midst of transition. Yet, many would say that the cultural transitions of which we are a part are unique in that they signify a kind of radical discontinuity with foundational assumptions that have formed both our epistemological and our anthropological starting places. Many would talk about these shifts as a move from modernity into postmodernity. According to Kenneth Gergen, a contemporary social constructionist, modern society was built around the need to contain disruptive forces and to build walls around chaos. Behavior modification and its offshoots would be an example of "the need to render chaos predictable."[1] One of the fundamental beliefs of the modern era is that objective truth exists and is knowable. In contrast, a postmodern perspective is characterized by the awareness of multiple perspectives on truth. Gergen suggests that we are "populated by others" in such a way that we are exposed to countless opinions, personalities, and doubts.[2] The result is that there is no single organizing truth but multiple perspectives. Consequently, postmodernism means that who we are, how we relate to various power systems in the culture, and what our past experiences have been all shape the way we understand reality and the way we construct it. As Bonnie Miller-McLemore points out, this is a confusing time of transition because "it is after modern trust in universal truths but before what we do not know."[3]

Feminist liberation perspectives have been both a contributing force to postmodernism and a consequence of these shifting boundaries around knowledge. Gerda Lerner suggests that from time to time women have "come into consciousness" about their exclusion from the meaning-making processes of the culture and these awarenesses have become a dynamic force for change.[4] During the past twenty-five years of this wave of the feminist movement, women (and some men) have become increasingly aware of the destructive impact of patriarchy, especially on women's lives. And they have also become aware of how our assumptions, our cherished bodies of knowledge, our institutions, and the very fabric of the society are distorted by a patriarchal orientation that has been a part of Western culture from our earliest historical records.[5] Consequently, there has been much effort in recent years to develop feminist methods that would accomplish several necessary purposes in the reorientation of knowledge and in the development of liberating practices. Deconstructive methods have emerged that bring a "hermeneutic of suspicion" to theories and practices previously held as "truths." Reclaiming methods have been developed in order to discover and record the experiences of those (women and members of other marginalized groups) whose perspectives were not considered or whose experiences were deliberately distorted as histories and bodies of knowledge were created and interpreted. Reconstructive approaches have also been created that look both at epistemological questions (how do we know what we know?) and at providing content that has been missing. And new practices have been proposed and instituted that give a wider range of options and rights to women and others who have been deprived of equal access to resources.

There have been extensive political implications arising out of these efforts, if we understand *political* to mean the nature of the power relationships of the culture. Roles for women (and to a degree for men) have been successfully challenged and changed. Biological determinism has been tempered by the awareness of the social construction of gender. And women and men have begun to find ways to relate to one another out of a fuller recognition of common humanity rather than out of the limited framework of sexual complementarity. These changes, of which we are in the midst, have not been smooth or linear. They have threatened much of what many hold dear and have often seemed overwhelming in the extensiveness of the challenge. There have been (and are) many forms of resistance to these perspectives, and there is considerable debate about how far we might go in reorienting knowledge and practices. There is, at this time, both a push to follow through even more radically on the implications of these liberation perspectives *and* a powerful conservative backlash to reverse or at least slow down many of the shifts in values and roles that have emerged from feminist thought.

Both of these somewhat polarized perspectives are reflected in the various men's movements as discussed in the introduction. However, in most of the men's movements there has been a clear effort to begin to look at what it means to be male in this culture and the implications of that for work, family, friendships, and spirituality. As is typical in liberation movements where those who have been denied or harmed the most are the ones who begin the challenge of the status quo, women have been the leaders in questioning the "truth" and claims of the culture; resisting those rules, roles, and practices that caused them harm and pain; and proposing new possibilities for a more just and liberating society. There were men who early on recognized the justice of these claims for women and who joined them as profeminists working for change. But, as feminism has developed, it has been better able to recognize the interlocking oppressions of a patriarchal system and the damaging effects this has on all members of the society. Consequently, feminist theory and practice is not just about women's experiences and women's rights but also about dismantling systems of power arrangements and stereotyped role limitations for women and men. A feminist/profeminist orientation is now a multicultural, multivalent analysis that includes the power dynamics around gender, class, race, sexual orientation, able-bodiedness, and age. As Rebecca Chopp says,

> Patriarchy is revealed not simply as a social arrangement nor as individual acts of cruelty toward women on the part of men but rather as a deep spiritual ordering that invades and spreads across the social order—through individual identity, to social practices, to lines of authority in institutions, to cultural images and representations.[6]

The implications of this understanding of patriarchy as a deep spiritual malaise is central to looking at some of the theological shifts that have been important in feminist/profeminist theory building in the past twenty-five years. If, indeed, patriarchy harms all of us and interferes with God's lure toward wholeness and justice for creation, then it is important to build proposals for the care of men on a foundation of liberation-based theology. In other words, feminist theology is not just about what theological positions are harmful or helpful for women. Rather, feminist theology is about the dismantling of narrow and distorted claims about God and creation that have resulted from attempting to understand God through a patriarchal framework and that have worked against God's intentions for humanity. Thus, the questions and methods of feminist theology are essential to looking at issues related to the care of men. There is much at stake for men, as the following chapters indicate, in the dismantling of patriarchy. As Rosemary Radford Ruether has said, "Patriarchy is itself the original men's movement, and the struggle to overthrow it must be a movement of men as well as women."[7]

THEOLOGY AND CULTURE: A FORMATIVE DIALOGUE

Patriarchy is a complex and interwoven system that organizes perspectives, relationships, institutions, and the rules that govern them around a set of dualistic and hierarchical assumptions. As pointed out above, patriarchy is a "conceptual error of vast proportions"[8] or, maybe more accurately, a "conceptual trap."[9] In other words, human reality has been built out of a set of faulty premises at its foundation. As Nelle Morton has said, "The partial has paraded as the whole."[10] As it has become evident that much "truth" is dependent on standpoint and experience, it has also become evident that our constructions of reality are problematic for most people. The construction of social reality, based on the perceptions and experiences of a ruling class (white, economically viable, heterosexual males in our culture) disadvantages those who have not actively participated in that construction and, ultimately, it damages all of humanity and creation.

Much of feminist theology has been motivated by the conviction that theological interpretation has a radically formative relationship

26

to culture and that the shape of the culture guides our ongoing interpretations of God and God's intention for creation. From the beginning, feminist theology recognized that women's reflections had been largely left out of the "human" interpretation of religious experience and that women had not been acknowledged as active "meaning-makers" for the culture's myth and symbol systems. In addition, the perspectives, purposes, traits, and needs of women (and others) had been assigned by the dominant culture and then had been devalued.

A dualistic understanding of the world emerged out of this process. Dualism takes dualities (a recognition of difference without a value judgment) and assigns dominant and subordinate status to the differences. So, those realities that could be seen as unities or as equally valuable parts of a whole, are separated and given differing value. These dualistic splits between things like mind and body, spirit and matter, thinking and feeling, male and female have been given theological significance in their valuing. The first of each of these pairs has been seen as more valuable, closer to God, and associated with men. The second of each pair was associated with nature and with women and devalued.

A corresponding hierarchy based on this dualistic starting place and descending from the most male to the least male has been used to structure society. God, seen as the top of this hierarchy and most male, has been understood to be the source of the hierarchy/natural order and the maleness of God has been sustained out of the cultural value system. So, a "sacred circle" has been established consisting of a God who is named, defined, and empowered through patriarchal assumptions and who, in turn, through human-created symbols and structures, names, defines and empowers (some) males. Women (and things and people more closely associated with nature), in this scheme, become defined as "other." Men (at least those who follow patriarchal rules for maleness) become defined as closer to God and as responsible for creating and maintaining systems of meaning. As Mary Daly once said so succinctly, "If God is male, then the male is God."[11] This dualistic system of valuing and devaluing does harm to the potential and diverse gifts of both women and men.

Originally, the impetus of feminist theology, then, was to empower and reclaim the importance of women's experience in both theological interpretation and in the liberative shaping of the culture. However, it soon became evident that if women's voices, in general, had been left out of the creative and interpretive processes, so had the voices of other groups who were marginalized by the value hierarchy of patriarchy. The experiences of the poor, the uneducated, people of color, gay men and lesbians, and others had been and continue to be excluded from the meaning-making processes of the culture. Consequently, issues of justice have become expanded beyond women's concerns and the enormity of the conceptual error of patriarchy has begun to be understood.

The importance of this relationship between religious symbols, and their interpretation, and human culture is at the heart of liberation/liberating theologies. As Rebecca Chopp and Mark Taylor suggest in the introduction to their text, *Reconstructing Christian Theology,*

> The problems of destruction, devastation, abuse, and imperialism have been reinforced and sustained, at least in part, by Christian practices and theological discoveries. For instance, rates of physical abuse of women are exorbitant in the United States. One of the justifications given by abusers (and sometimes the abused) is that women are inferior in God's hierarchy and must be submissive to men. Religiously sanctioned notions of women's obedience and service are often obstacles to women's freedom from exploitation.[12]

The vast network of social evils are of deep interest to liberation theologies. The concerns of feminist and other liberation theologies range from a focus on right relationships between men and women to the implications of atonement theories for the experiences of abuse in women's and children's lives to a revisioning of the relationship between humanity and the rest of creation.

A primary focus is still on the process of naming around questions such as who has the right to name, what does it mean to name, and how do we name the unnameable. The power of naming, especially naming God, continues to be a high-stake task for the theological enterprise. As a World Council of Churches study group, representing seventeen countries, said in 1980, "We have discovered that an almost exclusively male image of God in the Christian tradition has helped cause the affirmation of male, white, Western superiority and has led to a sense of inferiority of women and of people from non-Western cultures."[13]

It is important to recognize that the distortions that have emerged from a patriarchal mind-set in terms of religious symbol systems, theological interpretations, and the structuring of culture have harmed everyone. When a culture exists within a conceptual error like that of patriarchy and builds rules, roles, and rituals around that error, no one can truly flourish. If the goal of theology is "faith seeking understanding" for the sake of responding to God's ever present lure toward wholeness/salvation, then it is crucial that all voices are heard and that society is built to reflect those voices in the fullness of their humanity. Collaboration, collegiality, and honest partnership is required across various patterns of difference and diversity if we are to dismantle the oppressive systems that seek to empower only the few and to silence the rest.

CONTEMPORARY THEMES IN
FEMINIST LIBERATION THEOLOGY

It is useful, then, to look at some of the important and enduring themes in feminist liberation theology so that we might see how these themes affect the pastoral care of men. Although these themes are identified as contemporary feminist foci, they are also themes that have been integral to the theological enterprise for all time. Exploring the names and images of God, for example, has always been considered a central task for theology in general, not just for feminist theology. However, the critical links between the way we name God and the way we name (and value) the people, relationships, and institutions of the culture are a key element in feminist and other liberation theologies.

We will identify five theological themes that have been central to the work of feminist theology and social justice. These themes, in keeping with the above discussion, have obvious and deep interconnections with the way we have constructed our relationships and the rules that govern the exercise of power in the culture. Thus, there are significant implications for the care of men to be drawn from this work.

THE NATURE AND IMAGE OF GOD

For virtually all feminist theologians, language and imagery for God have been of central importance. This focus reflects what we have discussed above: that language does not just describe cultural reality but also informs, influences, and, to a certain extent, determines that culture. The fact that the dominant male power structure has had chief responsibility for developing and defining language as well as for interpreting primary symbols and metaphors results in a language and symbol system that discounts and devalues women's experience. Consequently, it has become a central focus for feminist theologians to take seriously the power of language, imagery and metaphors, especially about God.

Several male theologians have also taken on the theological task of exploring dominant language and imagery for God. Brian Wren, in a study examining the primary images and language used in hymnody, suggests that God imagery has almost exclusively portrayed the divine as male, all-powerful, in control, father, and king. He says,

> Language is my particular concern. The systematic and almost exclusive use of male God-language, in a faith in which God is revealed as incarnate in a male human being, gives a distorted vision of God and supports male dominance in church and society. The distortion goes deep, in liturgies, creeds, hymns, and the language of the Bible. Some agree and find Christianity so steeped in male dominance that they bid farewell to Bible and church. Others say either that God intends men to dominate women, or that the distortion stems from the Fall and will only end in heaven. My hunch is that many are unhappy with those choices and would like to find a way forward that enlarges our knowledge of God, rejects male dominance and the hegemony of male god language, and names God anew in recognizable continuity with classic Christianity.[14]

Sallie McFague suggests that there are two significant problems with the exclusivity of male God language as reflected in our theological traditions. Those problems are idolatry and irrelevance. Most authors would agree that the reality of the divine presence is beyond any kind of image that we can create and thus we must speak about

God through metaphors and analogies if we are going to be able to speak about God at all. The name that God gave when Moses asked for a name was *YHWH*—which probably means being or becoming. It is unpronounceable and creates the image of a God beyond our control. However, McFague suggests that we have needed to contain God by collapsing the metaphorical quality of the images we use and equating the divine reality with those names. This kind of containment is the essence of idolatry.

Irrelevance is also at stake here because we have frozen the meaning of God in a time not our own. When we do (rarely) break out of the idolatrous exclusive image of father, we tend to draw on images that do not reflect the significance of our own culture. In addition, the father image of God is always somewhat irrelevant to women in that they cannot reflect having been created in the divine image, as can men, when God is exclusively named father.

McFague suggests that

> the issues of idolatry and irrelevance come together in the image of God as father, for more than any other dominant model in Christianity, this one has been both absolutized by some and, in recent times, found meaningless by others. . . . The feminist critique of God as father centers on the dominance of this model to the exclusion of others and on the failure of this model to deal with the anomaly presented by those whose experience is not included by this model.[15]

These core critiques of idolatry and irrelevance proposed by many feminist theologians have more recently been joined by those of male theologians looking at the religious concerns of men. In a book edited by Richard Holloway, a variety of male theologians respond to issues of sexism in the church both as these issues affect women and also as they negatively affect men. Images of God that combine authority, power, rationality, protectiveness of others, kingship, dependability, righteous anger, maleness, and fatherhood have a formative and normative impact on definitions of manhood and masculinity. Philip Sheldrake captures this concern when he writes:

> Images of God as self-possessed, invulnerable and perfect tended to reinforce this (over-valuing of objectivity and emotional control). It was difficult to accept vulnerability and incompleteness and easy to

be guiltily preoccupied with lack of perfection and sin. To become an "adult" male, you freed yourself from natural weaknesses, gained certain desirable powers, and took up specific roles. The greatest anxiety was about loss of self-possession. This was especially threatened by sexuality and the vulnerability inherent in intimacy with people and God.[16]

Feminist and liberation theologies have engaged in significant and compelling critiques of dominant traditional God language on both theological and social justice grounds. It seems useful, then, to follow Brian Wren's proposal given under his chapter heading of "Bring Many Names." He suggests that there are several things we can do to reconstruct liturgy, prayer, and even doctrine out of these theological critiques. His first proposal is that we develop names, metaphors, and images for God and creation out of the lived experience of our own time. Following the Hebrew Bible principle that God is unnameable, he proposes creating a variety of images so that we don't try to contain God by equating the divine with one name or image.

His second proposal is that we reclaim the vast diversity of names and images within our traditions, including the biblical tradition, and reintroduce those to our worship and to our theological constructions. In this he suggests mixing biblical images for God with new images that are biblically compatible but emerge out of contemporary experience. The intent of this mix would be to avoid the traditional king, father, control-type images as much as possible until we have been able to appreciate the richness of these reclaimed images for God.

Wren's third proposal is that we counteract our tendency to separate humanity from the rest of creation by developing metaphors for God that demonstrate the deep interrelatedness of all of creation. He suggests that we are more likely to do God justice if we see God's love moving deep within nature. He also reminds us that the dominant use of the concept of human dominion over nature has contributed to the serious ecological crises before us. Again, the link between our theology and our human relationships and rules is demonstrated by the lack of a theology that finds God equally at work in nature as in the human community.

The fourth proposal for new God imagery suggests speaking of God as she. Wren proposes this, not because *she* is any more accurate for God than *he,* but because the shock value helps us recognize that God is more than our imagery and because we may see important aspects of the divine that we have missed by not using female imagery. He writes:

> Speaking to God in female terms may prove to be revelatory, liberating, daring, or frightening, but is unlikely to pass unnoticed. By speaking of God as She and naming the whole being of God anew, we are going against the grain of the society that has formed us. Since that society downgrades and disvalues what it labels "feminine," naming God as She means facing that downgrading head-on and hoping to break through it.[17]

Wren's final proposal brings gender and class issues together when he proposes that we name God after the image of the "bag-lady." This image (and genre of images) for God asks us to look at that which makes us uncomfortable and to experience a call toward deep social justice as part of our response to God. This kind of naming provides both the turning around and the sharp insight that good metaphors provide and also seems deeply in keeping with a central Christian message.

It is clear through this review of feminist and profeminist explorations about God-talk and the theology of God's image that there is much at stake in this work for men, for women, and for the culture in rethinking who God is in our systems of faith. Some common themes have emerged in this work in terms of an understanding of God. Marjorie Suchocki suggests that there are five such themes that reflect a shift in the contemporary doctrine of God. Those are (1) an emphasis on the relationality of God over the immutability of God; (2) a focus on God's immanence more than on God's transcendence; (3) a movement away from God's maleness toward both female images and nongendered images; (4) a commitment to God's active engagement in liberation through empowerment rather than a more passive understanding of God (Suchocki suggests that liberation has replaced salvation as a primary theme); and (5) an antidualistic emphasis which affirms that to transform the role of women in the society is to transform the society itself.[18] Suchocki says that these take different forms in different theological constructions but that they have become focal themes for much feminist work.

CHRISTOLOGY

As Rosemary Radford Ruether says, "The doctrine of Christ should be the most comprehensive way that Christians express their belief in redemption from all sin and evil in human life, the doctrine that embraces the authentic humanity and fulfilled hopes of all persons." "And, yet," as she goes on to say, "this once fully inclusive approach for all persons has become, the doctrine . . . that has been most frequently used to exclude women from full participation in the Christian church."[19] Who theology understands Jesus to have been and the Christ to be is of primary concern in feminist theology precisely because this doctrine has been so influential in excluding and devaluing women throughout Christian history. There have been five primary approaches to Christology in feminist theology over the past twenty-five years. The first approach, represented by people like Letty Russell and Elisabeth Schüssler Fiorenza, has been to reclaim Jesus' relationship to women and the importance of women in the early church so that gender negative Christology could be refuted. In this perspective, one can't go as far as to say that Jesus was an early feminist, but women's roles in Jesus' life and in the early church are reclaimed and Jesus' positive attitudes and culture-defying advocacy for women are lifted up. This perspective does not focus on the issue of Jesus' essential maleness as part of the salvific plan.

However, a second approach, represented by someone like Patricia Wilson Kastner, looks at Jesus in relationship to his participation in the Trinitarian godhead, and suggests that Jesus' maleness was incidental, not essential, to his participation in the divine intent. Most of these positions suggest that Jesus was male because it was culturally expedient for him to be so, not because only maleness (which supposedly mirrors God's maleness) can be salvific. This marginalizing of the maleness of Jesus is important since much of the Christological formulation that has excluded (and continues to exclude) women from full participation in the church has been based on the need for the priest to be able to represent Christ to the people, which thus necessitates human maleness in the clergy.

A third approach is best represented by womanist scholarship where the focus is on the historical Jesus as one who suffered and one who liberates. As Jacquelyn Grant writes, "The condition of Black people today reflects the cross of Jesus. Yet, the resurrection brings the hope that liberation from oppression is imminent. The resurrected Black Christ signifies this hope."[20] As Grant suggests, white feminist theologizing about Christology cannot assume black women's agreement because of the gulf that both slavery and segregation have caused between the two sets of experience. According to Susan Brooks Thistlethwaite, African American women focus on Jesus as the most accessible and relevant person of the trinity and, as such, find Jesus' presence powerfully relevant to their spiritual needs.[21] Jesus offers evidence that God both suffers with and liberates those who are oppressed.

A fourth approach has been to place less focus on the divine-human tensions of the historical Jesus and move instead to the notion of the Christ that was made fully manifest in Jesus but not exclusively so. This takes a variety of forms and focuses primarily on the liberating, empowering, and saving work of God in Jesus. Carter Heyward talks about Jesus as manifesting fully the power of God *(dunamis)* for right relationship. Rita Nakashima Brock talks about the power of Christa/community, which has again to do with the relational power of God made manifest in human community. The possibility of imaging Christ as female (Christa) is very real in this position, although this reimaging can also be a part of the other positions listed above. The shift identified in this fourth perspective is fundamentally a theological move from Christology to Christopraxis. Christine Smith identifies this position well where she writes,

> Wherever people live in the power of right relation, or enter into radical acts of love, or give witness to justice, there is the Christ. Wherever individuals are liberated, oppressive structures are transformed, and the power of evil is confronted, we stand in the presence of the Christ, God incarnate, God made manifest among us.[22]

A final approach taken by some feminists is to discard the notion of Christ (and the Trinity) as central to understanding the divine. This, again, takes a number of forms but tends to see God as a life-giving force found in immanent ways among all creation. The need for a vehicle of that immanence is found to be unnecessary. One might argue that this has moved too far away from the tradition to be called Christian theology.

THEOLOGIES OF ATONEMENT

Feminist theology has demonstrated a heavy investment in exploring, deconstructing, and reimagining Christian understandings of Jesus' death and resurrection. The investment has hinged, at least in part, on the recognition by many women of the epidemic levels of abuse against women and children and the use to which Christian theology has been put in allowing that abuse to occur. Feminist theorists have long been aware that abused women and children frequently receive messages from their pastors, from Christian husbands and parents, and from "well-meaning" Christian neighbors that there is divine meaning in their experience of abuse, that the abuse itself is salvific or a means to deeper spirituality, that it is their place to suffer, that husbands or parents know best, that they are somehow at fault, or that it is a sign of deep Christian charity to tolerate being abused by a "loved one." The stories about these kinds of messages, told by battered women, incest survivors, and others, are legion. Karen, in Jim Poling's book *The Abuse of Power,* tells of being sexually abused by her father one Saturday night and having to memorize the commandment to honor your father and mother the next morning in church school. Annie Imbens and Ineke Jonker conducted a study in the Netherlands of eighteen women who had experienced childhood sexual abuse and who had been raised in Christian homes as to how the abuse and the Christian upbringing might be related. They heard over and over again that Christian images of women, the God-given authority of fathers, and the mandates of humility, forgiveness, and submission were contributing factors to both the occurrence of the abuse and the difficulty they had in recovering from it. They also heard, in these interviews, of the correlation sometimes made by these women between God's

36

relationship with Jesus and their fathers' relationship with themselves. Imbens and Jonker recount the following.

> Several of the incest survivors told us that, as children, they had been sad about Jesus' crucifixion; they did not understand why he had not come down from the cross, or why God, his Father, allowed him to be crucified. The combination of the way they often experienced Jesus (as loving, good, close by, and providing security) with this torturous death (often explained as God's will in order to redeem the sins of humankind) gave these survivors a terrifying image of God: the image of a sadistic father, someone hungry for power. "God and my father were a lot alike," says Joan.[23]

These studies and stories convey some of the motivation behind feminist and profeminist theologians' exploration into theories of atonement. James Poling introduces his study into theories of atonement by acknowledging the centrality of the crucifixion to Christian doctrine. But he then writes, "The idea that there is any justification for a parent to sacrifice a child is difficult to accept in light of the testimonies of victims of abuse."[24] After exploring the theories of substitutionary atonement and incarnational atonement, Poling concludes that in these theories of atonement "God is a powerful figure who has the freedom to be wrathful or compassionate without considering the moral claims of the creation. . . . Like the perpetrator of sexual violence, such images of God assume prerogatives of unilateral power over those who are unprotected." Poling's proposal is to develop an image of God as one who is "relational and ambiguous" and who is, then, "a God we can worship."[25]

Rita Nakashima Brock argues similarly against traditional theories of atonement in her book, *Journeys by Heart.* She also reviews the various traditional atonement theologies and suggests that they all revolve around the notion of original sin—humanity born with a tragic flaw. In order for that flaw to be redeemed, the perfect and flawless one must suffer. Human beings are, then, the passive recipients of this transcendent God's gift—a gift delivered through another's suffering. Brock moves from there to make the connection with abusing fathers even clearer when she writes:

Such doctrines of salvation reflect by analogy, I believe, images of the neglect of children or, even worse, child abuse, making it acceptable as divine behavior—cosmic child abuse, as it were. The father allows, or even inflicts, the death of his only perfect son. The emphasis is on the goodness and power of the father and the unworthiness and powerlessness of his children, so that the father's punishment is just, and children are to blame. While atonement doctrines emphasize the father's grace and forgiveness, making it seem as if he accepts all persons whole without the demand that they be good and free of sin, such acceptance is contingent upon the suffering of the one perfect child.[26]

There are a number of other feminist theologians who have struggled with these issues of violence at the heart of the Christian tradition and the impact they may have on women's and children's experiences of abuse by those with whom they are intimately and vulnerably involved.[27] Their analyses of the problems are similar although they propose a variety of theological solutions. For the most part, though, there is strong resistance to traditional formulations of atonement as appropriate or helpful for women, and proposals generally see Jesus' death as cultural retribution for his commitment to just and liberating relationships and his consequent flouting of the deeply held convictions of his time. This reformulation of Jesus' life and death, as the result of resisting evil rather than as part of God's design to redeem humanity, contributes to a theology constructed around themes of liberation and empowerment of those who are marginalized and oppressed.

SIN AND EVIL

Some would say that this wave of feminist theology was born in the article written by Valerie Saiving in April 1960 entitled "The Human Situation: A Feminine View." In this article Saiving critiques Anders Nygren and Reinhold Niebuhr for their representative description of "man's [sic] predicament as rising from his separateness and the anxiety occasioned by it and [identifying] sin with self-assertion and love with selflessness."[28] Saiving went on from that point to suggest that women's experience is fundamentally different from men's in that their sin is less that of self-assertion and more of self-abnegation. This was a radical departure in theology because it sought to demonstrate the particularities of experience and their impact on the construction of theology and to make one of those particularities that of gender.

It is telling that this initiation point in feminist theology was around the issue of sin and evil. Feminist theology and feminist ethics are deeply related as the object of their study is the relationship between the formulation of theology and the structures and behaviors of the culture. Constructions of sin and evil have been some of the most radically challenged doctrines in liberation theologies in general.

In traditional theology sin was conceived primarily in individualistic terms—sin was "missing the mark," alienation, and separation. The root cause of sin, traditionally, was either pride or disobedience, both of which were seen as the human setting himself or herself up as god-like and thus being separated from authentic relationship with either God or neighbor. Feminist theology, as discussed in Saiving's article (and nineteen years later in Judith Plaskow's critique of Niebuhr and Tillich), began to critique this so-called universal experience of alienation through pride and suggested that women's sin is closer to a denial of the self or an unwillingness to respond to vocation. As a feminist revisioning of sin continued, connections between sin and distorted social structures and relationships began to emerge as foundational. Consequently, in feminist thought, sin and evil are generally seen together. Evil is the systemic manifestation of human sin and these manifestations always take place concretely in particular contexts. Thus feminist thought does not tend to deal with abstractions about sin and evil but about concrete realities in which sin and evil are made manifest.

Christine Smith, in a recent article entitled "Sin and Evil in Feminist Thought," reviewed the contributions of five feminist positions, including her own, on this topic. Although she notes that feminists have diverse positions on sin and evil, she does suggest four emerging commonalities shared by feminist theologians. First, most feminists are suspicious and critical of individualistic or privatized conceptualizations of sin. Second, there has been a shift from sin understood as pride or disobedience to sin and evil as a violation of relationship or a misuse of power against another. Third, there is more focus on the systemic dimensions of evil than on the more narrow or personal category of sin. And, fourth, there is a greatly increased focus on particularity, context, and social location for both the theologian and the situation being considered.[29]

Sin and evil are seen increasingly as belonging to the relational and communal realms over against the more private and individual ones. Patriarchy, as a form of systemic evil, has become a focus for communal action and judgment. The theological themes work together for the liberation and empowerment of creation, not just for the personal salvation of its members.

THEOLOGICAL REFLECTION

As one can see through the exploration of the above themes, theological reflection itself has undergone significant shifts over the past twenty-five years. Theology has become much more tied to the realities of particular contexts and has increasingly focused on the implications of doctrinal theology for concrete situations. Chopp and Taylor propose that there have been five major shifts in theological discourse over this period of time. These discursive shifts reflect the paradigm changes that have emerged out of both the postmodern and liberation contexts.

The first proposed shift is a change in cultural image from melting pot to collage. The melting pot metaphor was never accurate for those who couldn't look like those of the dominant population. That means anyone who wasn't white and male could never hope to be joined into the cultural image of community. The melting pot image also tends to play into the dualistic assumptions that those who can't fit into the melting pot are then less valuable than ones who can. This cultural shift is also reflected in contemporary theology according to Chopp and Taylor, who say,

> Black theologies, Asian-American theologies, feminist theologies, womanist theologies, theologies from gay men and lesbian women, and theologies offered from the perspectives of the disabled are all presented on the scene today. Where once such differences were either ignored or belittled as "special interests," theology today is increasingly understood as having its vitality *only insofar as its traditional resources embrace new voices and their differences.*[30] (italics added)

It is important to note that, according to this assessment, diverse theological perspectives spoken out of various perspectives are not in competition for the "truth" or for the validation of "orthodoxy." Rather, the truth comes by hearing the broad range of formulations and constructing meaning out of the many "truths."[31]

A second shift suggested by Chopp and Taylor is a move to speaking out of the realities of particular and global crises rather than out of a position of security or strength. This means that much of today's theology focuses on a new naming of sin and evil as those systems and beliefs that pose concrete threats to the survival of people—especially those people who have been persistently marginalized by dominant perspectives and structures.

This is a particularly important shift to note for a pastoral theology for the care of men. The flourishing of men is linked to the flourishing of all people. Only with the sharp critique of patriarchy and the reconstruction of both theology and culture around the salvific norms of liberation and empowerment will men, women, and children be able to live into the fullness of life. Liberation theology, if it is real, means liberation for all people.

The third shift that Chopp and Taylor name has been discussed at some length above, and that has to do with the inherent ambiguity of a postmodern perspective. The changes in theological orientation are significant because "postmodernity, as a challenge to theology, consists of finding ways to address a culture with a penchant for the fragmentary, the open, the ambiguous, and the different."[32]

The fourth shift relates to the breakdown of dualistic assumptions in that there is a shift away from seeing the modern beliefs, economics, and structures of the "First World" as superior to the other cultures previously seen as "Third World." This "postcolonial sensibility" means that part of the theological task is to analyze how Christianity has been used to justify a view of the First World as superior and to transform and restructure those destructive and devaluing orientations so that an understanding of the world as a global community might emerge.

The fifth shift has to do with the tensions that emerge when Christianity is placed in the context with other religions (both major world religions and particular indigenous religions). The result of this shift is the ability to respect other religions alongside of Christianity as "authentic expressions of the sacred for diverse peoples."[33] Chopp and Taylor quote John Cobb, a highly respected process theologian, as he addresses the tension of this shift saying, "The more deeply we trust Christ, the more openly receptive we will be to wisdom from any source, and the more responsibly critical we will be both of our own received habits of mind and of the limitations and distortions of others."[34]

These shifts in theology—from universal to particular, from dogma to praxis, and from security to survival—are central in building a pastoral theology for the care of men. Our work as pastoral theologians is to develop a base that allows us to break through the conceptual trap of patriarchy so that men and women can be helped to respond to God's invitation for justice, for a fullness of life for everyone, and for a true partnership in the work of liberation. We need to listen to one another very carefully in order that we might reveal the destructive traps of dualistic and hierarchical theology and the consequent oppressiveness of a patriarchal society.

IMPLICATIONS FOR THE PASTORAL CARE OF MEN

It is important that pastoral caregivers take the issues discussed above directly into the care of men and women. One of the primary implications of this material for the work of pastoral care is the important task we have of helping the members of our congregations learn to do theological reflection that is self-consciously in dialogue with the intense sociocultural changes of our time. It seems clear that the social changes over the past twenty-five or more years have been moving faster than the changes in our theological methods and doctrines. This makes sense as one of the purposes of the church has been to safeguard the traditions from capricious shifts. However, the consequences of that conservatism are significant in the increasing irrelevance of the church in the lives of many people.

We propose that one of the main tasks facing pastors and pastoral caregivers today is that of educating congregations to do relevant and adequate theological reflection. This reflection needs to be able to help congregations to develop interpretive principles and useful methods for maintaining the trialogue between their own life experiences, the theological traditions, and the radical cultural shifts.

The move into a postmodern consciousness has come more easily and naturally into the secular lifestyles of our congregations than it has into their religious and theological lives. There seems to be more of an awareness of both the diversity of perspectives and their appropriate truth claims in the culture than in our religious reflections. We need to help congregations find ways to bring their cultural lenses into the process of meaning-making that is at the heart of theology.

Chopp and Taylor propose three tasks for theological reflection today that are helpful as we work to empower our congregations. The first task they suggest is an "analysis of the key features and immense structural problems of the current challenges to contemporary Christians and their communities."[35] This includes paying attention to the variety of perspectives available, especially those perspectives that have not been easily or respectfully heard in the past. It also means a careful study of the contradictions and challenges to traditional theology without an abandonment of the theological task altogether. The connections between theology and culture need to be explored nondefensively in order for the other tasks of theological reflection to proceed.

The second task proposed by Chopp and Taylor is the work of bringing the new insights from a thorough and fearless analysis back into the traditions. This is the reconstructive task. This work includes reformulating doctrines, developing new liturgies, finding new ways to reach the spiritual needs of people and communities, and experimenting with the meaning of religious experience.

These first two tasks join with a third (and this is not necessarily a linear process) that Chopp and Taylor label "envisioning emancipatory practice."[36] This is a key feature of this proposal for theological reflection. Theological reflection must not only analyze the issues and propose theological reconstructions but also lead to the kinds of reflective practices that liberate and empower people and communities. As Chopp and Taylor conclude,

Amid today's structural evil and crisis—which drive many to despair because of the blatant and subtle realities of racial injustice, sexism, militarist spirals of violence, class exploitation, handicappism, and discrimination against gay and lesbian people—we may have a special challenge to point toward a grace abiding in history that promises nothing short of new *corporate* empowerment and flourishing.[37]

These three tasks of analysis, reconstruction, and building emancipatory praxis are not just the task of professional theologians, clergy, and pastoral caregivers. These tasks belong to the people inside and outside of churches in the hopes that they can fully participate in the formative dialogues and the crucial issues at stake.

There are other implications we would name that are more specific to the pastoral care of men. First, it is important to help men to explore their experiences in the context of both the anxieties and the possibilities of the changes going on around them. Men report to their pastors that this is a confusing time for them in terms of their roles in families, their commitments to paid employment, and the rules for masculinity in general (see chapter 2). Men, like women, have been raised with the confusing and double-binding messages of patriarchy about what it means to be a man. The paradoxical and destructive implications of these gender messages are becoming clearer to men, but it is unclear to most what the appropriate norms should be for "masculinity."

It is important for pastors to be able to understand the dynamics of patriarchy and its contradictory and damaging messages for men's lives and to be able to help men sort out what is true and faithful for their lives in community. This also means that pastors need to be engaged in this work for their own lives as well.

A second direct implication for the pastoral care of men is the need to help men make constructive changes in their own personal lives while always understanding that the personal and the political are inseparable. The kinds of issues that men are dealing with in their lives (the nature of work, their role in families, getting in touch with their own identities and feelings) are deeply related to the cultural shifts of our time. In helping men to gain clarity and purpose in their lives, pastoral caregivers are contributing, in one way or another, to the changes in the culture. Consequently, pastors need to be fully aware of the issues of liberation and empowerment at stake in men's and women's lives as they move into the twenty-first century. The issues raised above are not abstractions but deeply significant concerns for each person and community today. If we attempt to go

44

backward, to close ourselves and one another off from hearing the voices of those who have not been heard, we will work against the creation of a liberating and empowering global community. We need to keep before us the large communal issues even as we work with individuals in pastoral care.

And, finally, it is important to recognize the nature of this collaborative effort of deconstructing and dismantling a patriarchal culture that has been destructive for all of creation. Given the nature of our tendency to polarize issues in this society, it will be important for pastoral caregivers to model and teach a message of collaboration and collegiality in this work. We are at risk for developing (and already have to a certain extent) polarized and competitive "his and her" movements that work against each other. We are committed to the belief that, although it is important to carefully hear the experiences and interpretations of every voice, it does no good to set those voices against each other in competition. The task is massive and requires cooperation.

CONCLUSION

This book attempts to model that commitment in its diversity. We have worked as male and female co-editors and as male and female, black and white, gay and straight scholars in addressing the issues before us in the pastoral care of men. We recognize the fact that varieties of viewpoints obscure a common and unambiguous direction for our work. Nonetheless, it is that very diversity and ambiguity that will allow us to eventually build an approach to the pastoral care of people that is just, empowering, and liberating for all. The theological task must be at the heart of this vision. Without our self-conscious theological work, the task of empowering justice may fail and we may return to the hierarchical and dualistic premises of our past. It is important to carry into our task the recognition that we are in the midst of extreme and frightening crises in our world even as we seek for the hope that lies in God's persistent invitation to fullness of life for all of creation.

CHAPTER TWO

MEN'S ISSUES IN THE LOCAL CHURCH: WHAT CLERGYMEN HAVE TO SAY

Christie Cozad Neuger

The feminist movement, along with other economic and social changes of the past twenty-five years, has created new understandings of gender roles, family life, and the nature and meaning of work. It has become especially clear that assumptions about the "essential" nature of femaleness and maleness must be called into question and that old models of gender complementarity are no longer adequate for structuring relationships between women and men. For the past twenty-five years women, especially, have been trying to understand what these changes that come from the challenging and dismantling of patriarchy might mean for their lives. From the consciousness-raising groups of the sixties and seventies to the ongoing conversations in homes, over fences, and in academia, there has been a great deal of deconstruction and reconstruction about women's lives and about the bodies of knowledge that have sought to explain and understand the worlds of women (and of men).

Alongside the women who were working to make sense of these radical changes in how and what we know were men—men who worked with women for justice and in support of women as they reconstructed their own stories and traditions. Some men also worked against these challenges and the re-membering work in which women and some men were engaged. As time went on, men began to form working groups and movements within which to understand the changes and challenges that women were bringing and to understand the implications of those for their own lives. As the introduction to this book suggests, several kinds of men's groups and several kinds of men's literatures are the result of the past twenty-five, and especially the last fifteen, years.

But what is the actual impact of these movements, these challenges, these new life style proposals on the lives of women and men in the church? More specifically, for the purpose of this book, what difference has all of this work made in the everyday lives of men in their families, their workplaces, their friendships, and their churches? And what kind of pastoral care is emerging that best speaks to the current needs of men in our congregations?

This chapter was born out of three sets of questions arising from what might be called the "gender revolution" of the past twenty-five years. The first question has to do with the kinds of issues and concerns that men in the church are experiencing and with which of those concerns they are bringing to their clergy for pastoral care. Have the questions and issues that men face changed in recent years and are we, as caregivers, helping both to facilitate the bringing of those concerns and to give appropriate care to the men who bring them? How are the issues that men struggle with framed when presented to their caregivers, and are caregivers able to hear them and respond helpfully? In what contexts do men present their concerns to clergy? Are they more likely to initiate formal pastoral care or counseling than they were in the past? These are the questions about men's pastoral care needs that form the main agenda for this chapter.

However, there is a second set of questions. Do clergy find ways to invite ongoing conversation about these radical changes so that individual women and men feel free to seek care in this time of role transition? Are congregations working to provide leadership or are they counting on secular resources to provide direction? And, if churches are providing leadership around issues of the "gender revolution," how are they going about it?

The third set of questions behind this research has to do with clergymen. How have clergymen addressed issues of male identity, role changes, and new forms of collegiality with women in their own lives? And, does an individual clergyman's work with these issues make a difference in the way he goes about doing his pastoral care with men in the church?

These are the three sets of research questions that I attempted to address in a series of twenty structured one-hour interviews with clergymen about the nature of their pastoral care with men, the issues the men in their congregations were facing, and about their own "gender journeys." The interviews took place across three "mainline" denominations (Presbyterian, United Methodist, and United Church of Christ), in two regions (New Jersey and Minnesota), and within a variety of pastoral contexts.[1] In each case I sat down for a face-to-face interview with a clergyman lasting between an hour and an one and one-half hours and asked each of them the same set of questions. The interviews were taped and later transcribed. The material from the interviews was then used for this chapter to assess trends as well as particular issues and approaches. It is always risky to generalize, especially from such a small sample. Yet, there were some important similarities in the answers given, often with interviewees using the same words. I describe both these similarities and the differences in perspectives and proposals below.

MEN AND PASTORAL CARE IN THE CHURCH

Contexts of Care

The pastors who were interviewed were clear that men in their congregations rarely come for formal counseling or even make formal contacts for care. In fact, with one exception, those pastors who made any comparisons felt that the number of men who come in for pastoral care or counseling has stayed the same or (more often) declined in the past fifteen years. Although this contradicts Phil Culbertson's experience, the twenty pastors were almost unanimous on this point.[2] The one exception, who felt that more men were coming to him for counseling than in the ten years before, attributed it to a style change he has made that is more explicitly invitational for men. This unanimity about formal counseling does not mean, however, that men are not seeking pastoral care. For the pastor who is attuned to men's needs, there are a variety of ways that men in the parish bring themselves to the caregiver's attention.

The primary approach men seem to take in seeking care is through the casual drop-in to the pastor's office. Generally they come in during times when they are at the church for another purpose—dropping off a child for youth group, after a meeting, or doing a church errand. In these settings, a man most often seems to make either a casual or a light-hearted/humorous reference to a possible concern he has as a way to test out the acceptability of his need. If the pastor responds invitationally and nonjudgmentally, the careseeker will often continue by elaborating on the concern. If the pastor jokes back or treats the remark as a passing comment, the man tends not to pursue the issue. This means that it is easy to miss or dismiss the needs being tentatively raised. As one pastor said, "Pastors who are overworked and tired are in parallel to these anxious, overworked men and it's easy to miss their need."

A second place that pastors encounter pastoral care needs of men is in crisis situations. Men tend to ask most directly for help from their pastors in times of health crisis.[3] This still involves active invitational work on the part of the pastor, but it is often in the midst of a hospital or home visit that a man will begin to talk about some of the deeper concerns of his life—family worries, job issues, unresolved grief, and so on. Many of the pastors said that the first response that hospitalized men tend to make is the question about whether they are going to recover, and the second response tends to be about how much better off they are than someone else. One pastor said, "It's really hard for a man in my church, especially an older man, to acknowledge the fact that he can be wounded or his fears about that." However, many men seem to be willing to move to revealing their fears as they discover that it is safe to do so—that they won't be disparaged as being "weak" or "feminine" for talking about their vulnerabilities.[4] The expectations about care that have been established in the church prior to the particular crisis determine much of what men ask for. For example, in one church where there was an active lay caregiving program that involved a number of men, those men who were in health crises tended to be more willing to share their own feelings and fears. Again, though, the pastors noted that they did not see a shift toward more openness to feelings and sharing vulnerabilities in men in a crisis of health than they had seen fifteen years before. However, since most pastors noted that any increased sensitivities they were seeing were generationally divided, with younger men more likely to be more open, it may not be surprising that health crises, which were predominantly in older men, did not demonstrate an increased openness to care.

A third way that men came to the attention of their pastors was through referrals by their wives. Since the pastors had fewer marital counseling situations than they had in the past, this was no longer a primary means of access to men. However, several pastors noted that they occasionally received calls from women asking the pastor to call their husbands or engage in conversation with them when the man was around the church because of a problem that she perceived he was facing. Pastors found this to be helpful and usually quite accurate in terms of the husband's need.

Finally, the pastors who had men's groups operating in the church, especially men's groups organized around support, spirituality, or a mix of study and support, found that they knew a lot about the men in those groups and that the men were more likely to come to the pastor directly in a time of need. These groups also created supportive relationships among the men that functioned outside of the group structure itself. I will talk more about the group work later on in the chapter.

Men's Concerns

The most striking experience of these interviews for me was the almost unanimous agreement on the primary problem that men face. One pastor, in a small New York City commuting community put it well when he said:

> Men used to bring relational issues to me for care, especially issues around family and spouses. But, over the past eight years or so the major issue has been around jobs and their various stresses—especially loyalty, meaning, and security. As one of my parishioners said, "Everything I used to believe is no longer true. I was taught by my father that if you worked hard and stayed loyal, you would get ahead. I now know that this is no longer true." Men that are coming to me are in crisis because they no longer can find their primary identity in their work. There is enormous economic uncertainty and loss of meaning in work. And men who have thought of their work as a calling are going through faith crises around this too. Their self worth is challenged as well as their ability to be economically secure.

Over and over in these interviews pastors would spontaneously, and with almost identical language, identify the primary pastoral need of men around these issues of work. They were clearest about the economic and employment insecurities, but they were also in uniform agreement that the issues of identity and meaning and commitment were causing enormous stress. Pastors typically identified men as having to work more hours because fewer employees are expected to produce as much as when there were more employees and because of the fear of not measuring up and thus being fired. They also identified reduced meaning and identity in the workplace, which left men working harder than ever without the motivation of self-esteem and vocational satisfaction. Finally, pastors identified that men were talking to them about their discomfort with decisions being made in the workplace or decisions they were being asked to make that seemed morally questionable. Men wanted help in knowing how to think through these decisions in ways that would be consistent with their Christian belief systems. In the twenty interviews, there were only two exceptions to this as the primary topic of conversation and, even in these two interviews, the issue of work surfaced as a second- or third-level concern.

It is interesting to note that this concern about work, with different nuances, was consistent across regional differences, class differences, and racial differences. An inner city pastor in a multicultural church spoke very similarly to the pastor quoted above when he said,

> I think there's a loss of job security out there. Men worry about losing their jobs. They had bought into the idea that if you do a good job, the job will be there for you. That's not true anymore. They get laid off or fear getting laid off—they have mortgages, kids in college, all these commitments, and they are dependent on their jobs. Lots of men are very frightened. Even if it is something they enjoy doing, the fear of losing the job makes it so the satisfaction doesn't mean anything. People are confused. They're pedalling as fast as they can, but there's no guarantee. I sense a great deal of stress—they are trying to pedal faster than they can—and even as they do, they are attempting to question their lifestyles so that if they lose their job, they will still be able to live.

51

In the churches like the one above where there was a heavier African American population, the issue of racism was a key element of the discussion. As one pastor said, "These men are getting worn down from pervasive racism. When they are in managerial positions where they have to work extra hours to get respect, there is a tremendous disregard for their authority—a constant challenging of who they are. Racism in the workplace is increasing as economics continue to create increased anxiety." In the one church where there was a significant openly gay population, the pastor noted that there was a considerable amount of gay discrimination at work. Another pastor noted that there was a lot of job discrimination around disabilities in his congregation. These comments from pastors suggest that economic and employment insecurity puts a lot of pressure on all of the employees; but for those employees who are already culturally marginalized by race, lack of able-bodiedness, or sexual orientation, those pressures increase significantly.

These concerns about work as the number one anxiety that men face are striking in their intensity. I asked pastors how these issues affected women since most of the women in their congregations also were employed. Their response generally was that although women do experience concerns about layoffs, they do not have the same kind of identity investment or the single-minded focus on work as a source of meaning. This fits with much of the literature about men and work. Robert Pasick says:

> As family therapists, we see the changing expectations of men resulting in confusion and anger among many of our clients. They have been raised to regard work as their essential duty. For the entire period of development and training (during their youths), they were prepared to work hard and succeed at their jobs. Yet, when they reached the age where work is traditionally supposed to be their dominant concern, they found the old order had changed. What will replace the familiar structure is unknown. It is the stress of this dilemma that often requires therapy.[5]

I asked pastors what kinds of changes they had seen in the pastoral care needs of men, and they consistently suggested that these concerns regarding work (as well as other changes to be identified later) had become much more intense over that time period and had moved from being a peripheral or circumstantial concern to a dominant and pervasive one.

The second concern that these pastors raised had to do with raising children and men's roles as fathers. Named by all of the interviewees as a concern, only two pastors raised it as their primary observation, and most named it second. Probably the most significant change in men that this group of pastors noted was the amount of time that men spend with their children and the high quality of that time. One pastor said,

> What has changed in the past ten or so years is the degree of how much these men want to be good fathers—not just to look like good fathers. They are much more involved in their kids' lives, and their family lives revolve around their kids' schedules. They want to be more actively involved. They don't want to push that off on their spouse. Their job is not to bring money into the household only; it is to be involved in their children's lives. I see a lot of that.

For the most part the pastors saw this involvement as a positive change in the lives of men and families, but there were also some problems associated with it. At the same time that fathers are more involved with their children, they also carry a great number of concerns and worries about their children's well-being and future, chiefly: (1) success in school and the impact this would have on future plans and successes, (2) use of drugs and alcohol as a constant worry and as something the fathers had to work hard at keeping their children from, and (3) sexual acting out, sexually transmitted diseases, and pregnancies. As one pastor in an inner city, multiracial context said,

> Men in their midlife are really feeling stresses for their kids— especially teenagers. I don't think that my parents had the same kind of concerns for me as my generation has for our kids. There's a lack of predictability. Lots of fear. The kids are not turning out the way the parents expected, and this creates a lot of stress. Fathers worry especially that the kids are not succeeding—school, social relationships, kids living differently than they want them to in terms of values. It's a hard time for these fathers.

Another aspect of the fathering issue has to do with the role these children play in families where the fathers are active. Several of the pastors noted that the family schedule and focus is built around the activities of the youth. This in itself wasn't a problem as much as three trends they saw associated with this family structure. First, men experienced themselves as having no time for themselves because they were divided between their stressful work lives and their children's over-involved schedules. This issue of time is a significant one and the interviewees spent a lot of time talking about the time pressures for men. As a commuter town pastor said, "Men have no time. Between commutes and long work hours, men have no time for leisure, for their marital relationships, for the church, for themselves. Next to work, the next priority is fathering and that finishes off their time." A pastor in a small town church said, "Work, time, and stress dominate the pastoral care picture with men."

Second, men experienced a demand within themselves to provide everything that they could for their children. They feared that their children would be disadvantaged if they had to go without an activity or product that they wanted. And they worry that they won't be able to provide it all. As one pastor said about this recurring theme, "The men experience family stresses about how much the kids need and want—the fathers feel like failures because they can't give all of those things. Rather than question this adolescent entitlement, they feel like failures." The interviewees often suggested that the focus around the kids' needs seemed to be a way to try to keep them safe and ensure their success when they felt a lot of anxiety about their children's future. Another pastor said, "Fathers worry about their children—how much their children need and how they can support them. They worry that the kids won't be better off than they are. I hear a lot about keeping up with the schedules and how hard it is for them to set priorities—everything is extremely important and nothing can be left out."

The third issue has to do with the pastors' fears that men's intense focus on the lives of their children will have negative ramifications on marriages once the children leave home. Although they don't have hard evidence about this, they fear couple problems for these baby-boomer parents over the next few years.

This concern about marriages leads to a third major concern that these pastors had for the men in their congregations, crossing all race, class, and location lines. One pastor in an inner city church said it well when he exclaimed, "I'll tell you what they don't talk about—relationships with women. They do not talk about their marriages, and I don't know why. My wife and I try to model open communication, but they don't bring in issues around their marriages." Another pastor said, "I don't hear men talk about their spouses or marriages or see much marriage counseling. I've not talked with men about their spouses at all. I think that the family styles now are so focused on kids. When families miss church, it's usually because their kids' schedules conflict. It makes me nervous for when the kids leave home—what happens to the marriage?" And a third pastor said, "In terms of relationships with spouses, I don't get much of a reading on that. Men aren't talking about those relationships." Eighteen of the twenty pastors did not name issues around relationships with spouses or female partners to be a concern that men raised with them and, when asked, they consistently said that they didn't hear men talk about spouses. It is hard to know how to interpret this information, but given the divorce statistics of today, it would be important to try to find out what it means that men aren't talking about these primary relationships. This issue of spousal or partner relationships becomes a concern by its absence in these interviewees' pastoral care experiences.

Related to this, several pastors talked about the fact that men did not bring in for discussion typical midlife crisis issues—where they had become bored with spouses or lifestyle or job—nor did they see men acting out in the same ways that they used to with midlife crises. One pastor phrased it this way:

> I used to see a lot more traditional male midlife crises. I don't see this much anymore. There's still a lot of divorce, but I'm talking more about the old crises where nothing seemed to matter and they would go out and seek to find new stimulation. It used to come out of contentment and achievement, and that's rarer today. Maybe there isn't the luxury anymore to have midlife crises.

There were three other issues that arose for a number of the interviewees in their pastoral care of men but that weren't represented in all or even most of the interviews. The first of these issues has to do with identity as males. About one-third of the pastors suggested that shifting identity is an issue for the men in their churches. About an equal number felt that these issues about male identity really haven't surfaced in their local churches. The other third saw suggestions or glimmers that men may be struggling with their self-definitions, but it really hasn't come up in any explicit way. For those clergy who found that gender identity was a live issue for men, their observations indicated that men are in transition and in some confusion about what it means to be a man in today's changing world. These men are, for the most part, quite comfortable with women in the workforce and with the reality of shared domestic roles, according to their pastors.

Where they are less comfortable is in the meaning realm of these changes, and this was well articulated by the pastor of a small-town church when he said, "Men experience confusion about what it means to be male in today's world—especially with changes at work and at home—what gives value, what is 'safe' and 'trustworthy'? Men fear doing the wrong thing in terms of their gender roles and in their relationships with women, especially at work. They don't know what specifically defines maleness and what gives them meaning and worth." Another pastor said, "Men are asking, 'Who am I if it isn't my work that gives me value?' Some men are able to build lives that are more balanced, but right now there is a great deal of transition." These pastors did not identify many men who seemed to have been directly affected by the men's movements and the more deliberate search for "maleness." They were more aware of men who were experiencing a void of meaning and vaguely looking for ways to understand and fill that void. Most of the pastors were quite clear that they don't see many men who are willing to open up with their feelings or share their feelings with anyone, including the pastor.

Another element of identity that several of the pastors noted had to do with a vague level of resentment in the midst of these transitions: that they didn't really know what the rules were anymore about being male and, even more to the point, didn't seem to have much say in the creation of new rules. This related to their sense of uneasiness in dealing with women in the workforce. As one pastor said, "Men don't know what to do with women—women making demands or not accepting things the way they were. Men are afraid they are going to break rules they don't even know exist." Whereas most of the pastors said that men are generally comfortable with and respectful toward women in the workplace, there was at least a slight flavor of this resentment issue in many of the interviews.

The identity question led many of the pastors into a discussion of meaning and spirituality. Again, about one-third of the pastors talked about male spirituality as a focus in their congregations. Usually, they were referring to a dozen men or less who were intentionally beginning to talk about spirituality in their own lives and what that spirituality might mean as they seek new life foci. One pastor talked about the fact that in their large suburban church they had worked very hard to encourage men to begin to look at spiritual issues. They had a number of men who had attended the Walk to Emmaus program and who were helping other men become willing to make spirituality an acceptable topic of conversation. As a result, the pastor has had quite a few midlife men approach him about going to seminary—not necessarily to become clergy, but because their hunger for theological knowledge and access to their own spiritualities is so great. He suggests that the questions that are driving the men seeking renewed spirituality include: "Who is God?" "How can I find the hope that I need?" and "How can I take the risks that will help me challenge and rebuild my faith in the midst of my distrust of institutional religion?"

One of the interview questions asked about primary images for God among the men in the congregation. For most, the primary image of God was still Father and this was a dearly held image. The majority of pastors suggested that, although the men were spiritually hungry, they weren't particularly looking for *new* forms of spirituality. One pastor in a working-class suburban church put it this way, "Men want to hear that there really is a God—that there really is hope and meaning in the midst of this craziness. The men often call me 'spiritual leader' or 'my rabbi.' They don't want to be told to change—just to be reassured." He went on to say that the men want "a God who is secure and trustworthy and has things under control." Another pastor said, "There is mostly a desire to stay with the

57

traditional images and a fear of the challenges and changes about who God is. There is some willingness to talk about these theological issues but there is mostly fear and resistance."

There are generational differences around these issues, and around most of the gender changes, according to most of the interviewees. One pastor suggested, "Just as with men's identity concerns, this is very generational. Some men are finding a great deal of comfort and invitation in new images of God. For the older men, they want to hold on to the omnipotent, in-control, duty-oriented Father God. For some of the younger ones they like the mix of images but probably wouldn't like these new images to become the majority." And some of the pastors felt that changing images of God was an off-limits topic. One clergyman said, "Images of God are not forthcoming. Men here are not spiritually vulnerable. 'Dear Heavenly Father' is how men open their public prayers for the most part, and that's not open to challenge."

Several of the pastors said that the anxieties about work and about the future were driving a renewed search for meaning and that part of that meaning search could be called a spiritual quest. Pastors said that the culture itself has created a context where a deeper search for spirituality is necessary and that men are beginning to claim this for themselves. For a number of the churches these spirituality groups and individual spiritual seekers were fairly new but were growing much more rapidly than they had expected. Most of the pastors agreed that there is a spiritual hunger but a great deal of uncertainty and caution about how to address it. One exception to this caution is where there are spirituality groups for men that have taken hold and set a tone for vulnerability and spiritual growth in the congregation. Another exception is where there are a number of socially marginalized folks in the congregation where it is made clear that traditional theology has not been nurturing. So in one congregation where there are a number of gay men the pastor said, "The men respond well to challenging traditional theology. Much of it has felt oppressive to their marginalized experience. Many of the men are spiritually hungry and eager to re-imagine their spiritualities."

The conversations about identity and spirituality raised, in many of the conversations, the phenomenon of Promise Keepers. There were diverse opinions about this group/movement although the vast majority of the pastors interviewed for this study were suspicious. Five pastors felt that Promise Keepers had something very significant and positive to offer to men. They affirmed that men needed to be with men so that they could look together at what these cultural changes mean for their lives. Four of the congregations had sent men to a Promise Keepers' stadium event, and one of the churches had an ongoing group of Promise Keepers. Five of the pastors said that there were some positive aspects to Promise Keepers: bringing men together, helping men look at issues, offering men avenues to self-esteem, encouraging men to be responsible to families and communities, and rekindling men's Christian beliefs and commitment to the church. However, they were also suspicious of the political agendas behind the movement and of the potential rigidity of the definitions for maleness. Several were concerned at the movement's antigay stance. Eight of the pastors interviewed were almost entirely skeptical of Promise Keepers. As one pastor said:

> The whole philosophy of Promise Keepers is an expression of the reassertion of patriarchy, which has gotten us into trouble in the past—it's unhealthy and unnatural. However, Promise Keepers assumes that patriarchy is natural but that we lost it and need to reestablish it for things to work again. The question for all of us who are committed to justice for women and men is, How do we do men's groups without reestablishing patriarchy? How do we assist men in their lives without falling into that? I need help and consultation with these issues.

This articulates well what the majority of those interviewed felt about Promise Keepers.

There was a somewhat different understanding of the Million Man March. The three men of color who were interviewed, two of whom had attended the march, found it to be very exciting and important for both symbolic and social action reasons. They felt that the call to responsibility was an important message for African American men to hear. They also felt that what was most important about the march (and this was different from Promise Keepers) was what was happening among the participants much more than what was being said from the podium. These clergy also felt that lasting and important social action was going to be coming from this gathering and that this could already be seen in many of the communities. Several of the white pastors concurred with this view of the Million Man March although a few equated the general tenor of the March with that of Promise Keepers. In these cases, the content of the call to old forms of male responsibility felt more powerful than the racial context differences in which they were offered.

The third concern raised by several of the interviewees had to do with the lack of male friendships. They found that the men in their congregations felt a real lack of male friendship but didn't know how to go about forming those friendships due to both time pressures and lack of opportunities to meet new people. One of the pastors with a large African American population said that the men in his congregation paid a lot of attention to friendships but they didn't have enough of them. He also felt that, although men gathered with other men, they really didn't open up about issues that were important to each of them personally. The lack of friendships, the desire for more male friends, and the lack of initiative in finding male friends were named as problems by several of the pastors.

As these clergymen attempted to identify the primary issues that were confronting men in their congregations, they realized that they were primarily looking at the twenty-five to sixty-five age group. As we attempted, then, to look at the men outside of that group, the interviewees were able to identify certain other issues facing both the older and younger men of the congregation.

The majority of those interviewed identified health concerns as primary for older men, both fears of the future as well as fears of reduced capacities in the present. These older men are concerned about health problems that may arise in the future (and resources to deal with those health needs) as well as with diminished capacities that they are now experiencing. Along with the health concerns, interviewees tended to agree that life review and meaning-making also gained in intensity as the men aged and that several of the clergymen encountered these needs in their hospital visitation work. They also encountered these meaning-making needs among men who had taken early retirement or who had recently moved into a life phase where more time was available to them. A third need involved the drive to be productive. Many of the men expressing this drive had experienced success in their careers but now wanted a chance to contribute to something that felt more spiritually important. This may well be related to the search for meaning described above. Several of the clergymen said that groups of older men had sprung up rather spontaneously in the churches for the purpose of taking care of various projects in the church and missional priorities designed by the church. These groups seemed to be very dedicated, fulfilling an important need for these men. In contrast to this perspective, a few of the pastors felt that older men were primarily concerned with enjoying their retirement rewards of time and money after a hard work life. This was especially true of fairly recent retirees.

Among the younger men, especially among the adolescents, several of the interviewees suggested that adolescent boys have a deep need to be heard, even when they have trouble articulating their concerns and questions. They urged that clergy pay careful attention to adolescent boys as they seek to define adult manhood for themselves. Several clergy, especially (but not only) the men of color, suggested that adolescent boys need mentors and men need to be mentors as part of their own search for meaning. The two mentoring programs that had been established between the men and boys in congregations tended to work very well for both groups.

There was an almost equal split among those interviewed on whether young men and boys related in new, gender-fair and respectful ways to young women and girls in the churches. The responses ranged to both extremes with only a few answers in the center. The comments ranged from, "A lot of young men in my sons' age ranges (sixteen to twenty-one) haven't changed at all. I see them treating women quite badly. There's a backlash operating that may make it worse than it was ten years ago," to "I am really pleased at the way I see youth relate to one another. There is much more respect between the girls and the boys and many more deep cross-gender friendships. The friendships are important. We didn't have as many of that kind of deep friendships when I was growing up." There seems to be a split among youth as there is among adult men in terms of their responses to gender challenges and changes. As one pastor said, "There is quite a split—a group of men who have learned how to be more sensitive, trying to learn the "new" rules, who believe that it is right for the women in our lives and that it is right for us as men, *and* there is a large group of the traditional, macho, even backlash men."

The last specific population we explored in these interviews was couples in premarital preparation. Again, there was a significant split in responses about the issues facing couples preparing for marriage. Five pastors indicated that the egalitarian issues seem to have been worked out and are not much of an issue in premarital work. Four respondents suggested a real concern about egalitarian roles saying that things didn't seem to have changed much in the past fifteen years. Another three thought that there were generally concerns and conflicts about dual career and child-rearing responsibilities and about domestic work sharing. One pastor framed the premarital challenge in this way, "Overwhelmingly, the premarital issues have to do with gender concerns of who is in charge? who is going to do what? whose career will shape our lives? The deeper we go into how things are going to be in the marriage, the more problems seem to emerge even though the couple often thought that they had things worked out. Usually they are both willing to struggle with the patriarchal issues although both are often surprised at how deep their differences may be." I think this is a helpful reminder for pastors to not make assumptions about what it means to be "egalitarian." The split in pastoral experience around the primary issues in premarital work suggests that there is a considerable range of opinion about appropriate gender roles and task responsibilities among women and men today despite twenty years and more of cultural shifts.

Responses to the Gender Revolution

One of the questions asked of each of the interviewees was whether or not the so-called "gender revolution" had reached the churches themselves and, if so, what impact that had on the lives of men. The most dominant response to this question (five interviewees) was that there was a significant and dramatic generational dividing line around how the "gender revolution" had affected male church members. Pastors felt that the older men in the church had not experienced significant changes in the way they lived in their families, at their work, or in their personal approaches to life. The younger men, they suggested, showed some signs of increased sensitivity, much more acceptance of new gender roles, and a somewhat enhanced openness to new definitions of maleness for themselves. They also indicated that even with this generational difference, it was still only a small percentage of the younger men who demonstrated significant gender shifts other than gender role changes.

The other significant response to this question (five interviewees) was the conviction that the main impact of the gender revolution was that more strong women had moved into positions of church leadership, which meant fewer men involved in the church. One pastor commented, "A number of men only like the administrative, not the programmatic, aspects of the church. So, women are doing it all—just like in the home—and the men are missing." Another interviewee worried, "I think we have to be careful not to abandon the men in the church as women get more empowered in leadership. We need to find better ways to engage men."

Other responses to this question included several statements to the effect that this is a transitional and confusing time in the church (and culture) for men. Most believed that men would find their way through this time of transition in a healthy fashion if they weren't forced to make premature choices. Some feared that events like Promise Keepers get in the way of this healthy transition for men. Finally, one pastor expressed the ambivalence that was present in several interviews when he said, "If we asked the congregation whether a gender revolution had taken place in this church, the women would say 'no' and the men would say 'yes' and they would both be right."

Responses to These Ministry Needs

Most of the pastors are aware that if they are to address the needs of men in their congregations, they are going to have to meet them where they are. Pastors who are effective have learned to pay attention to the casual conversations, to allow themselves time for "interruptions" in the office, and to investigate seemingly lighthearted comments about family or work.

Interviewees gave a variety of responses to the question about how they attempt to meet the care needs of men. The most common response was that the pastors try to listen carefully to men in whatever context the encounter occurs. A second common response was that they try to model healthy gender behaviors and to use a variety of opportunities to appropriately raise issues that might be of concern to men. For example, one pastor said that he and his wife attempt to model gender-fair behaviors and open conversations in front of their congregation. A third response was that they try to offer a great deal of reassurance and encouragement in these times of stress and transition. This includes an attempt to join men in their worries and struggles and to engage in helpful relationships. One pastor said, "I basically invite them to be vulnerable and in relationship with me and with others. Men don't make or have friends around here. They are isolated. I invite them into relationship and openness. It's hard. They rarely respond."

This poignant response points to another ministry focus that the pastors named. Many of those interviewed try to help men get into relationships with one another. Several of the pastors said that one of the most significant problems in the lives of these men is their lack of friends or even companions. The African American males were seen as being somewhat better at building and keeping friends, as were the gay men; but all of the pastors said that the men in their congregations did not have adequate friendships. One major attempt at addressing this need has been the building of small groups for men in many of these churches.

Men's Groups in the Church

Almost half (nine) of the pastors interviewed did not have groups for men operating in their churches. However, eleven pastors had some sort of groups for men in the church. Those groups varied in type, attendance, and style; but each of them offered an opportunity for men to get together. As several of the pastors pointed out, different men feel comfortable and safe with different kinds of groups. Some are most comfortable with task groups where the conversations are oriented around the work. Others prefer programs that allow them to take in information without feeling pressured to actively share themselves with the other participants. Other men prefer support-oriented groups, and others are drawn toward study groups. No one type of group will work to attract all men to explore their lives in this time of change.

In looking at the interview responses, there appear to be three main types of groups. The first is the long-term group that meets monthly for breakfast or to accomplish tasks or for some sort of program. This group builds bonds of affection and camaraderie among its members, but does not appear to facilitate significant sharing or spiritual growth. The second type of group seems to be the support or growth group where men have contracted particularly to meet together and be open/vulnerable around their own life struggles. These groups tend to become very close and to facilitate relationships that often stretch meaningfully beyond the parameters of the group structure. The members of this type of group (which often operates around Bible or book study) may also serve as role models to other males in the congregation around taking risks in building relationships and sharing the self. The third type of group, that seems fairly new but popular in churches, is the support/employment networking group. Several churches had groups of this sort that had high attendance and interest. In this kind of group the members share some of their experiences of employment stress, and they work to resource each other with employment possibilities and options. Many also used these groups to discuss theological issues of vocation and various other dimensions of spirituality. Given the primary pastoral concerns in men's lives at this time, it is not surprising to hear one pastor say:

> We've just put out a cafeteria choice of groups for men in order to see what men might want in this church—support groups, illness support groups, a group about aging issues, study groups, and so on. The one group that is flooded is the Work in Transition Group. There is lots of networking and support for men who are temporarily out of work. There's a real hunger for spirituality in all of this. That's the good news.

Small groups in the church seem to meet a number of the needs that men have for support, reality testing, friendship, and spiritual growth. The challenge, of course, is finding ways to help fit group time into already overwhelmed and stress-filled schedules.

CLERGYMEN AND GENDER ISSUES

It was interesting, in the process of conducting these interviews, to see the connections between clergymen's own experiences and the ministries in which they were engaged. There were some rather striking similarities among the majority of the men interviewed. The similarity that was most interesting was how many of these men were raised with atypical gender self-understandings. Three-quarters of the men interviewed said that they grew up not fitting in with typical male stereotypes. They either told stories of growing up in families where they were expected to take on typically female roles or tasks, or they talked about self-understandings in the contexts of school sports or peer relationships where they did not feel as "masculine" as they were expected to. These experiences tended to be truer of the younger clergymen. The three clergymen who were over sixty said that they were raised with rather traditional gender roles but learned how to shift their gender expectations as adults, usually in relationship to spouses.

The men who talked about their sense of being "high on the feminine scale" made connections between that sense of self and their ready connections with justice issues for women and the feminist movement. Because of these connections, the majority of these interviewees were well into "men's issues" as they worked to integrate their "non-male" identities with "new male" identities. Each went about this in his own way, but it made the majority of these clergymen interested in working with men to help them break through unhealthy gender training toward more liberating identities.

These interviews weren't extensive enough to be able to make any more precise correlations between the clergymen's theology or developmental histories, but it was clear that the life experience of the clergyman was influential in his ministry interests and focus. Almost every interviewee at some point in the interview made a connection between his life stage or current life experience and the impressions he had about the needs of the men in his congregation. At the very least, his interests tended to be directed toward the age group he himself occupied. Certainly, his own training, value system, and loyalties influenced what he looked for as healthy and progressive.

IMPLICATIONS FOR MINISTRY

The implications of these connections between clergy experiences and lifestyles with ministry foci are twofold. First, and maybe most obviously, how seminaries and field experiences train clergy will deeply influence the kinds of ministries in which clergy will engage. This means that clergy who are intentionally exposed to liberating and just perspectives about gender (as well as about race, class, sexual orientation, and so on) will be more likely to guide congregational study in these areas. Seminaries need to train students to be able to be in dialogue with the major cultural questions that face today's women and men. Without having the tools to engage in these dialogues, clergy will most likely be unable or uninterested in helping their congregations move forward in these important matters.

The second implication is that since clergy tend to focus on ministry issues that mirror their own life experiences, it is important to help train them to pay careful and respectful attention to difference and to discount such a complete reliance on their own experience for leadership guidance. We do not help students when we teach them to trust their own experience as primary. In a culture that is frightened of diversity, clergy cannot help congregations to welcome that diversity, nor can they minister fully to diverse perspectives and experiences, unless they are educated beyond their own experience. They especially need to be trained to doubt their experience as guiding when it comes out of a culturally privileged standpoint. This means that one of the most important training areas for clergy and caregivers is in the justice issues and perspectives of those who are culturally marginalized by virtue of race, class, gender, sexual orientation, lack of able-bodiedness, and age.

There are other issues that might be teased out from these interviews, but a larger sample would be needed in order to test the connections.

Looking into the Future

There were two other questions in this interview that have implications for future ministries to men. The first question was a fantasy challenge asking what the pastor would do if he had unlimited financial resources (and a magic wand) but had to use those resources for one program in ministry to men. The responses to this question were often imaginative and touched at the heart of men's pastoral needs.

The vast majority of the responses had something to do with creating an environment where men could be with and talk with each other. In these proposals several clergy suggested rather specific topics: values, sexuality and masculinity, friendship, family values, and relationships with women. Some suggested retreat centers and various kinds of programs for men. Two of the men who suggested time for men to be with and talk with each other also suggested that they would use the money to pay off all the mortgages in order to relieve some of the stresses that the men experience. Others suggested training small group leaders and offering a variety of groups for all men in the church depending on their preferred modes of connecting with other men. In some of these proposals the interviewees suggested the need to teach men how to do self-reflection and sharing with one another—that these required a set of skills that couldn't be assumed. One man also suggested finding ways to market these groups and men's involvement possibilities in the church in ways that fit our media mind-sets. His only concern was that the church would get too big! Three clergymen suggested building projects—one a retreat center on the church grounds (built by the men and women of the church); another a communal center where men could find support and a safe haven (from homelessness, isolation, addictions, and so forth); and a third a gymnasium for men to be better in touch with their bodies and physical self-care. Another clergyman proposed a program of commuting buddies to counteract the loneliness and isolation of the east coast daily commute to work. Another interviewee proposed a mentoring system between the men in the congregation and the boys, with appropriate training and support for each group.

The enthusiasm, creativity, and commitment behind the programs suggested in this fantasy process encouraged both the pastors and me that there are ministry visions that are possible even without unlimited funds and magic wands. The need is for collaboration, cooperation, and commitment among pastors and congregations during this time of enormous stress and enormous possibility in the lives of men.

The other question asked of these interviewees was what they needed in order to carry out these ministries that they imagined. The responses focused primarily on their need for consultation with other clergy interested in men's ministries and on their desire for the seminaries to do a better job in training around gender issues and justice concerns. There was a general sense that these clergymen were not adequately exposed to the importance of gender specific groups nor were they exposed to the important role that culture, particularly gender training, plays in the lives of women and men. They also wanted better access to methods of cultural analysis around issues of economics, employment, and other social trends.

It is an important time for churches to provide leadership in helping women and men to continue to move through the radical cultural changes around us. We seem to be at a crossroads time in terms of women's rights and men's and women's partnerships—we will either move forward in justice-seeking ways or we will retrench in further actions of backlash and of narrowed options. The church needs to take a stand in the midst of these choices and facilitate the wholeness of individuals, families, and institutions. How we will go about this must become a primary and immediate agenda for our churches and seminaries.

CHAPTER THREE

HARD WORK, HARD LOVIN', HARD TIMES, HARDLY WORTH IT: CARE OF WORKING-CLASS MEN

Judith L. Orr

Tony saw Father Marcus across the parking lot and waved halfheartedly. Father Marcus walked toward him. In the midst of talking about the good haul on his latest fishing trip, Tony sighed, "Wish I was still out there—just me and the fish. They don't ask nothin' of me. Nothin' like the ol' lady. She's after me to go to night school to better myself. Sure, the week sometimes lasts longer than the paycheck, especially with two kids now. And the boss is a beast. But finally I told her, it won't get any better than this!"

Father Marcus knows that the expectation to move up the socioeconomic ladder is one that Tony's wife comes by honestly, since it is pervasive in American culture. She knows Tony works hard in the hospital maintenance department; but when she goes to her job as a typist at the local car dealer, she imagines other possibilities for Tony at which he might have more freedom on the job, make a little more money, and not have to do such dirty, back-breaking work. Tony sees it as one more person telling him he's not good enough, he's not man enough.

The church extends care to Tony and his family in a neighborhood and a world that is foreign to many seminary-educated, middle-class clergy. Even the pastor whose family of origin was working class may feel like an outsider. As Paul, who grew up working class and is now the pastor of a working-class congregation in small-town mid-America, said recently, "One guy asks me nearly every week when he shakes my hand after church and feels my callouses getting smoother, when I'm gonna get a *real* job again. I tell him it could be next week."[1]

CLASS: DEFINITIONS AND ASSUMPTIONS

There is no consensus among sociologists on the definition of class. As noted by Marie Haug,

> [There are] disagreements over whether class differentiation is a discrete or continuous variable, whether it takes different forms in large cities as against small towns, and whether it is a subjective phenomenon to be scaled by self-placement or an objective one to be scored by one or more independent indicators.[2]

The concept of socioeconomic class assumes a hierarchy. Karl Marx suggested that class is determined by economics—by relationships of ownership versus nonownership to the means of production by the bourgeoisie and proletariat respectively. Then a middle class of industrial managers arose. Still later Max Weber recognized that the increasingly complex nature of this class hierarchy included the factor of prestige as well as the economics of occupational income and the power of property ownership. Further, education and the consumption of goods and services have played a part in the determination of different classes and the divergent values held by each. The U.S. Census has similarly used occupation, income, and education in its determinations of class.[3] More recently, sociologists in the 1960s identified differential privilege[4] and the exercise of authority as additional factors in class relations.[5]

Father Marcus's encounter with Tony encourages us to understand socioeconomic class not positionally in discrete categories of occupation, income, or education, but in terms of social relations of control over work, over resources, over decision making.[6] A class is not a slot but a process of relations both structurally and historically, which includes the unequal distribution of rights, privileges, duties, and obligations in several arenas of life. Those in the working class take orders frequently and give orders rarely. They expect to give deference rather than receive it. Yet under patriarchy men expect to give orders and receive deference. Thus, working-class men live in the intersection of conflictual relations of economic production, reproduction, and consumption, which constitutes a nexus of power relations. Class is not merely a matter of having or not having power. It is an antagonistic field of struggle.

If we consider the political and economic changes in the last two decades that have caused decreasing numbers of industrial jobs as well as increasing numbers of clerical, technical, and service positions, as much as 59 percent of the American capitalist workforce could be considered working class.[7] In much the same way that the mass production of heavy industry prompted a de-skilling, fragmentation, and routinization of work, so now much technical and service work is becoming similarly structured. Job security and opportunities for advancement are limited, such that the ordinary American is struggling mightily.

However, the American myth of socioeconomic mobility suggests that those who are brightest and work hardest can move out of the class of their origins, as Tony's wife hopes.[8] For working-class men, the myth has often taken the form of getting promoted to supervisor, becoming a small businessman, or moving into a white-collar job, usually through additional education.[9] Given the American ideology of equality, or at least of equal opportunity, the myth suggests that class differences must, therefore, be due to individual differences in intelligence, talent, creativity, usefulness, or morality. Of course, the playing field is not level since some are more handicapped by circumstance than others, so many working-class folks feel like failures. The myth functions to justify and maintain inequalities of income, power, and self-esteem,[10] and class and status inheritance in the U.S. remain fairly stable.[11]

At least since the time of the Protestant Reformation when Luther and especially Calvin made theological connections between Christianity and capitalism, economic and social achievement have also been understood as moral issues. As suggested by Max Weber, the convergence of rationality, hard work, success, and morality on the basis of a calling, and the avoidance of emotionality, laziness, failure, and the other side of the tracks are characteristic of the capitalist system. These values are internalized by individuals who benefit from the system and resisted by many who are marginalized by it.

By individualizing failure to achieve upward mobility, the working-class man learns to choose more modest goals. He also believes he could and should have set them higher, so the discrepancy between what his aspirations are and what they should have been perpetuates a cycle of self-blame.[12] He may also cope with the myth

72

by blaming outside forces or groups (e.g., women or other racial/ethnic groups) and by deflating the achievements of others so as to inflate his own.[13] Tony's resistance to his wife's push for mobility is his own affirmation of being good enough despite what anyone thinks.

Tony's wife seeks what many of "the 59 percent" seek—to be members of the middle class, not because of the education or jobs they could have (they have no college degree and they are not managers and professionals), but because of the leisure they could buy and the neighborhood they could live in. This myth of upward mobility disguises their situation somewhat, because it proposes that "the system that screws 'em can save 'em."[14] Then the assaults on their dignity are harder to confront.

The working class is diverse. There is a range of economic comfort among working-class folk. Inequalities are related to variables of self-employment, level of skill, employment sector, sex, and race. The top segments may earn three or four times more than the most disprivileged full-time workers.[15] This working-class diversity is perhaps most helpfully described in Tex Sample's *Blue-Collar Ministry*, which distinguishes four working-class lifestyles.[16]

Winners are skilled craftsmen (carpenters, bricklayers, electricians) who have their own tools, have a good deal of control over their own work, and have often achieved a measure of financial success. *Respectables* are generally members of the lower middle class who seek self-respect through discipline and conformity to moral standards, such that they have a decent job, provide for their dependents, and can be trusted to work cooperatively. *Survivors* are semiskilled workers in dull and boring jobs and ongoing financial struggle, whose lives are centered away from the factory and whose hope lies in their children. *Hard-Living folks* are unskilled workers who don't strive for success, are underemployed or cyclically unemployed, and often are tough, drink too much, have unstable marriages and a degree of rootlessness. Lynne Segal calls them "fighters without a uniform."[17]

This diversity could explain many of the conflicting stereotypes of the working class, for example being both conformist[18] and impulsive.[19] Television has offered a fairly consistent stereotype, however, in Archie Bunker and Al Bundy. The working-class man is there portrayed as limited in perspective and ability to understand the world, limited in taste and refinement, lacking in discipline, and hostile to help. He is characterized as a drinker, overweight, hedonistic, licentious, violent, loud, boyish, inarticulate, boring, and stupid. His views are seen as parochial, authoritarian, and bigoted. According to Barbara Ehrenreich, in the 1970s "the working class became, for many middle-class liberals, a psychic dumping ground for such unstylish sentiments as racism, male chauvinism, and crude materialism."[20] There has not been a significant psychic cleanup since then.

GENDER: DEFINITIONS AND ASSUMPTIONS

In addition to multiple manifestations of working-class life, there are also multiple masculinities. A practice-based theory of power and gender relations helps us focus on what men do by way of constituting the social relations in which they live and work.[21]

In practice-based theory the structure of gender relations is seen as historically composed. Practices create a structure that constrains further practice, although practices may also resist those constraints. Practice-based theory posits that the construction of masculinity is both personal and social, requiring inventive action and reflexive knowledge at the same time that social rules, resources, and politics in any practice are engaged. It avoids the theoretical and practical limitations of voluntarism/pluralism and of determinism.

Thus, both class and gender are historically constructed relations among boss, worker, men, and women. They are grounded in material life of biology, family, work, and the structure of resources differentially available.[22] These are consensual and conflictual processes that both build and challenge social relations. Gender and class identities are therefore shifting realities involving inclusion and exclusion, affirmation and negation within histories, cultures, language, and community.[23]

The construction of gender, and of masculinity in particular, occurs through practices that shape three different but interrelated structures of relationship between men and women through history: the structure of labor, the structure of power, and the structure of desire. Each of these structures includes practices within both the family and the workplace.

The gendered structure of labor refers to the division of labor, the organization and practices of public/private and paid/unpaid work, of men's and women's jobs, of discriminatory training and promotion, of unequal wages, and of differential accumulation of resources. The structure of labor also influences control of the family budget and sharing of housework.

The gendered structure of power refers to a hierarchy of authority, control, and/or coercion. Power may be an imbalance of advantage or an inequality of resources. Social power is composed of force and of the ability to define a situation, to set the terms of understanding and discussion, to formulate ideas, and to assert morality. Within the family it includes control over decisions about the children's school or apprenticeship as well as personal independence from put-downs and violence. In the workplace it includes freedom from arbitrary authority, such as rough treatment by bosses as well as being heard by unions.

The main axis of power within culture aligns authority with masculinity. A second axis of power denies authority to *some* men. Hence, gender as well as race and class are formative constructions of a hierarchy among men resulting in hegemonic masculinity (white, heterosexual, professional class), marginalized/traditional masculinities (winner and respectable working class), and subordinated masculinities (poor and near-poor white men, racial minorities, and gay men).[24]

Finally, the gendered structure of desire refers to desirability of an other, to the structure of homosexual/heterosexual relations, to the antagonism of gender, to trust/distrust and solidarity/jealousy in relationships, and to the emotional relationship of child rearing. Given the emotional and erotic dimension to all social relations, constraints that prohibit actions have the intent to destroy those relations. The structure of desire within the family includes access to adequate contraception, the right to abortion, control of one's own sexuality, and the right to initiate and leave relationships. The structure of desire within the workplace is evident in freedom from sexual harassment and differential benefits to employees in differing family relationships.[25]

Given the practice-based construction of masculinity, there is no natural or necessary connection between masculinity and male bodies. Freud himself believed that masculinity is not best understood as the polar opposite to femininity.[26] Nor is the body a biological given, as Foucault has suggested, but the site of resistance and power over others, a material process occurring through everyday life of work, rest, diet, dress, sexual mores, and environmental stressors.[27]

The portrayal in popular culture of the working-class man as masculine and hard has been especially true since the 1930s' growth of trade unions.[28] The plant is seen as the last bastion of the male world with its hard/tough work, dirt, physical harshness, rough behavior, swearing, banter, male bonding, more-or-less serious fighting, release of anger and frustration, and rebellion against established authority.[29] This description is not unlike cultural masculinity expected in war and in sport: hard bodies, hard talk, hard bosses, hard work. Many of these men also drink hard and party hard, especially when younger. All see their bodies as their main source of power and esteem.

According to Lynne Segal, "working-class images of masculinity in terms of physical hardness [are] bound up with the requirements of manual labor and earning a wage."[30] Hardness is not only a way of acting but also a way of being, signifying a tough self-control in which working-class men are less focused on interiority (including fear, vulnerability, pain) and more focused on the concrete situation. It is true of celluloid working-class heroes such as those in *The Deer Hunter* and *Rambo*. The hard, cool pose of some working-class black men is an aggressive assertion of masculinity, a creative survival technique resisting domination in a hostile environment.[31] Such hardness also confers power on men by effectively withholding information about the self.[32] The kind of side-by-side male bonding and solidarity in the shop, the military, and in sports is different than face-to-face intimacy. It is also different from the competitive individualism of the middle class.[33]

Working-class kids who cannot afford to go to college and who resist the assembly line often go into the military[34] or aim for professional sports. "Put on a uniform and clothes don't matter," suggests Michael Messner.[35] All three settings—the shop, the military, and the world of team sports—have been homogender worlds of cultural masculinity, with much resistance to changing that fact. All three entail "practices through which men's separation from and power over women is embodied and naturalized at the same time that hegemonic masculinity is clearly differentiated from marginalized and subordinated masculinities."[36] In each of these settings working-class boys become men through the interaction of internal contexts such as psychological ambivalences (physical strength of manhood versus being judged a failure) and external contexts such as social, historical, and institutional realities of dominance and danger.

CULTURAL CONTEXT AND CARE: DEFINITIONS AND ASSUMPTIONS

Care of the working-class man in the 1990s is occurring in a time of rapid change. These changes are occurring on three fronts. First, economic changes have been remarkably swift. The shift from a blue-collar industrial economy to a service and information/technological economy over the last twenty years will eventually dislocate 15 to 45 million workers in urban America.[37] This makes workers more vulnerable due to the mobility of corporations (from core city to suburb as well as around the globe), the weakening of trade unions, the demeaning division of tasks with new technology, a decline in income and home ownership, and an increase in family poverty. Rural America is experiencing a decrease in the number of family farms from 600,000 in the mid-1950s to 100,000 in the mid-1990s,[38] the increased use of rural land for prisons and dangerous waste,[39] and a higher proportion of poverty than urban America.[40]

Second, cultural, political, and economic changes in sex equity have been remarkably swift and so has the backlash or resistance to them. There are fewer full-time jobs for white men and more part-time jobs for women and racial/ethnic minorities. Divorces are increasing, the modern family structure (breadwinning father and child-rearing mother) is declining, and the number of matri-focal or fatherless homes with men set adrift is on the rise.[41] There is also increased uncertainty about norms and responsibilities for these diverse families (for example sexual liberation, birth control, no-fault divorce, joint custody, shared parenting). Many men experience this as loss of authority within the family and being less of a man.

Third, changes in racial equality and the attendant backlash are also a reality of the last 30 years. Lillian Rubin observes that the structural basis for ethnicity has decreased (for example, persons of an ethnic group less frequently live in the same neighborhood, work in the same occupations, belong to the same social groups, and use the same manners and mores), but the psychological and political foundations of ethnicity have increased (cultural identity and affirmative action).[42] Unlike ethnicity, race is a socially and historically constructed ideology, with strong economic roots shaping it in America. Since the freeing of 4 million slaves after the Civil War, working-class whites have perceived competition for scarce resources and feared losing their jobs to blacks.[43] The fear behind racist backlash still functions today and weakens class consciousness and class solidarity.

Pastoral care of working-class men in this cultural context has not been a particular focus of study. Secular counseling literature suggests distinctive purposes and techniques in counseling with persons of other cultures[44] and with persons of poorer classes in American culture.[45] But cross-cultural pastoral counseling literature is still limited.[46] Most pastors of working-class men indicate that they do not often provide counseling, but they do have a number of occasions to see that the church extends care. Working-class men seek help through formal channels only when informal resources of family and friends are not available.[47] Like men of the middle class, the working-class man requesting formal assistance and counsel seeks someone trustworthy and willing to listen, expects to talk about personal issues, and wants the American dream of a decent job, suitable housing, and respect.[48]

Since the pioneering empirical study of A. B. Hollingshead and F. C. Redlich in 1958, the discriminatory psychiatric services received by persons of differing socioeconomic classes have been known and well documented.[49] According to Eric Bromley there is overwhelming evidence (in both simulation studies and studies of actual practices) that the working class is offered psychotherapy less often. There is little evidence, especially since the 1970s, that this is because the working class does not want it. There is equivocal evidence that they do not benefit from it.[50]

The working-class man seeks a place to belong, a place that provides collective expression and ritual resolution to his pain, his conflicts, and his dreams. Counseling that focuses on the individual in search of identity is a paradigm of limited use for care of working-class men. As noted by Larry Graham, what is needed is a paradigm shift from relational humanness to relational justice. What is needed is a paradigm that will create structures for accessible and diverse services, economic viability, and accountability.[51] What is needed is a focus on communal care that undercuts assumptions of individualism and the self-sufficiency of one's power and values.[52] What is needed is a politics of care such that care is "the activity of any person or community that supports the full and powerful participation in communities and societies of those who are suffering, excluded, objectified, and oppressed."[53] What is needed is care for those who may resist the very care they seek.

ISSUES WITH WHICH WORKING-CLASS MEN STRUGGLE

The economic, political, and cultural changes in the last two or three decades have helped to give shape to the issues with which working-class men struggle. These are usually presented as struggles with the pain of survival and making a living, with conflict in marriage, and with issues related to one's mortality and legacy.[54] The structures and practices of labor, power, and desire that construct masculinity in both the family and the workplace are claimed, resisted, and transformed as men experience the care of the church around these issues.

Sam is a computer terminal operator at the utility company, where he endures close monitoring, rotating shifts, and tedium. He doesn't make a lot of money, but what is most bothersome are the daily denials of his self-worth, intelligence, creativity, and cooperation.[55] Sam's wife told Pastor Henry she's worried about his irritability and his drinking.

Pastor Henry has heard it before and responded by asking two retired men, one a former utility worker and the other a five-year veteran in Alcoholics Anonymous, if they would be willing to be trained to co-lead an educational group called "Work, Stress, and Life." They consented. Only two men came to the group at first, including Sam, but it eventually grew to six men from various working-class jobs.

According to Michael Lerner, such groups among the working class are training groups rather than therapy groups.[56] The agenda is to identify stressors, learn relaxation techniques, learn communication skills, discuss inequalities of power, imagine redesigning one's work world, and making family connections to one's work. Pastor Henry found that men in the group increased in energy, acknowledged anger and fear more easily, decreased alcohol use, experienced increased social support and compassion, and took more appropriate responsibility. The men came to understand that stress itself did not determine their coping ability as much as economic, emotional, and marital resources to confront stress and manage functioning.[57]

Several men in the group who were heavy drinkers began to face the trouble it was causing them and their families. Some cut back with the support of the group, and one began attending AA. Drinking is especially common among hard-living men, but is not uncommon among others as well. As Ben Hamper points out, however, the six-pack of beer is merely the working-class version of the middle-class multiple martini lunch.[58] Alasuutari contends that drinking among working-class men reflects the tension between individual desires and societal constraint, such as those imposed by one's wife or boss. Drinking is a symbol and realization of personal freedom—a means of celebration. It also numbs the pain of not feeling man enough.[59]

In another congregation is Tom, a man who has just recently been laid off from the local mower factory in a county-seat town. He has been notified that the company is moving to Mexico within a year and gradual layoffs will be made until that time. He feels fearful and vulnerable, wondering how he will get by with all the payments he needs to make. His wife's job won't cover all the expenses, and he doesn't know yet how he will survive. He is also angry because he feels manipulated by a faceless corporation that cares about profit but not his loyalty.

Because work *is* the measure of the man in American culture, the economic crises of unemployment and underemployment shake the foundations of Tom's working-class masculine identity and self-worth. He never made a lot of money, but he provided the basics for his family and that accomplishment has now been stripped from him. The value of work in terms of pay and security is evaporating, and pain and shame are beginning to take its place.

Tom's shame prompts withdrawal interspersed with outbursts of temper, a common response to deal with the manifold grief and preoccupation with his problems. While he has spent more time at home while cyclically unemployed, he has not become much more involved in child rearing or housework, because of the increased stress he also experiences.[60] Interestingly, some who experience layoffs periodically come to anticipate them and may actually welcome the time off to rest, spend time with the family, pursue other interests, escape from a bad work situation, or investigate other work.[61] But this is a first for Tom. He doesn't yet know that he will survive it.

Depression, feelings of failure, and thoughts of suicide are not unheard of in the midst of job loss, especially if there is a sense that one is at fault and is powerless to do anything. Depression is the primary presenting problem in rural mental health centers, such that now there is proportionately more depression in rural areas than urban areas.[62] Tom's beliefs about the rewards of hard work are being challenged and his sense of vulnerability is increased. Tom's family has even begun to re-label essentials (for example eyeglasses, shoes, prescriptions, sleep) as nonessentials in order to protect his and the family's self-image.[63] His fear and anger struggle for constructive expression but are blocked in depression for a time. So far Tom and his family have been able to survive without asking for financial or other material assistance from anyone except family. To be on the public dole would be a *real* source of shame for Tom, since he has prided himself on his self-sufficiency. He remembers the time his brother was humiliated when a member of the Ministerial Alliance dropped by with a Thanksgiving basket when he was out of work. He slammed the door in his face and told him he never wanted anything to do with the church again. The minister was oblivious to the importance of giving control and decision making to those enduring hardship to say what they want and need.

Pastor Lillian has visited Tom and his family in their home a number of times since the layoffs. She has suggested Tom go to the mental health center to inquire about getting some antidepressants. But she also encourages him to work with her and the Evangelism Committee to begin planning a seminar on unemployment to be cosponsored by two other churches, the Chamber of Commerce, and the school where the seminar will be held. Tom has not agreed to attend a meeting at the church yet. But he has shared some ideas for workshops (Family Counseling on Finances, Psychological Effects of Losing a Job, Children and Teen's Responsibilities, How to Pray, Services of the State Department of Human Resources, and Employer Booths). Pastor Lillian also hopes he'll meet with Ted Spratch, who chairs the Evangelism Committee and received retraining after being laid off from his job two years ago.

Working-class men not only struggle with the issues of making a living and survival, but also with marriage and divorce. David Halle discovered in his interviews of chemical plant workers in New Jersey that 35 percent were glad to be married, 25 percent have mixed feelings, and 40 percent are unhappily married.[64]

Level of marital satisfaction is somewhat related to life-cycle stage among working-class men. Young couples with preschoolers often experience the greatest stress with fewest resources, because expenses are high, the husband's wage is lower at the beginning of his work life, the wife may not work for pay, and there is little time for leisure.[65] As the children begin to progress through school, marital stress may have to do with decision making about the children and frustrations with the slow progress toward the American dream. When the children have left home, the working-class marriage is generally at its most satisfying since the wage is usually higher than earlier and there is more freedom to travel. Companionate marriages are not uncommon in this latter stage.

According to Halle, the most frequent conflicts in working-class marriages are related to the wife's complaints in three areas. First is the lack of leisure time her husband spends with her; he spends it instead with friends or working overtime. This is true in spite of the fact that working-class men do more housework than middle-class men and more than working-class men of the previous generation.[66] Second is his low social status and education. Third is his drinking, although alcoholism is no more frequent among the working class than the middle class.[67]

Why do men stay in troubled marriages? Many report fear of change and fear of independence—making it alone both psychologically and economically. Many believe that their wives rescued them from the wild life and that the responsibility of marriage has brought needed discipline and order to their lives. But responsibility also constrains.

Tony, whom we met at the beginning of this chapter, was struggling with his wife Karen's complaints about his social status and the nature of his work. Father Marcus listened carefully to the way in which Tony used his authority in the family to terminate the discussion with Karen—"it won't get any better than this"—case closed.

Father Marcus wanted to reopen the "case" to hear more of the story. His experience was that usually husbands did not call for marriage counseling although they might call for help coping with divorce. Two months later Tony called saying Karen was talking about leaving him. Father Marcus offered to meet with them or give them a referral to the mental health center. Karen agreed to come with Tony to see Father Marcus.

Together they learned some new behaviors in communication and conflict resolution. They also had to deal with the guilt and anger related to Karen's recent brief affair with a white-collar coworker and Tony's having hit her.[68] Father Marcus was clear with both of them that continued infidelity and continued violence would destroy what they were trying to rebuild. Tony and Karen had a number of stops and starts. Along the way they faced the unreality of some of their earliest dreams and began to reconstruct new ones.

Father Marcus knew that working-class men are not more violent in their marriages than middle-class men, but that they are more often arrested and punished.[69] Perhaps because of this, Father Marcus wanted Tony to attend a men's anger group. He explained that the group took a no-nonsense teaching approach to the prevention and healing of violence and blame. It assumed no person deserved to be hit and that persons who solve problems through hitting could learn new techniques to monitor their own anger state, develop role-taking abilities (to see himself as his victim sees him and to imagine how the victim feels), and develop new behaviors.[70] The goal of such work was to discover respect and fairness in relationships of mutual benefit and obligation. Tony completed the group work, and he and Karen are still together for now. They experience the church's ongoing care primarily through relationships with other couples on the church bowling league.

The third issue with which working-class men struggle is the issue of their legacy in relationship to their own mortality—what they leave behind after they're gone. For many this is through one's children. The capitalist class leaves its children property (the firm and securities), the petit bourgeois class leaves its children property (the business or land), and the manager and salaried professional class leaves its children education and property. Children of the working class, however, inherit a legacy of hard work and discipline, a way of life rather than things.[71] Working-class men who hate welfare hate admitting that hard work and discipline are not enough. Those who are open to welfare have accepted that making it requires more than hard work, and various skills of survival are what they leave those who come after.

In earlier times this legacy of hard work and discipline was lived out through participation in brotherhoods and trade unions, which facilitated the training of apprentices as craftsmen and tradesmen of the future.[72] The desire of workers to unionize and strike for better working conditions was not only to benefit current workers, but also to restructure work for workers of the future, including one's children and those in one's neighborhood and ethnic group.

For others one's legacy is through patriotism—the willingness to fight, suffer, and die for one's country. Larry is a Vietnam veteran who is currently a bricklayer. He is still married to his high school sweetheart. Larry's father died while Larry was temporarily missing in action overseas, and he has only heard about the funeral from his wife and son. Larry's son Butch is a police officer, his daughter a beautician.

Larry has spent a number of years trying to make peace with his experience of the war and the devastating feeling that coming home was like a "wound that won't stop hemorrhaging."[73] Most helpful were the conversations that began at the V.A. hospital some years

84

ago to talk with others who had undergone the same experience. Some of his story, however, also began to receive a hearing about six months ago in the weekly Bible study, so that Larry began to try to put his war experience together with his faith. Rev. Waters has encouraged him to give a testimony, telling his story during worship. He's seriously considering it.

Legacy implies a loyalty to the future and a loyalty to the community. People need to belong or they blame themselves and others for their plight.[74] Communities based on ethnic bonds no longer exist in the way they did in old urban neighborhoods. Rural communities are undergoing a population loss as many of the young people leave those communities and leave the rural values behind, too. Then different folks move in with whom there is less interaction and seemingly less in common. According to Janet Fitchen, "What has broken down is community . . . no sense of belonging or oneness . . . a community to give the support—and criticism—that young people need."[75] Frank, the pastor of a small urban working-class congregation, has said that members of this younger generation are more focused on themselves than the previous one. They are worried about their own houses but not the neighborhood. The sense of community is gone. The challenge of the church is to help rebuild community on a *new* basis.

NEIGHBOR CARE WITH WORKING-CLASS MEN

Most working-class men see the church as a social group with resources to deal with a number of the transitions and crises of living.[76] They regularly experience care in the church at the communal gatherings of weddings and funerals, as well as leisure gatherings (bingo, fish fry, ice-cream social). They also increasingly are looking to the church for moral guidance for themselves and for teaching their children right from wrong. Bible study and preaching are important for these reasons.

Good neighbor care happens by "being there" (for example, visiting the sick, attending the tractor pull), by remembering anniversaries of births-marriages-deaths, by not judging him when he's out of work or going through a divorce, by encouraging the telling of his story, and by recognizing the many contributions he makes, since the culture recognizes him for very little. Working-class care happens in tangible ways—mentioning a job opening or offering a job to the unemployed, painting an elderly man's house, taking a man to work whose car got totalled. It is in these circumstances that working-class men come to know the care and direction of the church and God's providential care and direction in their lives.

There are occasions when social ministry is appropriate for extending care to working-class men. While such ministry is congregation based—ideally cosponsored by several congregations—issues are viewed through the prism of the community with needs-assessment and coordinating resources done by the churches.[77] Layoffs and plant closings affect whole communities. The countywide Unemployment Seminar coordinated by Pastor Lillian took an educational approach, offering such things as classes, workshops, a video library, and a technical competency lab. Another example is the support and advocacy group brought together by the Reverend Murray Schmechel in 1985 when twenty-five to thirty bankrupt farm families in Nebraska came together not for therapy but to make ties of hay-baling twine to which they attached an information sheet about the farm crisis to be sent to urban churches and to Congress. As they worked together, the families shared their experiences with one another.[78]

Political advocacy is also an important dimension of care as it creates new opportunities and rights some wrongs. Among the working class, political involvement usually means believing something is wrong in a moral sense.[79] While support groups are helpful to some, groups of advocacy or retraining were most sought during the 1980s farm crisis in Minnesota.[80] Michael Lerner suggests working for legislation that would prevent plant closures without fair reimbursement to the community.[81] One model for political advocacy is building bridges between labor unions and neighborhood organizations around shared agenda.[82]

Other forms of care for the working-class man happen in self-help groups. The model of twelve-step programs as a type of folk healing is congruent with working-class preferences for receiving help. Peer listening programs have been helpful during the Heartland rural crisis.[83] Working-class men do not easily trust telling their stories to outsiders or experts, but will do so among those with shared experience. The model of occupational stress groups suggested by Michael Lerner, mentioned above in the case of Sam and Pastor Henry, is such an example. Important here is the communal work of legitimizing their own stories told in their own words, recovering lost stories suppressed by dominant stories (myths), and making space for new stories. In the congregation this happens when families feel connected through the church's stories of resistance and hope and personal testimonials of victory over hardship.[84]

In addition to these communal or group models of care, there are also occasions for family and couple counseling. Psychoeducational family therapy is most helpful when family problems have a nonfamily cause, such as an economic downturn.[85] Structural Family Therapy is often used for training in communication, resolving disagreements, resolving power hierarchies and chronic conflict. It is a brief behavioral therapy (five to ten sessions) with the focus on the present. Problematic situations are enacted and solutions found in the interaction. The focus is on competence, the strength of the family, the transfer of skills used in other aspects of life, getting the family to communicate love and experience harmony.[86] This process helpfully focuses on working-class values of fairness, cooperation, and mutuality more than middle-class values of freedom, success, and self-actualization.[87]

In individual counseling working-class men generally have limited and simple counseling objectives related initially to relief from problems of living. This might include information on where to get needed services in the community, administrative help through bureaucracies, social intervention and advocacy when the problem is another person.[88] Crisis intervention also provides symptom relief and problem-solving with a short-term approach (three to four sessions) for the working-class man. He is encouraged to identify the crisis, the cause, the stress, and then to identify and use available resources, personal strengths, and coping behaviors. This keeps the focus on the present, on the least complex solution, and on action more than talking.

A variety of therapies based in learning and social learning theory, including behavioral therapy, are appropriate in many cases with the working-class man.[89] Generally the working-class man prefers to solve problems through deterrence (curbing or urging behavior) rather than finding causes and asking why. He doesn't see the point of probing the past unless it's to give some respite from the present. The effective therapist is active and directive in teaching and in applying reinforcements. She or he intervenes rather than prompts sharing of feelings. The working-class man hopes the counselor will sum up the presenting problem, give a recommendation, and send him (and his wife or family) away with something to *do* about the problem. He generally will not ask why a counselor does what she or he does. He simply wants results.

Brief therapy and solution-oriented therapy are also quite helpful with working-class men. They focus on strengths and competencies, helping people access resources, using techniques like role-play, reframing, acknowledgment, humor, and storytelling. They are interactional, task-focused, and future-oriented rather than intra-psychic, insight-focused, and past-oriented.[90]

ISSUES FACING PASTORS OF WORKING-CLASS MEN

There are several issues facing pastors and counselors of working-class men, according to Richard Voss. First, one must shift from clinical indifference and dissociation to an empathic embrace of the working-class man as one with dignity rather than one judged as inferior. Such a pastor thus becomes intimately familiar with working-class pain and the shame of indignity, disrespect, and powerlessness in contemporary culture. One also recognizes the enormous strengths of working-class culture in family, tradition, storytelling, and cooperative action. One learns to appreciate that working-class men share their feelings, questions, and concerns only after a trusting relationship is built, which regular visitation prior to any crisis helps accomplish.

Second, one must shift from an individualized, private model of counseling to an inclusive, collective, systemic model that can attend to problems of living, such as economic vulnerability, physical violence, and substance abuse. To experience the vulnerability and powerlessness engendered by the culture also helps one to understand some behaviors as resistive responses to powerlessness. For example, joking behavior among working-class men expresses values of friendship, generosity, and masculinity. It mediates disputes by allowing quarreling while working together. And it expresses a struggle for power in which working-class men distinguish themselves primarily by interpersonal skill.[91] Also significant are various forms of active resistance (threats, insults, obscenities, menacing behavior and words) or masked resistance to dominance (foot dragging, dissimulation, desertion, sabotage, false compliance, noncompliance, pilfering, feigned ignorance).[92] To understand the resistant function and meaning of these behaviors is to aid in acceptance and understanding of the working-class man.

Finally, one must shift from being a community observer to being a community participant. Middle-class pastors who engage the working class and the working poor often experience shame and guilt for damaging social policy and for one's own powerlessness to change things.[93] Being a participant also moves the pastor into caring action rather than merely caring conversation. Those in ministry with working-class men must be able to provide dual-focus counseling, including psychosocial counseling (systemic interventions requiring an advocate or advisor) as well as time-limited, supportive, direct counseling that might lead into longer-term counseling at some point.[94] Hence, flexibility and discernment are a must.

THEOLOGICAL THEMES IN WORKING-CLASS LIFE

A number of pastors believe that working-class men do not reflect on their lives to discern theological meaning. But many of these men do have religious experiences that provide strength and hope for them. Tex Sample suggests that three theological themes are common in oral cultures, such as that of many American Christian working-class men. These themes are being born again, being washed in the blood of Jesus, and going to heaven.

To be born again is to give up the living death of numbness that covers the powerlessness and meaninglessness of one's life. The working-class man comes to expect that his actions cannot effect the changes he seeks. Or he knows he's hurt lots of folks with his wild life. Bourgeois culture numbs his mind and heart into believing that having more will satisfy him and that violence may be necessary to protect what money, position of privilege, and need for order he does have. Resisting that numbness is a sign that all is not well, that

89

one seeks a new life. His sin may be rebelling against God's will; but it also may be his collaboration with the structures that oppress him and his despair about changing them. The "flesh" that is to be rejected are the principalities and powers of society's seduction to have, to dominate, to feel no pain, and to be unblemished that become irresistible to us. To be born again is to take Jesus' hand and let him take one away from all those destructive powers for a new life with him. No matter what—the working-class man has a friend and has a home.

To be washed in the blood of Jesus is to experience the great cost of this new life. To love as Jesus did is to stand with the broken, suffering world we created, calling for accountability and forgiveness, willing to give both in the midst of our failure to do so. This kind of love, in fact, ends upon the cross. The bloodshed of the cross is the world's answer to standing with those who suffer oppression from the principalities and powers. Christ on the cross agonizes over broken creation. Amid the loss in working-class life Christ says "I cry too, but together we will restore it, and in God's kin-dom nothing will be lost."[95] The working-class man understands the sacrifice of one's body. He understands the willingness to give up his own life-blood for a cause greater than himself (for example war). He knows what it means to suffer so that his children won't have to.

To go to heaven is to be free of the cares of this world—no more weeping and no more dying. It is the miracle of life after death, the renewal of this broken material world. It is the great hope not accomplished by any power but God's. There is still work in heaven (Isaiah 65:21-22), but it contributes to the general welfare of all. And it is restructured so that we also rest in God's abundance. Christ brings work and rest together when he says, "Come to me all who labor, and I will give you rest."[96] We rest because we are weary. We rest because we need it and we need God. We work and rest because it is the way of justice and peace. Such is the yearning of the working-class man. It is the way the world is supposed to be. It is a sacred place, set apart from the numbing oppressiveness. In such a hope is the ultimate care of God experienced.

These are hard times for the working-class man. Work and family life are hard, and at times it hardly seems worth it. The church's challenge is to be a caring community that embodies an alternative life, meaning for his suffering, and hope of a new day to come. The pastoral challenge is great. But the working-class man needs the hope the church can provide. We must respond for his sake and for heaven's.

CHAPTER FOUR

LOVE AND WORK AMONG AFRICAN AMERICAN MEN

Donald H. Matthews

L ove and work are intimately and dialectically connected. The economic health and welfare of black males has important effects on their capacities to enjoy satisfactory relationships as lovers, husbands, and fathers. African American males have the same psychological and spiritual needs as other males in our culture. Freud's famous aphorism about love and work is more than true for black males. The difficulty is that black males must also deal with the effects of historical and institutional racism that has left its distinct social and psychological marks.

Psychology, particularly pastoral psychology, is too often guilty of wanting to treat the psyche without addressing the social realities that affect the body, mind, and soul. In order to develop an adequate pastoral theology for African American males, it is necessary to consider the ways in which the economic structure affects the African American male. Recent works in pastoral theology are moving in this direction, but they are still too theoretical to be of much help to the spiritual care provider in the African American community. By contrast, the perspective developed in this paper agrees with Gustafson's call for the development of a descriptive theology that would recognize and describe the life dangers and life chances of African American males.[1]

Due to space limitations, only some of the socioeconomic conditions of African American males will be explored. This chapter will discuss how African American religion serves as a counterresistance to the negative aspects of social life for African American males. These negative social indicators, if left without intervention, can easily lead to alcohol and drug dependency as well as other maladaptive responses to the stresses incurred in a racist society.

SPIRITUAL CARE

I use the term "spiritual care" as a culturally sensitive alternative to the term "pastoral care." The object of African American religion is to produce "spiritual" persons. Therefore, persons are judged and stimulated by the spiritual standards first explicated in the "Negro Spirituals." I regard spirituality as the normative goal of African American religious praxis as defined by the African American Spirituals, which I contend are the indigenous center of African American religion. The analysis of this spirituality reveals a fourfold theological and ethical framework for the expression of African American religion, which consists of the dialectics of faith and feeling, family and freedom.[2]

Faith and Feeling

African American religion is characterized by African traditional religion's emphasis on direct modes of spiritual experience with the divine. Their emphasis on the divination process, by which religious leaders are in direct contact with spiritual entities, was suppressed by Euro-Americans until the advent of the Revivalist movements that placed a premium on the conversion experience. This confluence of African and European religious experience reinforced African patterns of religiosity and served as the building blocks for the development of African American Christianity.

Modern psychology recognizes how vital it is in normal mental functioning for persons to stay in contact with their deepest feelings. Through worship and prayer the very structure of African American religion facilitates regular experience of emotional depth.

Family and Freedom

Africans in their homeland experienced their lives within the framework of their extended families. Reverence for familial and tribal ancestors was and still is an integral part of the religious

93

experience of African people. The African American spiritual also shows this emphasis on family relationships.

American slavery was an economic system that paid little respect to black family stability and in fact undermined it as slave owners controlled the sexual and family lives of their slaves. Along with the constant possibility of being sold from their families, slave owners and overseers exercised sexual privileges with captive African women and men.

African American religion has placed a premium on the stability of the black family. After emancipation, black churches preached the necessity of developing and maintaining a stable family life. Even political and ideological opponents within the black community, like Booker T. Washington and W. E. B. DuBois at the turn of the twentieth century, were adamant in their desire to see black family stability increase in the face of the continued racist discrimination that blacks experienced.

Freedom did not involve abstract theological or ethical formulations but was intimately involved with the welfare of black families and children. Hence, a pastoral theology for the African American community must concern itself with this traditional and continuing emphasis on black family stability, for even in modern times the black family continues to undergo attack by the dominant society. The recent so-called "welfare reforms" are examples of how the state attempts to restructure the African American family.

THE RELATIONSHIP BETWEEN LOVE AND WORK: NO FINANCE—NO ROMANCE

Working

The recent debates on social policy issues affecting black males have been illuminated by the research of contemporary sociologists. One such study has been especially helpful in demonstrating the dialectical relationship between love and work, or, to put it in the language of the black community: "no finance—no romance."[3]

Neckerman and Wilson's development of marriage viability indexes for black males based on income reveals how difficult it has become for black males to successfully maintain stable families. Their research demonstrates that the basis of black family instability

94

lies in the lack of employment opportunities for black males. The so-called "feminization of poverty" in the black community is directly related to the lack of black male income; lack of income results in inability to create stable families:

> According to figures compiled by Wilson and Neckerman, black women face a shrinking pool of stably employed, or "marriageable," men. Trends in joblessness, incarceration, and mortality show that the number of employed black men per 100 black women of the same age has decreased over the past twenty years. Trends in employment and family structure, they argue, support the hypothesis that the rise of never married parenthood among blacks is directly related to increasing black male joblessness.[4]

The researchers also confirmed Wilson and Neckerman's findings and emphasized the structural relationship between stable family life and economic viability. Clearly, it is not enough for religious leaders to depend solely on counseling for the creation of stable black families.

In another well-known text that discusses the impact of racism on the African American community, sociologist Andrew Hacker also discusses the relationship between social factors and successful family life in the black community:

> The pool of "marriageable" black men gets smaller every year. A traditional requisite for marriage has been having a steady job or the prospect of one, a status not readily achieved given current unemployment rates. At the time of this writing, over half a million black men are in jails or prisons, and as many more could be sent or returned there if they violate their parole or probation. And perhaps as many as a million more have records as felons, not the best credential for employment. Another large group is debilitated by drugs or alcohol or mental illness. In addition, the death rates for younger men have reached terrifying levels. In the fifteen to twenty-five age group, the mortality rate for black men is now 3.25 times that for black women, with the principal cause of being gunned down by a member of their own race. The fact that in some areas as many as 20 percent of the men are missed by the census would point up their lack of even a settled address. And of those who were contacted by

the census, fewer than half held full-time employment during the previous year.[5]

Loving

The recent, supposedly most comprehensive, survey on sexual attitudes and behavior in America has revealed a distressing pattern in sexual attitudes among African American men and women. The great pains taken to include a representative sample of African Americans[6] make it particularly noteworthy for the black community.

The survey included a section in which sexual attitudes were categorized as traditional, relational, and recreational. The traditional category represented persons who stated that their sexual behavior is always guided by religious beliefs. They also stated that homosexuality is always wrong, that there should be restrictions on legal abortions, and that premarital sex, teenage sex, and extramarital sex are wrong. The relational category represented persons who believed that sex should be part of a loving relationship, but not necessarily reserved for marriage. Such persons would disagree that premarital sex is always wrong, but they would not have sex with someone they did not love. The recreational category represented persons who believed that sex need not have anything to do with love. This group also opposed laws that prohibited the sale of pornography to adults.

In comparison with white and Hispanic subjects, the survey revealed that African American men and women differed the most. Black males numbered 42.3 percent in the recreational category, as compared to 8.9 percent of black women. In the relational category, black males numbered 25.4 percent as compared to 45.8 percent of black females. Finally, black males numbered 32.3 percent in the traditional category and black females numbered 45.3 percent.

This data reflects that black females are more heavily influenced by religious beliefs in their sexual ethics. More significantly, it reveals that black women associate sex with commitment in far greater numbers than black men. Black males were over four times more likely than black females to fall into the recreational category.

This tremendous discrepancy gives statistical evidence to the growing alienation between black men and women. The authors quote the work of black sociologist Elijah Anderson in partial explanation of this discrepancy. Anderson believes that black males are involved in a contest in which a woman's body is the prize in a sexual game. The young woman, however, has ideas of a traditional relationship resulting in a stable family life. The male may act in ways that he knows the woman approves of until sexual gratification is gained. After this occurs, the male then moves on to new conquests.

These research statistics reveal the impact of what Cornel West terms "Black Nihilism" within the black male community. Such loss of values by black males when it comes to sexual relationships can only lead to increased jeopardy for black families. Not only do black males face decreased chances of employment and therefore a lack of the economic necessities for stable family life, but this data reveals the increasing presence of the impoverishment of the spirit as black males begin to accept and act out the sexual stereotypes that have been attributed to them.[7]

These sexual stereotypes emphasize the bodily and sexual nature of both African American males and females. Stereotypical holdovers from slavery still have cultural power as black males adopt a carefree attitude toward sexuality—an especially troubling state of affairs given the high risk sexual behavior that accompanies this ideology. The rising incidence of AIDS in black lower-class communities means that this population should be especially careful to limit multiple sexual partners and be more willing to commit to long-term relationships. The devastating economic and spiritual disempowerment of African American males calls for a realistic and practical theology for the spiritual care of black males.

It is also important to note that homosexuality is viewed in negative terms by most black clergy. In general, the black church has stood staunchly against the legitimation of gay relationships, while at the same time it has taken a very forgiving attitude toward black males who have been charged with sexual abuse. The cases of Mike Tyson and Clarence Thomas are paradigmatic of the patriarchal nature of black sexual ethics: Black males are supported in traditional negative patriarchal behavior, especially if the black community believes that its critics are acting out of traditional racist attitudes toward black males. The O. J. Simpson case is another example of how this defensive reaction by the black community kicks in when it is perceived that black males are the innocent victims of white racist activity.

The anti-gay reaction by the black church and community is not just due to conservative biblical interpretations; it is also buttressed by the social fact that black males and the black family are under attack. The approval of gay behavior is seen as another way in which the dominant white society is attempting to destroy the black male and black family. This is an unfortunate state of affairs since it obscures the real issues involved in same-sex relationships, namely, the desire by a traditional patriarchal society to maintain power through the creation of narrowly defined sex roles and relationships.

The black church has been very capable of reinterpreting scriptures that justified slavery or taught obedience to unjust social situations, but it has had a much more difficult time reinterpreting scripture that deals with traditional patriarchal sex roles. The mainstream black Baptist and Pentecostal churches have lagged behind mainstream white and newer black religious movements that have offered wholehearted, or at the very least, grudging support of female religious leadership. While the question of gay relationships remains an object of heated discourse by most denominations, the black church has been reluctant to even enter the dialogue.

COMPONENTS OF AFRICAN AMERICAN SPIRITUAL CARE

Theological Bases: Cultural and Structural African-Centered Religious Practice

Pastoral care for African American males must take into account issues of cultural identity. Some of the most successful contemporary African American churches are finding that black males respond positively to spiritual care when the pastor is able to communicate the gospel from an Afrocentric perspective. This includes disciplined and thorough programs that detail the relationships between classical African/Egyptian thought and the Judeo-Christian-Islamic faith.[8]

African American pastors and religious scholars alike are slowly awakening to the ways in which racism has hidden and distorted the contributions of African people to the great world religions. Whether it involves research and teaching about the

98

Egyptian Maatian foundation of modern ethical codes, or the celebration of Kwanzaa based on West African festivals, African American males are hungry to receive accurate information about the
religious history and contributions of Africans and African Americans.

Spiritual Praxis—The Ministry Circle: Personal
and Social Transformation

Contemporary theology has become convinced by liberation
theologians of the necessity of the hermeneutical circle. Pastoral
psychology must also take a radically different turn in order to
maximize pastoral practice with African American males. What I
term the "ministry circle" is a recommendation for religious leaders
to go beyond the standard mode of practice and move into the realm
of hermeneutical and practical engagement. Just as faith is necessary
for understanding in the hermeneutical circle, involvement is necessary for ministry in the ministry circle.

This view incorporates the aforementioned reliance on an Afri-
can-centered practice and uses that perspective to lend guidance to
personal and social transformation. It is also incarnational as it
recognizes that the Spirit of God has been at work in the history and
lives of African people. It gives value to the community-centered
praxis of the black church when it has been an advocate for personal
and social transformation in the African American community. It
also critiques the black church when it no longer recognizes its
divine call to be an agent of personal and social transformation.

In the hermeneutical circle, one believes in order to understand and
understands in order to believe. In the ministry circle, one ministers in
order to transform and one transforms in order to minister. The goal
and means of ministry is transformational. Care and belief are not
defined in terms of rational apologetic and expository doctrinal forms.
They take second place to the desire for a transformed life and
transformed world. God is involved in this transformation and wishes
the church to be involved in this process "lest the rocks cry out," and
others take up the mantle of transformation.

The black church has sometimes forgotten its genesis as a "spiritual" church—a church that was concerned with faith and freedom,

feeling and family. In the spiritual we have a folk example of a theological position that values personal and social transformation. The Million Man March, with its dual emphases on atonement and reconciliation with the development of economic and political resources, is a living example of the spiritual ministry circle at work.

MALCOLM X AS MINISTRY MODEL

The Autobiography of Malcolm X serves as a classic statement of the life of African American males. In contemporary times, the life and legacy of Malcolm X loom large as theological and political alternatives for black America. Malcolm's theological and political leadership was built on his religious leadership role as the primary evangelist and interpreter of the Nation of Islam. What is seldom highlighted, however, is Malcolm's role as a pastoral, or spiritual, leader. His life serves as a model of a religious leader who has completed the ministry circle.

The Autobiography of Malcolm X as told to Alex Haley has fast become a classic in American literature. The continued rise of Islam in African American communities, demonstrated in the leadership of Minister Louis Farrakhan in the Million Man March on Washington, emphasizes the importance of the religious leadership of Malcolm X. Black ethicists and theologians have also considered important the role of Malcolm X in black religious leadership although they often point instead to Martin Luther King, Jr. as the paradigmatic role model for black spiritual praxis. Important events, attitudes, and ideas of Malcolm X demonstrate how his ministry completes the ministry circle.

Malcolm's Early Ministry: Fishing

Malcolm's early life was spent suffering under the effects of racism and oppression. His father, a Baptist minister and follower of the black nationalist Marcus Garvey, was murdered by white hate groups while Malcolm was a child. Malcolm later went to prison after engaging in excessive alcohol and drug use and other criminal activity.

During his time in prison, Malcolm became a convert to the Nation of Islam, which was founded by the Honorable Elijah

Muhammad in Detroit, Michigan. After his conversion, Malcolm began a program of historical and religious study that anchored his black nationalist and Islamic beliefs. After Malcolm was released from prison, he began a program of conversion he termed *fishing*. It is unknown whether he borrowed the term from the sayings of Jesus recorded in the Gospel of John concerning the disciples becoming fishers of men. In any case, Malcolm initiated a program to rescue black males who had degenerated morally due to the societal effects of racism. He spent time with drug addicts, thieves, pimps, and prostitutes on their own turf and attempted to persuade them of the need to lead transformed personal lives by educating them about their neglected African religious and historical past.

Malcolm linked their need for personal transformation with the racist social conditions that contributed to their plight. Once these men were transformed, he challenged them to go after others who were also involved in morally irresponsible actions. Unlike the dominant black church model, which emphasizes that the saved should separate themselves from the sinful world, Malcolm emphasized the need for his converted brothers to serve as role models and catalysts for others in need of moral regeneration. By doing so, they would complete the personal transformative ministry circle.

Later Ministry: Social Consciousness

Malcolm's later ministry is marked by his attention to the social conditions that deleteriously affected black America. After his break with the Nation of Islam, he moved from being an evangelist who emphasized personal moral transformation to becoming concerned with leading his followers to greater involvement in combating racism and social injustice. By making this move, Malcolm completed the ministry circle as an advocate of personal and social transformation. As a devout Muslim, he continued to practice high personal moral standards, but at this point he understood his religious duty as a minister to include involvement in the social sins that afflicted his people.

Malcolm also had to overcome his attitudes and feelings of misogyny. He had accepted the Nation's view of the "true nature" of men and women:

> Islam has very strict teachings and laws about women, the core of them being that the true nature of a man is to be strong, and a woman's true nature is to be weak, and while a man must at all times respect his woman, at the same time he needs to understand that he must control her if he expects to get her respect.[9]

Malcolm's break from the Nation of Islam was spurred by his awareness that his leader, Elijah Muhammad, had engaged in sexual activity with his female assistants and had in fact fathered several children by these young women. It is interesting to note that after Malcolm made the break from Elijah Muhammad and the Nation of Islam, women, especially his family members, played key roles in his ministry.

Completion of the Ministry Cycle

In referring back to the spiritual, Malcolm's early religious life was dominated by the dialectic of faith and feeling as he gave his life wholeheartedly in devotion to God. He was deeply convicted of his own sinfulness and his need to lead a personally transformed life. Malcolm turned from being called "Satan" (a name earned for his irreverent views about God and his disregard for moral standards), to becoming a model and exhorter of personal integrity.

In his later ministry, he completed the ministry circle by becoming involved in the spiritual dialectical praxis of family and freedom. His religious leadership included the building of black families through emphasizing the need for his followers to become involved in the struggle for social freedom. He recognized that in addition to teaching black Americans to personally care for their families, blacks also needed to care about the social conditions that affected their ability to maintain stable family life.

CONCLUSION

This chapter has attempted to demonstrate a practical theological model that addresses the particular needs of African American males. It stresses the need for an indigenous black theological starting point that correlates the cultural structures of African American religion with the particular social and psychological needs of African American men. This methodology emphasizes the importance of grounding African American men in the cultural history of African people. It also emphasizes the relationship between present oppressive social conditions experienced by black males and the lack of family stability. The ministry of Malcolm X is put forward as an example showing a religious leader who was able to combine a knowledge of African and African American religion and history with a practical ministry approach that engaged in personal and social transformation. It is this kind of personal and spiritual transformative care that African American males need in the midst of our current social crisis. Any theological practice that does not seek to build up the African American male's self-esteem through a true knowledge of the African American historical and theological self, or neglects the very real presence of racism and social oppression, will not advance the care of African American males.

The goal of care to black males is the production of spiritual persons. This means that the dialectics of faith and feeling, and family and freedom, result in what Christians have traditionally called the love of God and love of neighbor. Nothing less than the inner and outer expressions of the Spirit are the goals of the spiritual care of African American males.

CHAPTER FIVE

THE MEN'S MOVEMENT AND PASTORAL CARE OF AFRICAN AMERICAN MEN

Edward P. Wimberly

The emasculating influences of racism and racial discrimination toward African American men have meant that the men's movement among African American men has taken a different direction than that among white men. The white men's movement is geared to helping men move beyond the stereotypical images of masculinity and femininity held out by wider society in order to develop new definitions of human wholeness that are liberating both to women and men. In contrast, the men's movement among African American men often imitates the dominant images of masculinity and femininity held out in wider society. The white men's movement is often perceived as a threat to African American men's sense of manhood, given the emasculating influences of racism in the United States. As a result, the African American men's movement is rooted in traditional and patriarchal understandings of what it means to be a man and a woman.

This chapter has several goals: first, to provide a sociopsychological context for understanding the pressures that African American men face in the United States as they try to develop into full maturity; second, to explore existing approaches of the African American men's movement as they appear in the literature; and finally, to present a narrative approach to the pastoral care and counseling of African American men along with the cultural resources needed to help them grow.[1]

The thesis of this chapter is that constructions of African American masculinity should be rooted fundamentally in the egalitarian, androgynous, and spiritual impulses that characterized African American maturity of the past. There is a long egalitarian and androgynous tradition of African Americans rooted deeply in Africa and in the black experience in the United States. African American women often embody these equalitarian and androgynous impulses; African American men need to cultivate the capacity to see the world through the eyes of African American women if they are to recover what has been lost from the past.

This chapter is intended for those who are engaged in ministries of care and education to African American boys and men. Its major purpose is to suggest one avenue for promoting wholeness, maturity, and hope in African American boys and men as well as for the African American community and society as a whole.

A SOCIOPSYCHOLOGICAL CONTEXT

The dominant sociopsychological images, rules, and expectations in society define what it means to become a man. There are at least two contradictory pressures that African American boys and men must face in growing up in the United States: the dominant images of masculinity held out for *all* men, and the sometimes subtle and often blatant pressures on African American boys and men to adopt alternative images of masculinity. The dominant images held out for all men to achieve are generally patriarchal, with the man as the center of the universe defining for all people what it means to be human. Becoming a man has meant having a sense of self and purpose, taking on the responsible roles of husband and father, and taking one's rightful place in society by defining one's own destiny.[2] However, white men have been given the privilege and authority to define what it means to be a man in the United States. This definitional privilege and assumption has been emasculating for African American men and has cut off the avenues for their achieving stereotypical images of manhood.

When the defining of manhood is restricted to a privileged set of men in a patriarchal system, entitled men take for granted their right to define the place and destiny of others, and others who are not so advantaged are expected to be passive and compliant in accepting their assigned role and place.

Within the psychological literature on identity formation, Romney Moseley has explored the roles and places in society that have been assigned to African Americans.[3] He posited that the wider society holds out a negative rather than a positive identity for African American youth.[4] Key to developing a positive identity is to become an active agent in meaning-making and to create one's own identity in interaction with others and the environment.

In forming a negative identity the self is passive in the meaning-making process. However, positive identity presupposes not only active participation in meaning-making activity, but also a positive cultural response to meaning-making. This cultural response involves the provision of viable roles, rituals, economic avenues, and job opportunities that concretely confirm and affirm the identities of meaning-makers.[5] However, in negative identity, acquisition of positive roles and the provision of societal supports for meaning-making are restricted.

One example of how society fosters and supports the formation of negative identity has been explored by the psychologist Erik Erikson. He has pointed out that African American male youth are forced by social expectations to limit themselves to three historic roles in culture that often result in a permanent loss of identity.[6] These historic roles are: (1) Mammy's oral-sensual "honey-child"— tender, expressive, rhythmical; (2) the evil identity of the dirty, anal-sadistic, phallic-rapist "nigger"; and (3) the clean, anal-compulsive, restrained, friendly, but always sad "white man's Negro."[7] Erikson went on to say that the only real identity allowed African Americans is that of the slave.

While Erikson's concept of negative identity is dated, there is evidence that negative identity is still a viable way to explore African American identity-formation today. This becomes evident when the narrative metaphors undergirding the formation of negative identity are explored. The dreams of unlimited opportunity and self-actualization have been deep metaphors undergirding the narrative tradition of positive male identity in the U.S. However, there is an alternative narrative tradition undergirding negative identity that I call the Sisyphus narrative.[8]

The Greek Sisyphus myth tells of a tragic figure who was condemned "to repeatedly roll a stone up a hill only to have the stone roll back down the hill just as it neared its destination."[9] Moreover, "the Sisyphus myth is the fate held out by the wider society for African

American males and females. Covert and overt messages push and pull for African Americans to adopt this role."[10]

The significance of negative identity and the Sisyphus mythology for the growth and development of African Americans cannot be underestimated. In fact, the high proportion of African American men that are incarcerated and involved in the criminal justice system, the spread of AIDS, growing drug abuse, and violence are all, in part, due to the sociopsychological factors associated with negative identity and the Sisyphus mythology for African American men. Negative identity and Sisyphus mythology push African American males into exaggerated masculine postures that often are acted out in violence.[11] Other contributing factors are undereducation and miseducation of youth, low teacher expectations, tracking in schools, placement in special education classes, and school dropout problems. The growing criminal population among African American young men is precisely a fulfillment of the negative identity. These young males often feel that the only viable identity open to them is that of criminal. This notion is reinforced by culture's distorted images of manhood for African American men in particular.

In response to the influences of negative identities held out to African Americans, there is recent literature that focuses on how negative identities can be turned into positive ones. Victor De La Cancela, for example, examines "cool pose" as such an act of transformation. It is

> defined as a ritualized masculinity entailing scripts, posturing, impression management and other carefully constructed performances that present the male as proud, strong and in control. "Cool pose" makes African American males visible and empowers them, yet it can also hide doubt, insecurity, rage and vulnerability, leaving males aloof from others and alienated from their deeper emotions.[12]

Cancela traces "cool pose" to practices in West African tribes as part of the rebellion against colonialization.[13] The positives of this legacy are seen in rap music, graffiti art, and break dancing. Such cultural transformation of the negative identities lend themselves to transcending poverty, correcting a lack of formal education, and creating new ways of expressing self. Often the transformation of negative identities into creative forms of self and community expression lead away from violence and into ways of participating constructively in society. They also serve to produce pride, dignity, and respect[14] and provide rites of passage for males, group solidarity, and group identity. However, there is also an underside to such cultural expression that Cancela identifies as sexism, criminal activity, homophobia, and expressions of an antisocial nature.[15]

I have explored negative identity and Sisyphus mythology in order to describe the limited avenues for personality growth and development for African American boys and men. The implication for pastoral care and counseling with African American men is that developing selfhood means tapping into sources of personhood that transcend the negative images of masculinity and identity prescribed for them.[16] This means that the sources of positive identity must be found in other places. Historically, these sources are found by retrieving racial and archetypal images of African personhood in prehistory, attending to oral styles of relating, remembering stories and myths, using Scripture as an important source of personhood, seeing the world through the eyes of women, and attending to stirrings from within the spiritual core of persons.

FORMS OF THE AFRICAN AMERICAN MEN'S MOVEMENT

Critiques of the White Men's Movement

Before exploring the sources of African American personhood and maturity beyond negative identity, it is important to examine the contemporary models of the African American men's movement. The first task is to explore why African American men have rejected the dominant men's movements. The second task is to present divergent approaches to the African American male maturity.

De La Cancela provides a critical understanding of why Latino men and African American men do not get involved in the white men's movement, especially the mythopoetic movement. He points to the class limitations of the movement as well as their appropriation of symbols belonging to ethnic groups. He says:

The generally affluent urban Caucasian men's movement can examine how its concepts of experiencing the wild man within, dancing the warrior's dance, and other mythopoetic/metaphoric weekend gatherings may be failing Latino and African American men. Critical to this examination is how the movement could be "ripping off" the cultural myths, rituals and practices of indigenous peoples globally such as sweat lodges, dancing, drumming, and council fires, and dangerously fashioning them into some pop, ersatz masculinity. The movement has also ignored current social conditions such as the fact that the majority of homeless people are men and the perpetuation of police brutality and harassment against both men of color and gay men.[17]

He concludes that the Bly-influenced men's movement demonstrates some male emasculating tendencies and "men of color do not need to be further exposed to Caucasian males' unique form of male-bashing, racism, heterosexism and misogyny that has historically claimed that African American women castrate or feminize their men."[18]

Wayne Davis, another critic of the white men's movement suggests that it does not address racism and sexism, it does not deal with skin color as the major source of brokenness, and it reinforces black male invisibility and isolation.[19]

In an age where the academic emphasis for African Americans has been on cultural difference and uniqueness, it is not appropriate for them to seek salvation from copying the white men's movement. There are diverse cultural expressions among ethnic people, and these differences are not deviant nor inferior to what exists in the dominant culture. Given this emphasis on cultural uniqueness, it is easy to see why there are not too many African American men involved in the dominant men's movement.

The Alternative of the African American Men's Movement

There is, indeed, a contemporary African American men's movement in this country. Its genesis was in the Civil Rights movement, and it found philosophical and practical underpinnings in the Black Power movement. A more contemporary expression of this movement is the "boys to men movement," which seeks to mentor black

109

boys into men and is an attempt to insure full participation and survival in wider culture. Most forms of this men's movement do not question dominant images of masculinity nor do they raise critical issues about patriarchy. Other more recent approaches assume that black males do not have access to fulfilling the normative images of masculinity, which is defined as autonomy over and mastery of one's environment and dominance in the nuclear family.[20] There are at least five approaches to enabling African American male maturity, and all but one assume a patriarchal view of manhood, along with dominant images of masculinity. These five approaches include (1) the Liberation, Civil Rights, and Anti-sexist form, (2) the Evangelical Biblical form, (3) the Full Participation/Integration form, (4) the Humanistic Rites of Passage form, and (5) the Narrative form. Each is explained briefly below.

THE LIBERATION, CIVIL RIGHTS, ANTI-SEXIST FORM   This sociopolitical approach to the African American male movement focuses on being "cool" as a behavioral and attitudinal script.[21] It emphasizes responding to the social circumstances that African American men face and challenging the economic and political conditions that keep them and their communities oppressed. Its central focus is on all people of color courageously asserting their rights. It is critical of sexism, racism, selfish consumerism, hedonistic sexual attitudes, homophobia, and classism. Though with origins in the Civil Rights movement, it is critical of the sexual exclusiveness of the Civil Rights and Black Power movements. It is sensitive to the cultural rites of passage that assist both males and females to actualize their possibilities through modes of verbal expression and styles of dress, music, and dancing. It addresses the problems facing the African American community including AIDS, violence, teen pregnancy, and black on black crime.

From a mental health perspective this approach focuses on helping people explore the negative side of the cool pose. It helps people explore their positive individual and group histories, and lifts up the significance of perpetuating an oral history of the survival skills used by African Americans. The goal is to improve the mental health of men and to help them respect both themselves and women of color.

EVANGELICAL BIBLICAL FORM   This form of the men's movement is built on the biblical understanding of men as heads of their homes (Ephesians 5), and of examples of males who were raised by their mothers and grandmothers (such as in 2 Timothy), coupled with providing positive models of leadership for other males.[22] In this biblical approach, the male head of the household accepts the patriarchal model of male leadership. However, from Ephesians 5 some evangelicals have interpreted male headship as a form of mutual leadership by both males and females rather than the lethal form of patriarchal leadership where the man dominates. Leadership of men is based on the principle of selfless love that was demonstrated by Jesus. However, some African American evangelical Christians, both male and female, take the traditional patriarchal interpretation as normative and attempt to live it out.

FULL PARTICIPATION/INTEGRATION FORM   This approach envisages as normative full participation of African American men in wider society. It seeks to use the dominant institution of society, namely school, as the central means for facilitating this full participation. Full participation in every aspect of society is called integration, and this is not necessarily social integration. This form of integration means that each person has the opportunity to fulfill his or her full potential as human beings without being hindered by racial oppression or segregation. It is possible to live in racially homogeneous communities in this form of integration as long as these communities are completely voluntary and not legislated or coerced into existence. Unfortunately, integration has come to mean social integration, where even voluntary homogeneous communities are suspect. This full participation approach assumes that sufficient involvement in American society can be accomplished either by predominantly African American or socially integrated schools. The full involvement approach helps visualize how African American institutions such as the church, fraternities, African American colleges, and public and private schools serve the ends of full participation in society.

Perhaps the best representative of this full participation approach is Jawanza Kunjufu, who has written and lectured throughout the United States on black boys becoming men.[23] His particular model assumes the marginality of African American boys and men, particularly their systematic exclusion from full participation beginning in the fourth grade. He believes that by the fourth grade level black boys become threats to teachers because of teachers' fears of behavioral problems. He believes that teachers begin to lower their educational expectations at this point and become disinterested in their African American male students. This contributes to the boys feeling marginal and isolated. To counter this trend toward marginality and exclusion, emphasis is placed on a holistic approach to the empowerment of black boys by including spirituality, understanding racism, improving time management, developing skills and talent development, paying attention to nutrition, diet, and physical fitness, creating an understanding of economics, being members of positive peer groups, and participating in service organizations.[24] Moreover, this approach focuses on the developmental needs of boys and the related psychological, emotional, social, and practical tasks that must be accomplished at each developmental stage.

Kunjufu also lifts up the central role that Sunday school and church have played within the African American community, citing studies that show that boys who are reared in Sunday school are less likely to go to prison. He concludes: "In the first barometer, we are in trouble if a large number of children, specifically male children, are not developing spiritually."[25] He feels that a relationship with God will reduce the self-hatred and destructive behaviors that exist within the African American community.

THE HUMANISTIC RITES OF PASSAGE FORM   This approach focuses on rites of passage or ceremonies of transition from boyhood to manhood in African traditions. It views the loss of the "ceremonial of etiquette" evident in pre-European Africa as a major problem for African Americans.

Nathan and Julia Hare indicate that the function of rites of passage are to provide customs, traditions, rituals, and ceremonies for the socialization of boys into their roles and place in society.[26] They look to African culture for these traditions as well as to the boys' connectedness to family and community.

This Humanistic Rites approach highlights the significance of patriarchy. They say:

112

There can be no viable race without a viable patriarch in a patriarchal society. In the patriarchal world of the past and the foreseeable future, it is the male and his performance that constitute the missing link to family stability and racial survival.[27]

I contend that it is possible for African American men to grow and develop into mature manhood without becoming patriarchs whose growth might well come at the expense of African American women.

THE NARRATIVE FORM   This narrative form capitalizes on the role of Scripture as the vision-shaping force in the lives of many African American men. Na'im Akbar in *Visions for Black Men* points to the symbolic universality of biblical mythology and its potential for helping African American men to become mature.[28] He highlights the significance of Scripture and its history in providing a liberating vision for African Americans, and suggests it holds out the same potential for African American men today.

This brief presentation of the literature is an attempt to show that African American men's movements exist. There is no one approach. There are many. Consequently, there are many attempts being made to address the needs that African American boys and men have.

A NARRATIVE APPROACH TO PASTORAL CARE

Pastoral care with African American men emphasizes a holistic understanding of the maturing process of selfhood rooted in the deepest inner feelings, values, intentions, and spirituality emerging from a man's life.[29]

Through pastoral counseling, the African American male discovers his unique self, his true emotions and feelings, his meaning and purpose for life, and his unique contribution and vocation to the world. He is able to engage in all aspects of life, including the formation of close and intimate relationships with significant others, while taking full responsibility for his own growth and development. Pastoral counseling identifies the sources of his manhood as including his African heritage, the African American tradition of equali-

113

tarian relationships and androgynous roles, the penchant for oral styles of communication, the use of Bible stories and characters, and the capacity to be empathic with African American women.[30]

One spiritual source of a man's sense of selfhood can be found in Genesis 1:26 where human worth is grounded in God's image and likeness. Within each person there is a push from within to realize this God-given image and the infinite worth and value of each person that is inherent in being God's creation. Pastoral care recognizes this divine urge in each human being and attempts to help African American men claim their creature roots and their innermost spiritual push toward selfhood. Pastoral counseling uses the counseling relationship between the evolving person, the person's relationships with others, and the pastoral counselor to facilitate the emergence of the person's full identity and selfhood.

Not only are the spiritual roots of African American identity found in being created in the image of God, they are also rooted in the ongoing activity of God establishing God's reign on earth. God's reign has been characterized as the unfolding of a story to which Scripture points and to which persons are called. All human beings are visualized as being called to a significant work and a unique place in God's unfolding drama of salvation. When one embraces this call, one's life and community take on significance and meaning—the significance of God's narrative salvation—and personal identity is linked to participation in God's life and work. Each person, whether lay or clergy, has his or her special vocation in God's salvation drama. Pastoral care within this narrative context helps people to discover God's claim on their lives, how this call brings significance to their individual and collective lives, and how it should be carried out to bring personal meaning and fulfillment.

Being created in the image of God and finding personal significance and vocation in God's unfolding drama of salvation are the spiritual roots to becoming a mature person. Mature persons also grow in context as they participate with others, their sociocultural surroundings, and their historical roots. Consequently, there are contextual sources of the identity and maturity that must be explored along with the spiritual roots. Below are some of these contextual sources of African American male identity.[31]

Racial and Archetypal Sources of Personhood in Africa

Egypt and Africa avoided the split between matriarchy and patriarchy that dominated the rest of the world. According to Charles S. Finch there was a creative reconciliation between matriarchy and patriarchy in lower cultures of the Nile.[32] The archetypal and racial source of African American manhood is found in the creative tension between matriarchy and patriarchy. The racial and archetypal inheritance of African Americans is a creative synthesis between the masculine and feminine cultural dimensions. It is part of our African past.

There is an abundance of evidence that the creative reconciliation between the masculine and the feminine has survived in the United States. A review of the literature on black male and female sex role imagery reveals that equalitarian roles and androgynous learning of roles were very common within the African American community.[33] From this alone, it is clear how helpful it is for pastoral counselors to be aware of the cultural heritage of African American males and to employ this awareness in pastoral counseling.

The Oral and Cultural Style of Communication

Emerging out of the creative synthesis between matriarchy and patriarchy is the African American male's inclination for storytelling. Historically, oral skills were highly prized in Africa and in the African American community.[34] This indigenous style of relating was comfortable for African American men and women. It is of immense importance when doing pastoral care with African American men and their families, for the men especially are more apt to participate when a style of relating is comfortable for them.

My discovery of the importance of oral styles of communication came when my wife and I did marital enrichment with African American couples. In the early 1980s many African American men were afraid of marital enrichment because they felt that this was women's turf, and they felt at a disadvantage in the area of intimacy. My wife and I tried a variety of things with the couples, but we were careful not to go straight into working on methods of intimacy. Much of what we did was modeling, where my wife and I shared information from our lives that we felt the couples needed to share with each other. In the process we told stories about our marital life, particularly stories about our meeting, our courtship, our marriage ceremony and related events, our ideal images or mate expectations, and our ideal images of marital life. We also shared how the ideal images had to be modified when encountering the real mate. The men seemed to be greatly interested in the stories we told and in the method of storytelling itself. From this we discovered the importance of storytelling as a major method of enabling African American men to participate in a nonthreatening way in marital enrichment, and, by extension, other forms of counseling.

Exploring the Stories That African American Men Use

Given the bent to use oral styles of communicating, it is critical to explore the stories that African American men tell. Are the plots tragic and growth-hindering (akin to the Sisyphus story) or hopeful and growth facilitating? Offering alternative stories that challenge existing negative or tragic stories is essential in pastoral counseling.

An example is instructive. A young African American male actually referred to his life as resembling that of Sisyphus.[35] This young man was bright. Though he was college and seminary trained, he saw his life as a life of tragedy and dead ends. From him I learned that counselees often see their lives in terms of central stories. In fact, many not only identify with the characters in these stories, they also mimic or imitate the plot that lies behind the story and find it hard to embrace any alternative plot for their lives.

This young man was not an isolated case. Many African American males between the ages of sixteen and twenty-six are finding themselves caught up in the Sisyphus myth with no way out. Pastoral counseling with African American males must identify and explore in depth the stories that undergird their lives, for example, by imagining how the plot will unravel if they continue to follow it. Another goal is to help them discover alternative stories that are growth-producing.

Editing Stories of African American Males

Pastoral counseling with African American males means providing a context for them to edit their personal stories in light of divine
116

Scriptures. Scriptural stories in the Old and New Testaments provide a vision and future hope for many African American males.[36] It is important to explore with them the biblical characters and stories with which they have identified. Bible stories and characters still permeate the lives of African Americans, and they are important resources for pastoral care.

The narrative story that undergirds Scripture challenges such stories with tragic plots like the myth of Sisyphus. The goal of pastoral counseling is to help African American men find a deeper reason for living meaningful lives in the present rooted in a hopeful Scriptural vision of the future.

By helping African American males in counseling to compare their own personal stories with that of the larger vision of biblical stories, one can help them to edit or reauthor their stories in light of a larger vision of reality. The case of a homeless African American man is a good example of this. The man was in his early thirties and the oldest of several children. At fifteen he had had to go to work as a crane operator to support his five younger brothers and sisters. His parents had both died, and there were no relatives for him to fall back on for support. Consequently, he raised his younger brothers and sisters himself.

When I explored with him his homeless situation, he said that he had made his contribution to society by successfully providing for his brothers and sisters. He was proud of the fact that he had only lost one brother to crime; the rest were living productive lives. However, he also felt that it was time for someone to take care of him for a change and that, although it was a hard life, being homeless was a way to be taken care of and supported.

The scriptural story that made the most sense to him in our counseling time was told in a movie he saw. He pointed out that in the movie there was a small boy who followed Jesus, but Jesus would not let him join up with him, saying he should go home and mature some more. The counselee felt like the little boy; he was not ready for life but had some growing left to do.

This story was very instructive to me because it told me that he needed to be in a community where he could be nurtured; it pointed to the possibilities of what he might become if he found that nurturing community. The movie was a beacon in his life pointing

117

to what his future could be like as a follower of Jesus. It was a metaphor and hope to which we returned in counseling as we struggled with his homeless situation.

*Developing the Capacity to See the World Through
the Eyes of African American Women*

In addition to helping African American males edit the stories of their lives in light of the larger spiritual vision of the faith tradition, pastoral counseling also needs to help African American men to be more empathic with the world perceived by African American women. Masculinity in the wider culture connotes the separation from the influence of mothers and the relational culture that the mother represents, as well as becoming free from external control. African American boys and men develop these pushes toward autonomy in an exaggerated sense because of the emasculation they experience due to the legacy of slavery and reality of racism. Therefore, African American males have less access to masculinity-conforming settings than many white males.[37] Consequently, compulsive masculinity is a result of the psychological push for autonomy and for mastery of self by separation from the control of others. Compulsive masculinity is defined as masculine behavior characterized by toughness, sexual conquest, manipulation, and thrill-seeking.[38] It is "the belief that toughness—physical prowess, emotional detachment, and willingness to resort to violence to resolve interpersonal conflicts—is an omnipresent characteristic of masculinity."[39]

While the emphasis in the above definition is on lower-class black men, no African American male escapes these influences. Added to this masculine orientation is the idea of being a "player of women," in short, of the sexual, emotional, and economic exploitation of females.[40] In other words, the end result of compulsive masculinity is complete alienation from women and the cultural connectedness needed to survive in a hostile society.

In pastoral counseling one remedy for this alienation is assisting African American males to have more empathy by seeing the world through the eyes of African American women. Beyond increasing empathy, this also helps to keep black males connected to their cross-generational roots. Womanist theologians have indicated that African American women are concerned with relational and cultural roots of their personhood, and men could benefit greatly from learning this perspective of black women.[41] The capacity for empathy with African American women does not make a man less masculine, but helps him to tap into the inner resources of his manhood rooted deeply in his racial and cultural heritage.

Many African American males fear getting too close to the world experienced by African American females. For some of us it exposes our own vulnerability. Yet, African American men feel better about themselves if they allow themselves to feel what their female partners feel.

One African American male was terrified at his wife's fear of abandonment. He was a problem solver, and he didn't know how to make her feel better. He would stay home, but this did not seem to work, so he gave up and started to distance himself from her. Their relationship worsened.

From watching my responses to her in pastoral counseling, he learned that his wife seemed satisfied by my attention to her feelings and to her view of reality. He began to see that his attention to her seemed to reduce his wife's anxiety, and so he began to abandon the problem-solving approach. He learned to be more emotionally present, and he also began to realize that attending to the feelings was not as frightening as he thought. He began to feel better about himself and his marriage.

Cross-Generational Connectedness

Closely related to seeing the world through the relational eyes of women is the notion of cross-generational relatedness. This means being connected to at least three generations of extended family members. Masculinity in the culture of the United States usually means cutting off generational roots for the sake of competition and advancement. Consequently, all men, whether African American or not, have difficulty maintaining cross-generational roots. Therefore, assisting men to return to extended family roots is a major function of pastoral counseling. This is especially the case when marital and family discord seems to stem from unresolved family-of-origin issues.

119

Learning to do family-of-origin work with African American males and teaching them to reconnect with the extended family are efforts crucial to their ability to survive and develop creative lives.

An example of this diagnostic and creative work is found in Byron. As he felt like he was being controlled by his wife, he would withdraw from her emotionally and go into his own world. He was raised by an overprotective mother who frequently intruded on his life and relationships. He responded by distancing himself from his mother. Consequently, he and his wife were having severe marital problems as he repeated the distancing strategy with her.

As a result of counseling, Byron established more frequent contact with his mother as a means to learn to be less intimidated by her intrusiveness. He worked on controlling his anxiety while he was with his mother, and he also worked on not overreacting by running to or giving in to his mother. As time went on, the relationship between him and his wife began to improve because he was dealing successfully with a pattern that he developed when he was very young.

Attending to Hurt Feelings

Violence associated with compulsive masculinity makes it especially important that pastoral counselors attend to the feelings of hurt and shame of African American males. Violence always masks feelings associated with being less than a man and having one's vulnerability exposed. Showing empathy and sensitivity in this area by helping African American men examine these feelings is essential for the pastoral counselor.

Peter was very volatile. When arguing with his wife, he felt as if she undermined his manhood. Neither knew how to express anger in constructive ways. In counseling Peter would shut down and refuse to participate if his wife became too critical of him. Gently, I helped him to express what he was feeling. Slowly, he became more articulate about what he was feeling and this increased articulateness seemed to make him less threatened by what his wife said. I also helped his wife to explore what was behind her anger toward him. This helped to reduce some of the anxiety between them. As his wife explored some of her own feelings and as his ability to constructively express his feelings increased there was a decrease in the explosive volatility of their relationship.

Immediacy

Attending to feelings of hurt is important, and attending to the relationship between counselor and counselee is also vital. Immediacy means attending to the feelings and the relationships that exist between the pastoral counselor and the counselee at any particular moment in the counseling process. It is important here because of the cultural values placed on the relational style in the African American community.[42] This means that many African Americans are people-oriented and prefer direct styles of relating. This is especially important when counseling with African American males.

In counseling this means dealing with the moment no matter how explosive and difficult it may seem. Dealing with how people feel about the counselor is vital in a particular moment of counseling. Equally, exploring the counselee's feelings about the counselor is vital to developing a working counseling relationship and a healthy outcome of counseling.

CONCLUSION

The African American men's movement has taken many forms. These forms have been reviewed here, and a narrative model of pastoral counseling with men has been presented as a means of addressing the needs of African American men. Rather than drawing on wider cultural images of masculinity that have led to negative identity and compulsive masculinity, the model presented here focuses on indigenous sources of personhood rooted in African American spirituality, culture, and history. An important link to this rich heritage is reconnecting with African American women who are relational carriers of the African tradition.

CHAPTER SIX

THE SHAMAN SAYS... WOMANIST REFLECTION ON PASTORAL CARE OF AFRICAN AMERICAN MEN

Toinette M. Eugene

T he Million Man March was an eleventh hour cry and quest for a new way of being for black men in relation to black women, other black men, black families, the black church and community, and also with the dominant American culture and society. Held on October 16, 1995, in Washington, D.C., it was the largest assembly of African American men of this century. Hailed as a holy day by promoters Louis Farrakhan and Benjamin Chavis, it in many ways lived up to its billing. It was a ritual of renewal for black men. Passionate expressions of fraternity were common. Equally important was the expressed determination to make the fraternal feelings result in permanent changes in the communities in which black people live.

This essay is the reflection of one womanist[1] on the meaning of that epic and watershed historical event and its ethical implications for and impact on the pastoral care of black men. By focusing on the issues with which African American men are struggling, and by reflecting on the relationship of some black men to the Men's Movement in the dominant culture, issues of pastoral care emerge that in many ways demand a womanist ethical response. The competent pastoral care of black men in American culture and society requires the commentary and cooperation of black women if any lasting therapeutic, theological, and praxiological outcome is to transform life in communities in which black men and women lead, live, and fare.

The Million Man March capsulizes the neglect of and the need for pastoral care of African American men. Its noteworthiness has made known to a racist society the symptoms that that society has exacerbated for black men and boys. It hints at the capacity of real pastoral care to restore in the lives and communities of black men the ability to achieve their highest calling—to be in right relationship with all those with whom they are engaged.

The Million Man March has had an enormous, if delayed, response from the pulpits and men's organizations of the black church[2] in recruiting male leadership back to the congregational organizations that exist to give the nonordained black male some status in a pastorally dominated and female-populated congregation. The Million Man March offers an opportunity for a womanist ethical and pastoral care response to the potential for a new model of pastoral care for black men by and in the midst of all of the members of the community to whom they are most closely linked and committed. Edward P. Wimberly in his text, *Pastoral Care in the Black Church* insists that

> unlike the sustaining function in the healing tradition of mainstream Protestant pastoral care, sustaining in the black church tradition has not been the function of the pastor alone. The sustaining dimension of black pastoral care has been the function of the total church acting as the caring community. It was not just the pastor who looked after the spiritual and emotional needs of the church members; the whole caring community provided the sustenance for persons and families in crisis situation.[3]

The Million Man March also provides the opportunity to offer a womanist note of caution on the danger inherent in the lack of pastoral care and just ethical understandings that accompany the New Men's Movement in the dominant culture—a movement that has sought to mollify its racism by inviting and encouraging black men into its activities and ethos.

My response to the Million Man March and to the "New Men's Movement" is as an African American womanist and ethicist who sometimes identifies herself and employs herself as a shaman and an imam—gender neutral terms for spiritual guide and teacher/prayer leader. This response has four parts: (1) the Million Man March as a measure and means of womanist ethics and pastoral caregiving for black men; (2) an imamic rerun of what Sojourner

Truth said to the "New Men's Movement"; (3) a shamanic recollection for African American men and any others who are undecided about their place or role or relationship to the "New Men's Movement"; (4) an alternative "pastoral care" myth of the creation of humankind and familyhood that may have some relevance and hope for the consequences of the Million Man March and for follow-up movements aimed at inclusivity, integrity, empowerment, and equality among all peoples.

THE MARCH AS A MEASURE AND MEANS OF WOMANIST ETHICS AND PASTORAL CAREGIVING FOR BLACK MEN

Many prominent African American women argued that the Million Man March was a blatant throwback to the times when women were expected to stay on the sidelines to cheer the men on. For many women, the Million Man March was an attempt to reconstitute a kind of black patriarchy.[4] I argue that there is a difference between acknowledging the pains and problems of black men and their need for pastoral care and downplaying the lives of black women. I argue that the problems that black men face—drugs, homicide, gang violence—dramatically affect the health and character of their communities, especially affecting the lives of black women and children.[5]

The peaceful march succeeded in countering various stereotypes of black men—that they are violent, that they are bereft of mainstream values, that they have no interest in spiritual or moral matters, that they blame social structures or blind forces for their problems. But the message of atonement, including Farrakhan's disjointed and esoteric disquisition on the subject, failed to address squarely the issue of black men's treatment of black women. No strong note was sounded of repentance for the misogyny, sexism, patriarchy—and homophobia—that have plagued our communities, our churches and mosques.

I didn't expect Farrakhan to carry out this kind of pastoral care, but I did expect others to make the point. This did not happen. The appearance of Dorothy Height, Maya Angelou, and Betty Shabazz countered the organizers' insistence on a man-to-man affair, but their presence seemed a token gesture. If these women were allowed to come, then all women should have been invited. Pastoral care is not a ministry that is positioned as a gender-exclusive privilege and calling. Authentic pastoral care of black men in order to be success-ful is predicated, however, on how the results are received, recipro-cated, and respected by black women and black families who represent the healing ministry of the black church.[6]

The demonstration of strength and dignity of black men loving and learning from and listening to one another cleared a psychic space and a public arena for black men to confess their limitations and to clarify their suffering.[7] The signs of black male limitations and suffering are painfully apparent and in need of pastoral care. United States prisons are packed with black bodies. Unemployment lines swell with black males. AIDS and homicide are bitter prizes in a lottery of black male self-destruction. Racism incites acts of police brutality against black males. Ignorance fuels the fears of black men, even the well-educated, whose anger is an uncomfortable reminder of unfulfilled justice.

Yet even as this is a litany of ills that befall black males, we must be mindful of those that plague black females. Single females who head households experience economic trauma. Teen mothers strug-gle under emotional and financial hardships. Black women have an extraordinarily high incidence of breast and cervical cancer. Sexism and racism deliver a powerful punch to the social aspirations of black women. The sexual and domestic abuse of black females receives less attention than that of white women.[8] Perhaps most painful of all, black men reinvent the wheel of patriarchy by claiming a ques-tionable heritage of male privilege.

This abuse of male privilege happens because too often black men have criticized white racism while ignoring the harmful, even violent sexism and misogyny many white and black men endorse. That is because too often some black men resent or abandon black women thinking black women have it better in a white world that in reality taxes them three times over—for their gender, race, and economic situation. It is because too often black men's talk about redeeming or healing black families is a disguised attempt to subordinate black women and unfairly discipline black children.

Rhetoric about male leadership in black families is often joined to vicious homophobic beliefs that lead to purging the black family of "queers" and "queens." From rap to religion, black men have tried to patent authentic masculinity by excluding the pain and perspectives of gay males.[9] Such bigoted practices undermine ethical and moral male authority and enlist black men in just the sort of intolerance that womanist ethics and pastoral care seeks to oppose.

I argue that the kind of pastoral care that directly addresses and opposes the sickness, the evil, the injustice, and the pathology delineated above lies in the formation of a womanist ethical perspective and prophetic form of pastoral care that deals directly with the larger issues of the "New Men's Movement" as well as with the fallout, the failings, and the potentially positive future of the Million Man March.

THE FORMATION OF A WOMANIST ETHICAL PERSPECTIVE ON THE NEW MEN'S MOVEMENT

When I asked one male colleague what he thought the "New Men's Movement" was, he said, somewhat wryly and puckishly, "Why, woman, don't you know that it's a movement meant by menfolks to end patriarchy for good!" My own experience flashes a yellow warning light, blinking in the back of my brain, telling me differently. For my entire life, I have experienced all versions of the "Men's Movement" as the epitome of patriarchy. The "New Men's Movement" is "of white men, by white men, and for white men only"—period! There are to be absolutely "no women allowed," unless as guests or protégés and, preferably, "no boys allowed" either unless they are members of the most elite men's club in the world, that is the "Old Boys Club." By "no boys allowed," I mean, no admittance to those persons who are addressed euphemistically, either covertly or overtly, as *boys*—a substitute term for men of color, or men whose work is domestic, menial, demeaning, or dehumanizing. The "New Men's Movement" as I know it also denies admittance to those other boys, the "gay boys" whose sexual preference or orientation renders them unfit for the company of "real men."

It was the "Men's Movement" of the United States Senate that stood in judgment on both Clarence Thomas and Anita Hill. The other almost exclusive Men's Club on Capitol Hill, known as the House of Representatives, is well known for its decisions denying those women who wish to exercise their right to engage in combat duty, and thus to advance their rank and pay in the armed forces, because they are worried about demoralizing "the troops" and disrupting the "male bonding" that needs to go on. These are some major models, along with that most revered group known for many years as "the Brethren"—now including two white sisters and one African American brother to replace the retired former "colored" Justice among them—that I identify in these heady political times as premier paradigms of what the "New Men's Movement" is all about.

So, when I am asked for my response to this "Men's Movement" as I know it, my first reply is usually: "Get thee behind me!" When I hear that the "New Men's Movement" is not a patriarchal power-house, but a parallel movement to feminism and womanism, I am apt to respond like the person from Missouri who appears in the last section of the Gospel of John, and who makes a request for a true *semeion*. With doubting Thomas, I say boldly, "Give me a sign." Show me that the "New Men's Movement" is not patriarchal either as a means or as an end. Put my finger in the wounds, let me see, for in fact, I am very anxious to be shown. I am profoundly interested in both the process and the product of what is being promised and touted as such a revolutionary voluntary association of persons of the male persuasion who intend to end patriarchy now!

Give me a sign that it is not exclusive or only primarily meant for white, middle-class, middle-aged, middle-of-the-road to slightly left-of-center guys! Give me a sign that this movement is open to all, and not just "visitors welcome." Womanist ethics and theology, womanist club movements and womanist activists have rarely excluded our "brothers" (for example black male colleagues and associates), and have rarely excluded either "de facto" or "de jure" white people of either gender or of particular sexual preferences from our ranks or our gatherings or from helping us to attain our ends—justice, equality, and respectful mutuality in personal, family, and professional relationships. I need a convincing sign that the "New Men's Movement" is changing its closed position and its closed doors and its restricted list of with whom it will affiliate.

Womanists simply cannot afford what might be considered as optional luxuries often associated with the New Men's Movement, nor do most of us seek these kinds of exclusionary privileged forms of relationships or memberships in such rarified "country club" atmospheres. Our preference for more proletarian and egalitarian forms of association is known as "the solidarity of the oppressed." We learned it from the text known as the Good News and from Jesus, our Suffering Servant Leader, who had a preferential option for the disenfranchised, the weak, the abused, and the disinherited. This One is the only worthy Model of what it means to be King, Warrior, Lover, Magician—the buzzwords and power archetypes for the "New Man." From this countercultural and prophetic model I am open to learning a great deal of what I assume the "New Men's Movement" might also have to gain by way of imitation and affiliation.

I am constantly reminded by some of my male colleagues and the media that because our modern culture has avoided ritual process, particularly abdicating responsibility for mentoring African American boys into mature manhood, that we womanists have failed.[10] I am instructed and encouraged to believe that the "New Men's Movement" is seeking to redress perversions of mature, true masculinity. The "New Men's Movement" is seeking to access nurturing, generative, male people who are beyond the practices of patriarchy and who can relate well with everybody. I am open to the possibility of this evidence as I experience it "up close and personal." From my womanist ethicist perspective, I am also open at a more academic, discursive level of debate, to discussing the theory and theology that sustain it.

Womanists, and we include among our ranks African American men who welcome the opportunity to be with their sisters in the struggle to "lift as we climb," sincerely do want to know what the "New Men's Movement" has to offer us. We do want to know precisely and in depth what this new movement is willing to do for us and with us that is different than what has been detrimentally, negatively, and repeatedly done to us, for us, and on our behalf by the previous incarnation of this group before the New Age dawned.

WHAT THE IMAM SOJOURNER HAD TO SAY: PASTORAL CARE PERSPECTIVES FOR BLACK MEN

My response to the "Men's Movement" is a rerun of what Sojourner the Imam had to say on one occasion about liberation for all people. In reply to the derision of the "Men's Movement" that sought to silence the women at the Women's Rights Convention held in Akron, Ohio, in 1851, and that also sought to keep men of color and men without property disenfranchised by a patriarchal use of white power and privilege, Imam Sojourner said that "if the women were about trying to get the world right side up again, the men had better let them." Departing from her argument for women's rights and for African American emancipation, I want to rerun her radical theology of reconciliation as a reply to the movement we are discussing. Referring to the creation myth of patriarchal theology, Sojourner said that "if the first woman God ever made was strong enough to turn the world upside down all alone, these women together ought to be able to get it right side up again! And now they are asking to do it, the men better let them."[11]

Although I would take issue with Sojourner's acceptance and interpretation of the biblical creation myth, I do accept the deeper ethical principle of reconciliation that is inherent in her liberation theology and her notions of pastoral care for men and women.[19] Sojourner stressed the importance of getting on with getting the world right side up again. This is an implication and an invitation that I take to mean working together in creative, liberating ways. If her injunction to the men at that gathering can be applied to the nonpatriarchal "renewal of the earth" as it is theoretically intended by the "New Men's Movement," then I am willing to say, "If the folk in this men's movement really mean to do their part to get the world right side up, then I am not going to get in your way. I do believe we ought to help each other as much as we possibly can!"

Resisting the matrix of domination requires us to identify and to engage some revolutionary shifts on behalf of the New Age of equality. In order to know, and so to change, our sexist, racist, and classist ways of being and doing, then I affirm Alice Walker's implicit pastoral care claim that "what is always needed in the appreciation of art or life is the larger perspective: connections made, or at least attempted, where none existed before, the straining to encompass in one's glance at the varied world the common thread, the unifying theme through immense diversity."[13]

Partiality and not universality is the condition of being heard in the context of womanist pastoral care for black men and marginal others. The phrase "for all men" must yield to more than politically correct inclusive language, toward the adoption of morally courageous inclusive dialogue with all people, with persons of diverse sexual orientations, and those from different racial and geographic origins.

Dialogue is critical to the success of this approach in pastoral care, the type of dialogue long extant in the Afrocentric call-and-response tradition where power dynamics are fluid, everyone has a voice, but everyone must listen and respond to other voices in order to remain in the community. Sharing a common cause fosters dialogue and encourages groups to transcend their differences. However, existing power inequities among groups must be addressed before an alternative epistemology or theology such as those described by Sojourner Truth or Alice Walker can be used.

A SHAMANIC RECOLLECTION FOR MY
BROTHERS AND ANY OTHERS

Besides making journeys, seeing, and changing states of consciousness, the shaman is a person who, in a sense, is a public servant whose main work is for others. Shamanism is a kind of spiritual activism in which one works with powers that connect human beings to the incredible power of the universe, a work that involves sojourning and shifting back and forth between realities.[14] As a womanist ethicist, I claim this role and this responsibility, which also involves diagnosing the sicknesses one senses and participating in the healing process.

What follows is intended as a frank discussion of the roles and relationships that are possible for black women and men to have and to make together and in partnership with one another as aspects of a refinement of community pastoral caregiving.

My reply to my African American brothers and to others from the place where I stand is the same memorable reply Sojourner Truth is reputed to have drenched Frederick Douglass with when he despaired of any resolution to the problems of the oppressions experienced by abolitionist and feminist movements at the hands of the "Men's Movement." Douglass, the country's leading black abolitionist and the most prominent male advocate of women's emancipation in his time, had returned from Europe in despair concerning the prospects of liberation. At an antislavery convention attended mostly by persons who had found an alternative lifestyle to the "Men's Movement"—Quakers, pacifists, recovering racists, women, other people of color—he came forward with a doleful address. "The black man, excluded alike from the jury box and the ballot box, is at the mercy of his enemies," he said in dejection. "What will the colored people and their friends do now?" Shaman Sojourner could not tolerate such pessimistic talk. Rising slowly in the back of the room, she called out in tones to make the rafters ring and spirits lift, "Frederick, is God dead?" God most assuredly was not. Within eight months the war of union and emancipation had begun.[15] Shaman Sojourner had made the diagnosis of the diseases of fear, disharmony, and soul loss, and moved to pastorally engage her patients in their cure.

Shaman Sojourner took up her drum, since she had studied the sound of a decidedly different Drummer. She ordered Brother Douglass to follow the One who is resurrected, who is not dead, who neither slumbers nor sleeps until justice is done. If you, my brothers, and others are looking to drum out racism, sexism, classism, or ordained clericalism from our midst, be wise in the social movements with which you choose to associate and from whom you decide to take your direction and steady beat. To the ritual action and direction of Shaman Sojourner, I add the wisdom and the words of Doctor Martin Luther King, Jr. taken from his memorable sermon "The Drum Major Instinct."

And there is, deep down within all of us, an instinct. It's a kind of drum major instinct—a desire to be out front, a desire to lead the parade, a desire to be first. And it is something that runs a whole gamut of life.

And so before we condemn them, let us see that we all have the drum major instinct. We all want to be important, to surpass others, to achieve distinction, to lead the parade. Alfred Adler, the great psychoanalyst, contends that this is the dominant impulse.

And we have perverted the drum major instinct. But let me rush on to my conclusion, because I want you to see what Jesus was really saying. . . . He said in substance, "Oh, I see, you want to be first. You want to be great . . . significant. . . . Well you ought to be. If you're going to be my disciples, you must be." . . . I want you to be first in love. I want you to be first in moral excellence. I want you to be first in generosity. That is what I want you to do.". . .

And so Jesus gave us a new norm of greatness. . . . Recognize that he who is greatest among you shall be your servant. . . . You only need a heart full of grace. A soul generated by love. And you can be that servant.[16]

Martin Luther King, Jr., great shaman and imam that he was, knew the ritual meaning and the power that comes from marching by the drum and from stepping high as a drum major. He claimed and practiced that ritual process, and wrote about it in ritual language. It is available for us to refer to in deciding how important it is to be in fellowship with those others who are radically different drummers.

Yes, if you want to say that I was a drum major, say that I was a drum major for justice; say that I was a drum major for peace; I was a drum major for righteousness. And all of the other shallow things will not matter. . . . But I just want to leave a committed life behind.[17]

As a shaman, I deeply believe in the power of ritual process as an important part of womanist ethics and as pastoral care. I believe that it is possible that the new "Men's Movement" has, as one of its purposes, to cure or at least to actively respond to the experience of patriarchy. Nonetheless, like Shaman Sojourner, I say to my brothers and to their friends and to others who would listen, "Go where you are watching as well as watch where you are going" when you participate in such activities as the new "Men's Movement" and other movements that the "New Age" promotes and proposes. God will not be mocked by pseudo signs of "solidarity" and by weak, shallow attempts at creating integrated but elitist fraternities and sororities.

A NEW RENDITION OF AN OLD CREATION MYTH

My first response to the "Men's Movement" indicated my nonacceptance of the old creation myth that allows for the flaw of a woman as the reason for evil in the world, although I would accept larger implications of reconciliation/forgiveness as a hermeneutic that I do find useful as well as therapeutic. In closing my comments about the new "Men's Movements" as well as the potential outcome of the Million Man March, I offer a different rendition of a liberational vignette that is shaped by a myth recounted in *Daughters,*[18] by womanist writer, Paule Marshall.

Womanist movements or meetings do not resurrect the myths or the archetypes that exemplify and exercise pure and unbridled power and control over the lives of others and over the land and the means of production and the creation and maintenance of family, friendship, and community. This is not the myth of Iron John; nor of Tom Sawyer and Huck Finn and Jim, their Friendly Servant; nor of Hansel and Gretel; nor of Snow White and her Prince. Neither is it the myth of the convicted and dangerous rapist Willie Horton nor of *Boyz N the Hood.*

Instead, from Paule Marshall, we hear a womanist ethic of pastoral care and receive a profoundly moral imperative in a wonderfully complex tale. Marshall insists that to be a human being in relationships of integrity and mutuality with others, one must be of use. And that in order to be of use, men and women must work together—and that the relationship between the sexes is far more complicated than she has ever imagined. Pastoral care for black men in the novel by Marshall requires all who are involved in the family system, in the relationships that are intimate to engage in mutually supportive activity—to lift one another up to new heights of respect and reverence as a new identity is inspired.

Throughout *Daughters,* the principal character, Ursa, is regularly visited in her mind's eye by an image of profound significance. The image that is engraved in Ursa's earliest memory is of her mother lifting her up to touch the great stone toes of the statues of Congo Jane and Will Cudjoe, the two heroes of Triunion's rebellion. The new creation myth images call for Ursa to reach beyond her ordinary proportion and to stretch to meet it:

> See if you can touch her toes, Ursa-Bea! . . . Stretch all the way up . . . I'm not going to let you fall. . . . And make sure to touch Will Cudjoe's toes while you're at it. You can't leave him out. . . . Warmed by the sun, their toes had felt as alive as her own. Congo Jane and Will Cudjoe, co-leaders, co-conspirators . . . lovers, friends. You couldn't call her name without calling his, and vice-versa, they had been that close.[19]

Ursa never forgets the great stone couple. Years later in college, Congo Jane and Will Cudjoe inspire her to study the mutually supportive relations that existed between the bondmen and women and how these relations allowed them to resist slavery in the United States and the Caribbean. Through Ursa and her friends, author Paule Marshall states her belief that it is time for this new and more fortunate generation to make itself useful to others who still are struggling. They are now able to concentrate on the common good. They can and must afford idealism. Their imperative is no longer what it was. In a time when the "woods are on fire," they must be useful. The moral and pastoral care code of *Daughters* and of many womanists is strict: people who fail to be of use fail as human beings.

As I reflect on the many and diverse meanings of the "Men's Movements" and the Million Man March, my response remains largely a hermeneutic of healthy suspicion based on historical precedents and on my personal experience. However, I do have a criterion that helps me in changing my mind and my own approach when I need to. This criterion for my own conversion and *metanoia* is based on "truth-in-action," a praxis methodology that helps me to alter whatever it is that holds me back from practicing what I preach. This criterion is based on selected verses from the African American version of the family Bible, with its selection of Proverbs known as "Mama Saids" that begins with the text, "God don't like ugly. Ugly is as ugly does." The truth must be found ultimately in my deeds.

So I expect that this same criterion of "truth" and authenticity can be equally used to assess the validity and utility of the "Men's Movement" and the Million Man March. If the march and movement is, as I am told, about ending patriarchy and enhancing and empowering women and families, then you may be most assured that I am on the lookout for the ways in which it makes itself useful, and with whom. I am watching for "truth-in-action."[20]

AFTER THE MILLION MAN MARCH: THE NECESSITY OF A WOMANIST-BASED PASTORAL CARE

The Million Man March epic is over for America; the meaning of the march begins to materialize in the obvious and chronic need for pastoral care for the subjects and focus of that event—African

American men. A prophetic and poignant passage in Jeremiah 8:20 captures our predicament: "The harvest is past, the summer is ended, and we are not saved." For black men, this means that many of the beliefs that they have embraced and the passions that they have invested in those beliefs have come to a dead end.

This is not only an indictment of some black men's refusal to reform themselves. It also points to the nation's failure to fix the mess it has created. Black men came to the nation's capital to claim their share of moral responsibility for what they have made of their lives. But they also came to call our country to address the sexual, material, and racial ruin that rots the core of American democracy. The harvest of national and personal neglect is past, the summer of playing roulette with the unsatisfactory remedies is ended, but we are not saved or restored to right relationship. The meaning of manhood in its fullness, of the egalitarian African American history and tradition, is not nearly restored to its former splendor and glory.

I submit that the ethical imperative emerging from this event is not for a "New Men's Movement," but rather for developed forms of pastoral care based on womanist ethics and praxis. The implications of pastoral care for black men that is shaped by womanist-informed ethical paradigms is now more than ever a therapeutic and theological necessity as a means of redemption and resurrection of empowered and liberated new life.[21] Womanist ethicist Cheryl Sanders lifts up the challenge that a womanist-based pastoral care has to offer:

> The challenge is to identify and nurture a new generation of morally empowered African American male leaders who can demonstrate to others that power is available to restore African American males to a morally sound condition, to strengthen them in spirit, courage, discipline, and staying power, to enable them to solve their problems through restoration of mental clarity, and to bring order to the chaos of their lives. This is not exclusively the work of men, but if there is going to be any real possibility for ensuring the survival and wholeness of entire people, male and female, as womanist ethics would require, then men are going to have to play a special role in leading the whole community toward reconciliation because men have contributed mightily toward its brokenness and alienation.[22]

The essence and the possibility of a womanist-informed pastoral care for black men lies in the basis by which the Million Man March was initially conceived. The Million Man March is a majestic reminder of black men's willingness to speak their pain and to imagine a brighter future. They marched not to put anyone down but to lift up the sorrow and successes of men whose stories[23] are not often told in their rich diversity and complexity. Black men participated in the Million Man March not to create a "New Black Men's Movement," but to feel the power of black male unity. They marched not to fortify but to dismantle black patriarchy.

Black male seminarians and colleagues, pastors, and the proverbial "brother-on-the-street" have told me and other black women in insistent tones and in summary fashion of the need for and receptivity to a womanist-informed practice of pastoral care. They shared with me both in their tears and with strong testimony, "We marched to be better sons to our mothers, better husbands to our wives, and stronger mates to our partners. We have marched to be better fathers to our daughters. We have marched to tell our sons that we love them. We have marched to tell our brothers that we need them, our fathers that we admire them, our uncles that we respect them. . . ."

These telling phrases indicate the ethical basis and implicit need for and acceptance of the kind of pastoral care that effects change and transformation that can renew and restore the personal and the public soul of black America. This is the kind of readiness and receptivity for pastoral care that can renew the face of the earth. If only we begin to tell it like it is, as it is, then we can begin to practice the ministry of pastoral care of black men in such a way that we might all become the people and the community of faith that we long to be.

As we participate together in the common pastoral care task of working at getting the world "right side up again," I close with the powerful yet cautionary witness of Shaman Sojourner Truth who understood the effects of missed opportunities in the work of liberation, abolition, equal rights, and the development of right relationships based on justice-love. She reminds us and encourages us even though the hour is late, the harvest is passed, and we are not yet saved.

Shaman Sojourner, from her womanist perspective and ethic, speaks to the imminence of what may yet emerge in the wake of that walk into Washington by bold and brave black men. The Million Man March is the beginning and promise of new forms of pastoral care for black men that hints hopefully that the midnight hour is almost over and that in the parlance of the black church, "trouble don't last always, joy will come in the morning." My own womanist ethical perspective echoes the positive premise behind Imam Sojourner's eschatological words:

> I know that it feel a kind o' hissin' and ticklin' like to see a colored woman get up and tell you about things. . . . We will come up again, and now I am here. . . . I wanted to tell you a mite about Woman's [and Men's] Rights, and so I came out and said so. I am sittin' among you to watch; and every once in a while I will come out and tell you what time of night it is.[24]

CHAPTER SEVEN

MALE VIOLENCE AGAINST WOMEN AND CHILDREN

James Newton Poling

INTRODUCTION

Robert, a European American working-class man, sought pastoral counseling after he was arrested for child sexual abuse of his four-teen-year-old daughter. He wanted to stay out of prison, keep his marriage and family intact, and maintain his active membership in the Mormon Church. He considered his sexual abuse of his daughter to be a sin that he must face, and hoped that God and the church would forgive him over time and restore him to full membership.

Todd, an African American professional man, joined a psychoeducational group for men who batter after he was arrested for hitting his girlfriend. He wanted to avoid further legal difficulties and maintain his intimate relationship if possible. He also wanted to control his abuse of alcohol and stop the intergenerational cycle of physical and sexual abuse because he was becoming "just like my father." He recently returned to the Baptist Church where his mother attends because they have a program for recovering addicts.

These are two of the hopeful stories I have heard over the last ten years in my work as a pastoral counselor with men who have been convicted of violent offenses. Robert and Todd feel ashamed and guilty for their violence and are willing to do what is necessary to give themselves a future instead of risking more violence and the threat of imprisonment. However, they face many internal and external obstacles as they try to understand their history of physical, sexual, and emotional violence toward women and children. Their cultural, racial, and class locations influence how they perceive themselves as men and how they define the choices they have before them.

Robert and Todd are typical of some violent men who feel remorse and seek to avoid the consequences of their behaviors. They don't want to lose their marriages, their families, their jobs, or their freedom. While most violent men are encouraged to continue their violence by the lack of response of churches and the courts, a few violent men are learning from the legal system and from other family members that their violence is not acceptable behavior. While most men seek to avoid responsibility for their violence, a few are turning to pastors, pastoral counselors, and other professionals for help. It is imperative that the church become competent to provide assessment, referral, and care for men who genuinely want to overcome their violence and dominance over women and children.

How can violent men, many of whom are Christians, engage in violence against women and children and not seek help from pastors and other caregivers? Because the churches have not identified male violence as a pressing ethical and religious issue. Why do many churches refuse to see male violence as a major threat to the health of women, children, and families and instead call for a return to "family values" (the male-dominated, heterosexual nuclear family) as a solution to society's ills? Because the church's patriarchal theology gives priority to the rights of men over women and children.

The primary goal of this chapter is to identify male violence as an ethical and theological concern for the church and to suggest ways that pastoral care can respond to the needs of men who are violent. A secondary goal is to help the church be sensitive to the cultural, class, and racial contexts in which male violence against women and children occurs.[1]

REVIEW OF THE LITERATURE ON MALE
VIOLENCE AGAINST WOMEN AND CHILDREN

Male violence against women and children has many names: "wife abuse, marital assault, woman battery, spouse abuse, wife beating, conjugal violence, intimate violence, battering, partner abuse,"[2] child sexual abuse, child abuse, physical abuse, rape, emotional abuse. In this chapter, I will rely on the following definitions of male violence that focus on behaviors of perpetrators and consequences for victims/survivors. These definitions emphasize the presence of male power and control in intimate relationships as well as the discrete acts of behavior.

Definitions of Male Violence

> Male violence toward women encompasses physical, visual, verbal, or sexual acts that are experienced by a woman or girl as a threat, invasion, or assault and that have the effect of hurting her or degrading her and/or taking away her ability to control contact (intimate and otherwise) with another individual.[3]
>
> Domestic violence is a pattern of assaultive and coercive behaviors, including physical, sexual, and psychological attacks, as well as economic coercion, that adults or adolescents use against their intimate partners (including physical assault, sexual assaults, psychological assaults, threats of violence and harm, attacks against property or pets and other acts of intimidation, emotional abuse, isolation, use of children, and use of economics).[4]

How Much Interpersonal Violence Is Male Violence?

Because this book is about men and their issues, it is important to focus on this important moral and theological issue of male violence. Beyond that, there is much research that male violence against women and children makes up a majority of interpersonal violence. The most conservative figure I have seen comes from police reports, which indicate that 70 percent of domestic violence calls come from women.[5] However these figures are unreliable since men are learning to call the police to bring charges against their female partners in order to gain the advantage in court. Other studies suggest that 35 to 50 percent of women have experienced acts of violence from their male partners in their lifetime and that 95 percent of domestic violence calls to police are from women.

Based on the last seventeen years of empirical inquiry, experts now estimate that as many as 4 million women experience severe or life-threatening assault from a male partner in an average twelve-month period in the United States; and that one in every three women will experience at least one physical assault by an intimate partner during adulthood.[6]

140

Some researchers suggest that as many as 50 percent of women will experience a violent assault from an intimate partner in their lifetime. These statistics mean that women are in great danger of violence from men and with far greater prevalence and severity than men.

The position adopted by most authors is that a critical assessment of the present evidence indicates that men commit the bulk of the serious cases of physical violence toward women and children and are largely responsible for sexual aggression.[7]

What About Female Violence?

Some researchers believe that the violence of men and women is equal, and they argue for "sexual symmetry in marital violence." Support for this position has been derived from studies that show "that equal numbers of men and women commit acts of physical aggression to their partners, . . . and that spousal homicide statistics . . . show equivalent numbers of male and female victims."[8]

Counter to this argument about sexual symmetry is that crime statistics show a ratio of three to one or more between male and female violent crimes.[9] Most research shows that men are more physically aggressive than women on minor scales, such as having hostile feelings or engaging in verbal abuse. And when the consequences of violence are taken into account, "most acts of aggression that result in injury or death (and fear of these) are carried out by males, and in particular young males."[10]

There are at least two basic differences between female and male violence that must be understood: (1) Women are more frequently injured or killed by male partners than men. For example, 40 percent of all homicides of women are caused by male partners or ex-partners, whereas only 10 percent of male homicides are caused by female partners or ex-partners.[11] "Twenty to thirty-five percent of women who present to hospital emergency rooms or community-based practices are there because of symptoms related to assaults by a husband or other intimate partner."[12] Injury from battering is the leading cause of emergency room visits for younger women. (2) When women use violence, it is almost always a form of self-defense against male violence. That is, women use physical violence to

141

protect themselves from battering, whereas most men use violence for power and control of their partner.[13]

There are also serious problems of interpersonal violence within gay and lesbian relationships, which need to be acknowledged and addressed with forms of analysis and intervention appropriate to the dynamics.

Male violence against women in heterosexual relationships is a paradigm for intimate violence in gay and lesbian relationships: one partner is intimidating and controlling the other through the use of or threat of physical violence.[14]

More research needs to be done of gay and lesbian relationships to discern the particular patterns that need to be challenged.

Issues of Race and Class

Male violence against women and children occurs in every social class and all cultural groups in the United States, including European American, African American, Latino, Asian, and Native American. Inadequate research methods, such as "the use of clinical samples, data from official police and agency reports, and the failure to control for social class,"[15] make it nearly impossible to evaluate racial and class differences on domestic violence. We do know that, in most cultures in the world, severe male violence against women and children is more common and more often tolerated and rationalized than female violence against men. We also know that male perpetrators use all kinds of rationalizations for their destructive behaviors, including cultural differences, to justify their violence and that economic vulnerability contributes to the difficulty of protecting oneself against violence. However, neither cultural rationalizations nor the prejudices of the dominant culture should be allowed to justify the use of violence to coerce and terrorize those who are vulnerable. Methods of intervention to prevent male violence must be culturally sensitive to the needs of the victims. For example, the police and courts must be trained to be fair to ethnic and class differences so that interventions are effective.[16]

Prevalence of Male Violence

If we define male violence as physical or sexual behaviors that cause, or could cause, physical and psychological injury or death to someone else, how big a problem are we discussing? How many

142

victims of male violence are there, and how many violent men are there? This question is important because of the common public assumption that such violence is rare, especially within one's own social group. While the public is afraid of being mugged, robbed, burglarized, or killed by strangers from other groups, it is commonly assumed that people are unlikely to face violence within their own social group. Actually, the prevalence of violence is highest within social groups and within the family.

I have never seen a study that tries to estimate the number of men who have committed violent acts. The social denial of the problems and the refusal to face the vulnerability of women and children to male violence means that reliable statistics cannot be collected. Scientists have made some progress recently in studying the number of victims of male violence, especially the number of women and children who have experienced some form of male violence in their lifetime. The results of this research shows that society is facing a monumental problem that has been denied.

Prevalence of Rape

Using conservative definitions of rape and using conservative methods of collecting and interpreting data, Mary P. Ross reviews twenty empirical studies and estimates that at least 14 percent of all women have experienced a completed rape as adults in their lifetimes. Results of the studies range from 8 percent to over 20 percent.[17] This is an astounding percentage of the female population. Adding attempted rapes doubles the number of victims in most studies.

Prevalence of Child Abuse

Estimates of physical abuse of children range from 200,000 to 4,000,000 cases per year. The National Committee for the Prevention of Child Abuse estimates that over 1,000,000 children are seriously abused per year, including 2,000 to 5,000 murders of children.[18] Women are significantly involved in the physical abuse of young children where they are the primary caregivers. However, men often abuse young children and are responsible for the majority of abuse of older children and adolescents. Estimates of child sexual abuse

143

range from 12 to 28 percent of girls and 3 to 9 percent of boys. This means 210,000 cases per year of which 44,700 per year come to the attention of some professional person such as a teacher, pastor, physician, or social worker.[19] Most experts believe that a majority of physical and sexual abuse of children is never reported to authorities.

Prevalence of Battering

"We found that someone getting married runs greater than a one in four chance of being involved in marital violence at some time in the relationship."[20] In addition, live-in and dating relationships are also dangerous places because the rates of violence are almost as high.[21]

The credible research on male violence indicates that at least 25 percent of women and children will be victims of physical or sexual violence by men, with substantial physical and psychological injuries in their lifetime, either as children facing physical, sexual, or emotional abuse or as adults facing assault, battering, rape or psychological control. These statistics do not diminish with social class, race, religion, or faithful church attendance, although they do correlate with gender (women are more frequently victims than men). This means that 25 percent or more of the members of the typical congregation have experienced male violence, either as survivors of child abuse or adult-survivors of rape, battering, and psychological abuse. If this is true, then the silence of the church about interpersonal violence and its consequences is one of the most disturbing realities that must be faced. The additional problems of sexual harassment and exploitation at work and in professional relationships extend the forms of male abuse of women even further.

CAUSES OF MALE VIOLENCE

Competing Social Science Theories

There are several competing, but not necessarily incompatible, theories among scientists who accept the reality of male violence: genetic and hormonal theories, evolutionary theories, socialization theories, and womanist and feminist theories of power and control.[22] Those who prefer genetic and biochemical explanations study the influence of chromosomes and testosterone on human aggression and predict that a certain percentage of men will act out their imbalances in violent behaviors. Those who prefer historical explanations go back to prehistoric experiences of hunting and gathering societies and the survival of the fittest, which produced species of human beings that are not adaptable to the technological information age of postindustrial democracies. Others favor sociological explanations about the construction of masculinity within the culture of violence in news, film, television, pornography, sports, guns, cars, military training, and preparation for war.

I prefer womanist and feminist theories of male violence, which emphasize themes of power, control, and dominance of men over women, children, nature, and the competition of men for dominance over one another, which leads to racism, war, and economic oppression. This theory is not in competition with the other theories, which are true in their own ways. However, theories of power and control provide the active motive for individual men to continue their violence. When Gelles and Straus ask in their book *Intimate Violence* why men use violence against women and children, they find it is: "Because they can."[23] What they mean is this: men are violent because they can get by with it, because there are usually no serious consequences for being violent, because they are encouraged to be violent, and because it works as a method of power and control. Violence works if a man wants to control others, and it will continue to work until society decides that the use of violence by men to maintain dominance over women and children is unacceptable and must be changed.

Religious Interpretations of Male Violence

Our society, including the church, has not decided that male violence is a moral problem serious enough to be challenged and changed. There are at least three conflicting religious interpretations of male violence in our society: (1) male violence is a sign of the breakdown of God's natural hierarchy of the headship of men over women and children; (2) male violence is a problem of the sinfulness of human nature; (3) male violence is the use of force to enforce male dominance over women and children and to maintain other forms of oppression such as racism, classism, and heterosexism.

145

Some groups believe that male headship is a part of God's natural order and that God's hierarchy moves from men to women to children. This traditional conservative position promotes male dominance and hopes to limit the need for violence by educating women and men to certain family values. Violence occurs, in this view, when the natural hierarchy of men over women and children is threatened and needs to be reestablished. Male violence is unfortunate because some men are too immature to know how to assume their rightful place at the head of the family without resorting to violence and because many women have been led by womanism and feminism into rebellion against the leadership of men, which makes violence inevitable as men "rightfully" enforce their dominance.[24]

Some groups believe in abstract human rights including the right to be free from violence, but despair of changing human nature. This traditional liberal position is that violence against women and children is an unfortunate consequence of the fact that people who get attached to each other act out their individual pathologies and inflict all kinds of damage on each other. We need to maintain our educational programs and provide support and resources for people so they can grow out of their need to be violent toward one another, but this process will be agonizingly slow. In the meantime we should not be punitive toward the poor souls who mistreat one another, but we must be compassionate and help them to see that there are better ways to be partners, parents, and lovers. This view assumes that women and men are equally violent. It merely considers that it is too bad that men are so much stronger and inflict the most injuries on others. But the real problem is individual sin and immaturity, which can only be solved through the slow process of education.[25]

By contrast, the womanist and feminist view of male violence is that gender inequality is socially constructed as a hierarchy, that most men base their personal identities on being members of the dominant class, and that the purpose of male violence is to enforce male dominance over women and children like other forms of oppression such as racism, classism, and heterosexism. As women have become conscious of themselves as an oppressed class, although experiencing different kinds of oppression from one another depending on race, economic status, sexual orientation, religion, and nationality, they have challenged both the liberal and conservative views. They reject the conservative view that gender inequality is God-ordained and that restoration of male dominance will decrease male violence. They also reject the liberal view that violence is caused by individual sinfulness. Violence is not evenly distributed within society as it would be if its basis were a fallen human nature. Rather, women and children, especially girl-children, experience violence out of proportion to their numbers.

Womanists and feminists have developed complex theories of gender power relations that unmask the purpose of male violence—to maintain male dominance. Therefore, male violence will not be stopped until gender equality is written into the laws and social practices of our society and until there are adequate consequences for violence against women and children as there must be against other violent crimes. This requires a massive social change along all fronts, from religion to law, education, and economics.[26]

GUIDELINES FOR ASSESSMENT, REFERRAL, AND PASTORAL CARE OF MEN WHO ARE VIOLENT[27]

The consequences of conservative/evangelical and progressive/liberal views of male violence have been tragic for many women and children. The litany of inappropriate pastoral responses is legion: *What kind of wife are you to make him so mad? You should have more faith, and God will restore your marriage. What are you doing to create this kind of conflict? I think you need some marriage counseling to work out your problems.*

In these and similar ways, many churches advocate the unity of the family, the sanctity of the marriage, and the privacy of what happens in a Christian home. As a result, many survivors who have talked to their pastors say that they have stayed in violent marriages and other relationships for decades, blaming themselves, and taking responsibility for the behaviors of the men. Some pastors have tried couple counseling to mediate the conflict between them so the violence would stop, without analyzing the vulnerability and jeopardy of the women and children in the family. In most cases, Christian congregations have taken the side of the violent man because he is the head of the family or because they don't want to get involved in a "domestic dispute." One female pastor discovered that the congregation in which she was newly installed had witnessed three murders among their members and extended families without understanding the dynamics of male violence underlying the murders.

Because male violence has not been a designated area of research and training in the field of pastoral care and counseling, our field is unprepared to deal with the issues of male violence. Given the current state of ignorance about issues of male violence and gender injustice, pastors and pastoral counselors should not attempt to do care and counseling with men who are violent without specialized training and changed attitudes. In this section, I will suggest some guidelines for pastoral response to women who are victims and to men who are violent, and I will present some issues that require a revision of traditional pastoral care and counseling methods.[28]

The Priority of Safety and Pastoral Care for Victims of Abuse

I believe it is unethical to engage in pastoral care or counseling with a man who is violent without due consideration of the safety and pastoral care needs of his victims. Whenever a pastor or pastoral counselor identifies male violence as a potential problem in a relationship or family, past or present, she or he should begin an assessment of the safety of women and children around that man. For example, if the man has a history of abusing children, one must assume that any children he has access to are in potential danger, especially if no one else knows his history. If a man has a history of battering in previous relationships, one must assume that the current intimate partner is in jeopardy. As I will discuss later, I believe that the normal constraints of confidentiality do not apply when issues of violence are concerned. Men who have a history of engaging in violence should not be trusted to assess their own danger to others because they have a history of minimizing and rationalizing their behaviors and the consequences to others.

Ensuring the safety of potential victims requires contact with other professionals who have direct contact with the victims. In the case of child abuse, this may be the county department of social services or private agencies who specialize in child abuse. In the case of battering, this may be the local shelter, rape crisis services, or other agencies who provide support and services for battered women. Anyone who works regularly with men who are violent must have ongoing consultative relationships with community agencies who work with victims.[29]

Use Wider Community Structures of Accountability

One of the most dangerous things a pastor or pastoral counselor can do is to work in isolation with a man who has violent symptoms. This perpetuates the very structure of secrecy and deception that fosters violence. Acts of physical or sexual violence against a woman or child, within or outside the family, are crimes and violations of law. Most likely, a pastor or pastoral counselor will find out about domestic violence through the woman or child who is harmed or through an advocate. In a case of incest, I heard about the abuse from the aunt of the adolescent victim and was able to initiate an intervention in the family with supervision by the director of clinical services at the local mental health center.

In situations of child abuse, professional leaders such as teachers, social workers, and mental health workers have a legal mandate to report the suspicion to the authorities, either the local police or a city, county, or state hot line. Some states require religious leaders to report child abuse, while other states exempt clergy from this requirement. However, I believe pastors and pastoral counselors have an ethical mandate to report because it is the only way to protect endangered children.[30] Learning how to follow up such reports during the family crisis usually requires special training and supervision.

Through several decades of this dangerous work, the leaders of the domestic violence network have honed their assessment skills. Knowing how to support women when they are in danger is very complex and pastors should have supervision from community experts in each situation.

It is important to reiterate that most pastors and pastoral counselors are ill-equipped to deal with situations of domestic violence. We need to see ourselves as part of the response team of the larger community: directors of women's shelters, hot-line organizers, police and courts, and advocates for women and children. Unless we

149

work as members of the team, it is likely that our interventions will endanger those who are vulnerable.

Combat Secrecy and Deception of Abusers

One of the skills pastoral counselors need is compassionate confrontation; that is, the ability to form a therapeutic alliance with the healthy aspects of the man's personality by requiring accountability, but without being abusive or punitive in the process. This is necessary because of the internal structure of violence itself. The purpose of violent behavior is coercion of another's behavior to one's own will without consequences for one's own violent behavior. Violent men hide the true character of their violent interpersonal behavior and deceive those in authority about what is actually going on. In earlier patriarchal societies where men had the explicit right to beat their wives according to the "rule of thumb,"[31] such deception was not required. In the United States we must work toward a time when physical and sexual violence against women and children is no longer tolerated, either by law or by accepted practice.

Men's defensive rationalizations of violence are legion: *I hardly touched her. She bruises easily. I was trying to grab her and she fell. I was acting in self-defense. My daughter came into my bedroom when my wife was gone. She was only my stepdaughter.*

Pastoral counseling techniques that depend on ambivalence and guilt for destructive behaviors are totally inadequate for working with male abusers who have spent a lifetime rationalizing and justifying their violent behaviors and avoiding the consequences. For them it is a way of thinking and feeling that is ego-syntonic and not easily changed. This is why a pastoral counselor must have a larger context besides the intrapsychic world of the man in which to work. Unfortunately, most of our intrapsychic and family theories are also contaminated with male dominance and collude with male aggressive disorders. Thus contact with outside agencies and professionals with womanist and feminist orientations are absolutely crucial in order to counteract the secrecy and deception of abusers and create the means for accountability.[32]

Work Cooperatively with Other Professionals

I hope that pastoral counselors will eventually have adequate theories, attitudes, and skills to work with men with violent symptoms. Until then, we must work in consultation with, and with accountability to, community professionals who do have these skills. Through individual and group supervision, didactic sessions, and participation in regular networks of professionals who work with victims and abusers, pastoral counselors can make the changes necessary to do good work with this population.

Revision of Traditional Pastoral Care and Counseling Methods

Confidentiality. The purpose of the traditional emphasis on confidentiality within the churches is to provide safety for confession of sin to be addressed by the rituals of the church. Within the mental health field, confidentiality allows shame-based transference issues to emerge for therapeutic intervention. Without such confidentiality, little in-depth pastoral care or psychotherapy can be accomplished. This principle is true in work with male abusers except that issues of safety for his victims must be paramount. In working with a man who is violent or abusive, it is crucial not to collude with the destructive and self-destructive impulses of the personality at the expense of those who are vulnerable. For violent men, manipulating such collusion is often their greatest interpersonal skill.

The limits of confidentiality must be clearly negotiated at the beginning of a pastoral counseling relationship. Whenever the pastoral counseling contract identifies violence against others as a focus, the pastoral counselor must cooperate with others to provide accountability for acts of violence. As a pastoral counselor, I agree to keep confidential any matters that do not involve the safety of others, to keep the man informed of any contact I have outside of therapy, and to openly discuss any concerns the man has about my commitment to his health and safety. Two situations periodically occur: sometimes I hear from another professional that the man has been abusive or threatening to his partner or children and I use the information to confront him. Sometimes he gives me information during therapy that he is being abusive or threatening, and I warn the persons involved. In both of these cases, information is being exchanged with persons outside the therapeutic relationship, which contradicts the expectation that confidentiality equals secret-keeping.

I believe these are legitimate limits on confidentiality when working with violent men. As a pastoral counselor, I have a moral commitment to protect the safety of those who are vulnerable. I also have a moral commitment to join the healthy psychological development of the person and refuse to collude with his violent impulses and behaviors. This means helping him face the consequences of his behaviors and maintaining, if possible, a therapeutic alliance at the same time. The ability to sustain a positive therapeutic relationship during episodes of violence in the man's life may itself be the paramount healing moment.

There are some sacramental definitions of confidentiality that interfere with a pastor's ability to accept these suggested limits of confidentiality. In response one can clearly distinguish general pastoral counseling from the sacrament of confession and absolution of sins. It may be possible to maintain the Roman and Lutheran sacrament of confession in limited use but not extend it to all pastoral conversations. In this case, pastoral care and counseling would not be covered by the secrecy of sacramental confession. Another response is to rethink the theology of the sacrament of confession itself: I believe the safety of other people sets limits on the confidentiality of the confessional.[33]

Therapeutic neutrality. Among pastoral counselors using psychoanalytic and systems theories, neutrality is considered a high value. Certainly it is important for a pastoral counselor to seek to provide positive regard, empathy, and authenticity in every pastoral encounter, and to respect the process by which an individual seeks healing. It is also important that the pastoral counselor not be abusive or manipulative in seeking values and goals that are foreign to the person. But these legitimate forms of neutrality must not be confused with the lack of a moral context for pastoral care and counseling. Much research has been done on the moral horizon within which pastoral care and counseling is practiced.[34] But issues of violence challenge the definitions of what we usually mean by neutrality or fairness because the consequences for vulnerable persons requires constant monitoring.

In entering the treatment relationship, the therapist promises to respect the patient's autonomy by remaining disinterested and neutral. "Disinterested" means that the therapist abstains from using her power over the patient to gratify her personal needs. "Neutral" means that the therapist does not take sides in the patient's inner conflicts or try to direct the patient's life decisions. . . . The technical neutrality of the therapist is not the same as moral neutrality. Working with victimized people requires a committed moral stance. The therapist is called upon to bear witness to a crime. She must affirm a position of solidarity with the victim.[35]

In pastoral counseling of violent men, a pastoral counselor who takes a moral stance against violence in interpersonal, intimate relationships may be faced regularly with a person's attitudes and behaviors that are abusive and violent. The traditional "bracketing" of moral values for the sake of in-depth pastoral or therapeutic work is not appropriate because it represents a form of collusion against the best interests of the person. It risks forming a nontherapeutic alliance, what Robert Langs calls "lie therapy."[36] Learning how to bring clear moral principles of nonviolence into the therapeutic setting without being judgmental and moralistic is a test of therapeutic skill.

Couple and family counseling. Pastoral counselors frequently engage in couple and family counseling. However, under the influence of womanist and feminist therapies that focus on sexual and domestic violence, couple and family counseling in situations of violence is discouraged. Why? Because of the assumption of most systems theories that everyone in the room shares responsibility for the problem being discussed and because anything the partner of a violent man might say could become an occasion for future violence. Under the conditions of present theory and training of most counselors, these assumptions are formulas for disaster. "Safety for victims first" is always the motto in situations of interpersonal violence. This means that a report to the proper authorities that a crime has been committed, an effective safety plan for the partner, full confession and acceptance of responsibility, and a program of rehabilitation by the violent man must precede any couple therapy.[37]

Consultation with victims and other family members. There is some difference of opinion about whether a counselor working with a man

153

who batters should have direct contact with the victims and other family members. Some say yes, because it is the only way to know whether the man is a danger to his partner and children during therapy. Some say no, because asking the partner to disclose how she feels about him may further endanger her. The underlying principle seems to be that the counselor should never rely solely on the information received from a man who is violent, but must have other sources of information about his ongoing behaviors without further endangering family members.

Transference and countertransference. Very intense emotions are generated in the helping relationship when the man has a history of violence. Such a man is used to having his way, is an expert at manipulating, coercing, outsmarting, and threatening others, and feels justified in controlling others. This means that effective limits on his behavior will often generate rage and resistance. On the other hand, such men are singularly inept at meeting their emotional needs through vulnerability and mutuality and thus can be hurt and shamed. Managing these transference issues is a challenge to any therapist.

One of the main countertransference issues for the pastoral counselor is fear. Violent men know how to frighten others and play on their fears. They may have sustained family terror for years for the gratification of power and control needs. This predictably generates fear in the pastoral counselor. It is crucial that the pastoral counselor be intimately familiar with her or his fear response and have resources for using fear as a signal anxiety of what is going on in the therapeutic relationship. After all, when the pastoral counselor feels fear, there may be actual danger to women or children, or to the therapist. Thus fear must become a form of signal anxiety as a part of assessing the safety of other people. In some cases the pastoral counselor's fear means that the man also is afraid and is intimidating others in order to become more comfortable. It is important to ask why the man might be afraid at this moment and why he is resorting to power and control.

Another countertransference issue is rage. One way the counselor can defend against feeling afraid is to opt for power and control. Righteous anger can be tempting when in the presence of someone who is deserving of our anger. The public reaction to child molesters is instructive here: *lock them up, castrate them, let them be raped and see how they like it.* When one feels personally affronted by the violence of another, rage gives the illusion of power and superiority. Yet fear and rage show the risk that the counselor can become very similar to the violent man. A violent man is the expert at using anger to frighten others, at controlling and manipulating others into submission, at the games of domination and terror. While the counselor might have all of these human feelings, pastoral counseling depends on the ability to contain such feelings within a larger context of compassionate strength. These countertransference issues must become the subject of regular supervision when dealing with violent men.[38]

RELIGIOUS ISSUES OF MALE VIOLENCE[39]

Male violence against women and children raises many issues for theological reflection. The church's and theologians' long silence about male violence makes apparent the church's complicity. The following doctrines have bearing on the issues of male violence against women and children.

Salvation

It is remarkable to remember how many biblical stories focus on safety and freedom from violence. To be saved often means to be rescued from death and destruction: God rescues Hagar and Ishmael from the desert and starvation; God rescues Joseph from the pit and sends him to Egypt; God leads the Israelites to freedom from slavery; God rescues Jeremiah from the cistern; God raises Jesus from the tomb; God frees Paul and Silas from prison and other dangers. Yet there is a tendency among settled, wealthy communities of Christians to spiritualize the meaning of salvation into some kind of psychological inner freedom from shame and guilt. Victims of interpersonal violence are recovering the meaning of salvation as safety and freedom from violence.

Salvation as safety and freedom from violence can also be a spiritual resource for men who are violent. Without overstating the case and minimizing the differences between perpetrators and victims of violence, it is possible to see violent behavior as a kind of

155

prison, also. One who has chosen to be interpersonally violent may feel powerful for the moment and may be puffed up by the experience of control over others. But, ultimately, one who uses violence in interpersonal relationships is alone, in a prison of isolation from others, and alienated from the self.

I have worked with violent men over years of pastoral psychotherapy and have felt their imprisonment. When they come to themselves, they realize that they have never been able to love themselves or others. The violence they have inflicted on others comes back on themselves. Salvation from this inner prison can be a commitment to safety and freedom from violence. It is not an exaggeration to say that some men have prayed: *Save me from my own violence.* Parallels to Paul's conversion after killing Christians and to King David's repentance for the violence he did to Bathsheba and Uriah are useful. Salvation can mean safety and freedom from violence for victims, and it can also mean safety and freedom from the doing of harm to others.

Confession, Repentance, Sanctification, Restitution[40]

One of the deepest cries of some violent men is this: *Can I change? Will I ever be safe with my children and my partner again?* Fortunately, the Christian tradition has a strong emphasis on the necessity and possibility of human transformation. Jesus began his ministry by calling his followers to repent. Paul was struck with the blinding light and asked by Christ, "Why are you persecuting me?" This moment changed his life and initiated a reexamination and transformation of his identity. He spent the rest of his ministry calling others to repentance.

Unfortunately, established churches tend to spiritualize the basic concept of repentance so that it becomes a cheaply bought absolution of unnamed sin and evil. Many abusers turn religion into another form of manipulation and control. Caught and threatened by the criminal justice system, some abusers manufacture a conversion: *Judge, I've found Jesus; I'm a new man, and I promise you this will never happen again.*[41] Sometimes religious leaders, lacking an adequate understanding of the deep roots of violence in some personalities, mistake this formulaic response for genuine transformation.

156

As Marie Fortune says, "If it is a genuine experience, this conversion becomes an invaluable resource to the offender who faces incarceration and possibly months of treatment. . . . If it is not genuine, the pastor is virtually the only person who has the authority to call the offender's bluff."[42]

Confession, repentance, sanctification, and restitution are biblical terms that can describe the long road to healing and personal change required of men who are violent. *Confession* means complete openness and honesty about multiple offenses, the consequences for others, and the attitudes and beliefs that lie behind behaviors that harmed others. It means an end to secrecy, deception, lying, rationalization, minimization, and avoidance of the consequences of one's behavior. Full confession itself can be a major undertaking for men who have relied on violence in their lives.

Repentance means turning one's life around and going in a new direction. It means rooting out all the old patterns that made violence an option and seeking new values, beliefs, behaviors, and relationships. In many cases it means leaving one's subculture and circle of friends and seeking out peer groups, mentors, and spiritual directors who have the strength and skill to confront any laziness or self-deception.

Sanctification means practicing the new patterns of behavior with such faithfulness that they become second nature. The old self has died, and a new self is born. It usually takes many years before the new self is reliable.

Restitution means providing resources to victims for the harm that one has caused. In many cases the damage will have been so severe that a man who has been violent must be restrained from direct contact with victims. Most attempts by an abuser to pursue a relationship with a prior victim should be discouraged. This is so that the victim/survivor has the power to determine the nature of any future relationship. Pursuing an ongoing relationship is often experienced by the victim as additional harassment and is often terror-filled. By contrast, sometimes restitution can take the form of providing resources to the victim for therapy, for education, for beginning an independent life.

After child abuse or battering, a violent man has an incredible debt to that person, which may last for many years. Part of confession, repentance, and restitution is the willingness to do whatever it takes to restore the balance of justice in these relationships. In other cases, when support of the victim is impossible, a man in recovery from violence can provide financial and other kinds of support for other victims who seek healing from their experiences of violence. Contributions could be made to a local women's shelter, to organizations that provide low-cost therapy services for children and adult survivors of sexual abuse, and to educational programs to change the attitudes and practices of institutions such as churches, schools, business, and law. If substantial numbers of violent men would have such a change of heart and mind that they would be willing to dedicate their resources to the support of all women and children who suffer from violence, our society would begin to see a new day.

Forgiveness[43]

The meaning of forgiveness has been so cheapened by Christian churches that it is almost useless in terms of healing and reconciliation between people. Because forgiveness is automatically and unconditionally given to everyone without the work of repentance and restitution, this doctrine has become a part of the problem rather than part of the solution. For example, abusers have developed a reputation for going to their pastors after disclosure of their violence and asking for prayers and forgiveness. In too many cases, pastors are willing to engage in this empty ritual and send the abuser back to the family to continue his terror. As a result, many survivors have rejected forgiveness as an important part of their healing process. Rather than forgiveness as the restoration of a relationship with God, forgiveness has become a tool of abuse and stigma. Survivors who are angry are frequently told to stay out of the church until they are willing to forgive. Many survivors have left the church for their own spiritual health, while the men who abused them continue to serve in leadership positions, having interpreted the church's forgiveness as wiping clean all memories of the past.[44]

Yet, in spite of this false theology of forgiveness, some survivors are offering a reinterpretation of the true meaning of forgiveness. Rejecting forgiveness as forgetting, as false reconciliation, as covering up the past, as an obligation laid on those who are vulnerable,

158

some survivors are seeing forgiveness as one of the last steps in the healing process. After a former victim is safe from violence, after she has grieved the many losses caused by her experiences of violence, after she has reorganized her life to the way she wants it to be, after she has gained inner strength and a relationship with God, then the work of forgiveness can be considered.

For the victim, forgiveness is letting go of the immediacy of the trauma, the memory of which continues to terrorize the victim and limit possibilities. The memory is the lens through which the world is viewed. Forgiving involves putting that lens aside but keeping it close at hand. It is the choice to no longer allow the memory of the abuse to continue to abuse. But this step of healing must be carried out according to the victim's timetable.[45]

In this context, forgiveness is redefined as an aspect of healing: not only inner healing of the spirituality of the survivor but also healing of the relational web that includes other people. Violence rends God's web of relational love that holds people together. Forgiveness as healing creates new webs of relational love through solidarity between victim/survivors and their advocates.[46] This reinterpretation of forgiveness moves beyond a naive desire for forgetting or overlooking that many offenders wish for but which is often reabusive for the survivor. In this context, forgiveness does not mean one-to-one reconciliation, but it means that the internalized hatred that resulted from the violence has been overcome in the loving spirit of the survivor. Healing has progressed to a spiritual depth where hatred of abusers is no longer the primary force in one's life.[47]

Theology of Power and Sexuality

Some of the distortions about male violence come because of the church's confusion about power and sexuality. Historically, rape has often been blamed on the seductive woman, battering on the rebellious woman, and even child abuse on the responsibility of parents to instill discipline and respect for authority. When children and women complain of abuse and violence, church leaders often refuse to believe their stories, and side with the man whom they perceive as having authority in the situation. The blessing of heterosexual relationships within the family without regard for issues of power

159

and violence have created dangerous situations for women and children.

Fortunately, much good work has been done lately on issues of power and sexuality. Marie Fortune's *Sexual Violence*[48] was one of the first to identify this problem, and much other work has been done to revise this aspect of the church's theology.[49]

The Sin and Evil of Male Violence

Male violence against women and children must lead the church and its theologians to reconsider the questions of sin and evil.[50] A significant pastoral problem in working with violent men is that they don't know how to confront the reality that they have deliberately harmed someone they thought they loved. In spite of biblical passages about the slaughter of the firstborn sons of Egypt, the slaughter of people and animals in the time of the Judges, Herod's slaughter of all male infants in the region of Bethlehem, and the torture and murder of Jesus, the church has been virtually silent on the issue of male violence against women and children.

If more than 25 percent of Christians have experienced sexual and physical violence at the hands of men, what does this silence mean? It means that the church and its theologians have failed to address one of the most common expressions of evil in the experience of its own members. Violent men have a right to ask the church: *How could I be violent toward someone I love? How could the church allow me to engage in this behavior to the damnation of my soul and not confront me with God's judgment and grace?* Most men who have come to me for help are at a total loss to face these questions themselves. They have never heard sermons, Bible studies, prayers, or spiritual guidance on these questions. They have been left to their own rationalizations to figure out the religious importance of their experience and their thought processes have led them in even more destructive directions.

I dream of a time when male violence against women and children becomes a part of the church's theology of sin and evil. What would it look like? It would be a theology that refused to ignore the danger of tyrannical power in interpersonal relationships, whether enforced by physical strength, sexual abuse, male dominance, or threat

160

of violence. It would be a theology that was realistic about the spiritual dangers to one's soul of abusive power over those who are vulnerable. It would be a theology that squarely faced the evils of gender inequality, forced sexual abuse, male power and control, and exemption from accountability and consequences. Such a new theology of evil would acknowledge that the church perpetuates these dangers when it idolizes the family, when it idealizes parental authority, when it accedes to the male dominance of our culture, and when it contributes to the confusion of sexuality and power. I believe that facing the evil of male violence within the church requires a reinterpretation of much of the church's theology. The only way a massive evil such as this could be overlooked is by the church allowing the evil of male dominance to cloud its vision of the gospel, thus overlooking the presence of violent interpersonal relationships among Christians.

Jesus: Authority without Violence

Can the figure of Jesus be reconstructed as an image of authority without violence? In a culture where authority is patriarchal in structure, Christology has often been problematic. Some liberal Christologies project a docile Jesus who, though nonviolent, was hardly a figure of authority. Rather Jesus' virtues of submission, obedience, long-suffering, and meekness corresponded very closely to the nineteenth-century cult of true womanhood, which included piety, purity, submissiveness, and domesticity.[51] The Christian virtues of love were best preserved by women who stayed at home away from the brutality of the raging industrial economy. Conservative theologians have emphasized the imperial and victorious Jesus, the right hand of the Father-God, who wields power with terrible consequences for those who are lost. This Jesus bore the cross with full confidence in the victory afterwards and has full authority to reign on behalf of the almighty, omnipotent God.

Neither of these Christologies is helpful for men who want to recover from their violent patterns. They need a new Christology that reveals an image of internal strength to take responsibility for their violent tendencies and to accept accountability for those whom they have abused and controlled in the past. They need a new

Christology that reveals a different kind of authority, not only an authority that is nonviolent but one that also values mutuality, equality, and respect between all persons. Given the long history of patriarchal theology, a new Christology will take many years to emerge fully. Fortunately, the women's movement has already started the process of theological transformation, and Christian men need to join in.[52]

CONCLUSION

This chapter has summarized some of the pastoral care and counseling issues of male violence against women and children. Many women are coming to the church with complaints and lawsuits about male violence in Christian families and by Christian leaders. A few men are coming to the church and its pastors for guidance concerning their violent behaviors and attitudes. The church is not prepared to deal with these pastoral needs because they seem to be new and because the church has not faced its complicity in this problem.

In this chapter, I have summarized some of the current literature about male violence and suggested some ways that pastoral care and counseling must be revised to respond to this pastoral issue. Finally, I suggested some theological implications for the church's doctrine and practice. I hope that facing the issue of male violence against women and children will enable the church to fulfill its pastoral care responsibilities to all of God's people whether they are victims and survivors of violence or recovering perpetrators who seek redemption for their lives.

CHAPTER EIGHT

PASTORAL CARE OF GAY MEN

Randle Mixon

INTRODUCTION

This chapter addresses issues of suffering, healing, and wholeness in the lives of gay men living in the United States of America in the late-twentieth century. If the focus seems too much on suffering, it may be attributed to an assumption that a major function of pastoral care is to help careseekers deal with the difficulties that people face in living in the world. Some of the assumptions here about the difficulties faced by gay men are based on the author's experience, both personal and clinical, and some are based on clinical research in psychology and pastoral care and counseling. The chapter also recognizes that there are real strengths gay men bring to living in the world and that pastoral caregivers, in their function of facilitating growth and community, need to be aware of these as well.

This chapter also addresses some of the standard myths and stereotypes about gay men that are shaped by the dominant culture and how these shape the lives of gay men. These include beliefs that gay men are sex-obsessed and promiscuous; that gay men are effeminate and therefore less than adequate men; that gay men are determined recruiters and therefore a danger to children and adolescents; and that gay men are vain and preoccupied with maintaining their youth and beauty. Such myths and stereotypes are insidious, for not only are they imposed on gay men by the dominant culture, which insists that all gay men are like this, they also may creep into the self-understanding of gay men and become self-fulfilling prophecy as well as internalized sources of oppression.

These myths and stereotypes are often devastating to gay men as they struggle to adopt healthy lifestyles[1]—lifestyles that have integrity both for their gay being and for their personal values. This can be illustrated by the cries of frustration, anger, and pain from gay men attempting to reconcile their beliefs about love and faithfulness in relationship with the belief that in order to be gay one must immerse oneself in a particular gay subculture that does not support the former values. For example, a gay man desiring the intimacy and connection of a human relationship goes to a gay bar where, in a dark, noisy, smoky room, he seeks out other gay men in hopes of finding the perfect partner. What he often finds is that no one in the bar measures up to his ideal, so he settles for some form of disconnected sexual encounter or he experiences rejection and devaluing because he himself does not measure up to the physical ideal projected by a prospective partner.

Where is the support for healthy alternative lifestyles for gay men, many of whom hold the same traditional values as their heterosexual counterparts about love, fidelity, responsibility, caring, home, and relationship, though they have been told all their lives that they are incapable of holding these values? The author believes that pastoral care and counseling hold some answers to this question.

CONTEXT

The population with which this chapter is concerned is gay men living in the United States of America.[2] In some sense, this classification of human beings is a relatively recent phenomenon, even though the practice of men having sex with other men is as old as human being. It is only in the last 150 years or so that the notion of men actually forming same-sex, primary, and lasting relationships has come to be common, at least in this culture.[3] Still, it is not easy to be a gay man in this culture. There are many layers of suffering one must endure when claiming a gay identity and adopting a gay lifestyle.

ALIENATION FROM PASTORAL CARE AND COUNSELING

With few exceptions, gay men have not turned to pastoral care and counseling for resources of healing and comfort because they

164

have feared that they would not be understood or accepted.[4] The routes to pastoral care and counseling are either nonexistent or impassibly damaged due to real and/or perceived prejudice. This is a legacy of the antigay prejudice in religion, in psychology, and in the current culture. Stories abound of gay men rejected by families and churches—for example, the gifted seminary student whose father, on learning of his son's gayness, took him to the nearest freeway entrance and dumped him. Stories of gay men hiding in closets of pseudorespectability also abound, though they are not often shared publicly unless one of these men is caught in a compromising situation.

Gay men are no different than any other population in their need for pastoral care. The need for spiritual connection and pastoral care is profound for gay men, especially since most gay men live intimately with suffering and death in the age of AIDS. Yet gay men have consistently responded in one of two ways to the church and its function of pastoral caregiving: either they have rejected the church in pain and anger in the face of rampant heterosexism and homohatred,[5] or they have remained in the church, carefully hiding their identities and their needs. In both cases, adequate pastoral caregiving has been unavailable to gay men. This is true even—and sometimes especially—for those closeted gay men working as pastoral caregivers whose own internalized homophobia interferes with their ability to be present fully to other gay men in need.

Given this context of alienation, the task for pastoral caregivers is twofold: (1) to address the prejudices of their own traditions and discipline, and (2) to rethink how they offer pastoral care and counseling to gay men. It is not sufficient for pastoral caregivers to attend to the needs of gay men seeking care without also involving themselves in enlightening their disciplines and transforming their traditions, which have been guilty of perpetuating prejudice and injustice. To attempt to offer care and counsel while embracing a context that is negative toward gay men creates the kind of double bind that is troubling for careseeker and caregiver alike.

Pastoral caregivers must be conscious of the particular concerns of gay men. The best caregiving requires acceptance of men being gay, not just tolerance. "Love the sinner, hate the sin" is an inadequate, though common, pastoral response to the needs of gay men

165

for pastoral care. Gay men are underevaluated and underserved by pastoral care and counseling. Yet, they experience profound distress, sickness, pain, and death as well as deep joy, hope, caring, and healing—the stuff of which pastoral caregiving is made. Gay men need the support and healing that pastoral care and counseling, at its best, can provide. At the same time, gay men have much to teach the field of pastoral care and counseling about creatively shaping illness experience and gracefully plumbing the depths of suffering in search of human wholeness.

BASIC ASSUMPTIONS

Basic assumptions for this chapter come from theological,[6] psychological, and pastoral care and counseling[7] sources. These assumptions are encapsulated in the belief that all of life is God's good gift. The myths and stereotypes about gay men, most of which are created and/or sustained by religion in its various forms, have tended to distance gay men from the realization of their rightful role in God's creation and to deny them their human wholeness, which includes vital experiences of relationship and community. Though social and cultural change that would value gay men as part of God's good creation is highly desirable, healing, wholeness, care, and relationship are not totally dependent on such change. Gay men can and do come to wholeness and healing in the face of prejudice and suffering. The gracious assistance of skilled caregivers on both the sociocultural and personal fronts can greatly enhance these processes.

NEGATIVE PSYCHOSOCIAL EXPERIENCES OF GAY MEN

Stigmatization

Stigmatization is the process whereby someone or something is labeled wrong, bad, unclean, impure, inadequate, or "less than."[8] For gay men, stigmatization is often first experienced externally in antigay humor; in ridicule for nonconformity to accepted and expected sociocultural norms; in avoidance, neglect, or overconcern of and for children who are different by family, peers, and institutions; and in the heterosexism endemic to this culture that lifts up only heterosexual images and models as acceptable and valuable.

The clear message to a gay male growing up currently in the United States is that there is indeed something inherently wrong with him—that he is unclean, inadequate, and bad. For example, one sees virtually no positive role models for healthy homosexual relationships on television or in the movies. "Fag" jokes and gay bashing are still commonplace, socially sanctioned forms of violence, even in such "liberal" cities as San Francisco and New York. The religious right continues to press its agenda of homo hatred by actively opposing basic gay rights as "special rights" and advocating for antigay legislation throughout the country. In some courts of law in this country "homosexual panic" has been accepted as a defense in gay bashing and murder cases. Experiences of stigmatization lead to marginalization, a phenomenon with both external and internal roots for gay men.

Marginalization

As a result of stigmatization people find themselves confronted with a difficult choice: either they make some sort of "false self" adjustment to sociocultural expectations and try to live as someone they are not, or they openly confront discrimination and abuse and find themselves living on the margins of society. A self-affirming gay man will have difficulty finding acceptance in the workplace, in school, in church, and in various social interactions and institutions because of stigmatization. He will either spend a great amount of psychic and physical energy trying to make himself acceptable and accepted, or he will reject the institutions and lifestyles of the dominant culture and invest his energy in the creation of an alternative world. Even in a supposedly enlightened environment like the San Francisco Bay area, one hears stories of gay men reluctant to take a male date, or even a life partner, to an office party for fear that management will block further advancement for openly gay employees. Or one finds, even in supposedly welcoming and affirming congregations, that it is not permissible for two men to hold hands or otherwise show affection as their heterosexual counterparts do for fear of being accused of flaunting their lifestyle.

Often the alternative worlds have been seen as underworlds: seamy, mysterious, immoral, and illegal—for example, bars, bathhouses, sex clubs, and public parks and restrooms—or they have been seen as poor imitations of the dominant culture's institutions and lifestyles—that is, gay men playing house, engaged in acting out traditional male and female roles. John Reid's novel, *The Best Little Boy in the World*,[9] is an amusing tale of someone going to great lengths to pass as heterosexual. On the other hand, drag and leather scenes are ways in which gay men try to assert their distinctiveness. Both of these marginalizing resolutions to the problem of stigmatization can be linked to feeling shame and can involve acting out that shame.

Shame

Shame is the feeling that there is something wrong with oneself. It also serves the self-protective function of keeping the vulnerable aspects of oneself safe from attack by persons who, one believes, would not understand and, therefore, would not accept one's self-identity. There are times when it is appropriate to feel shame,[10] but the concern here is with what has been labeled a "toxic sense of shame,"[11] that deep-seated belief that one *is* fundamentally wrong or bad, a belief that shapes all the rest of one's feelings, thoughts, and behavior. Many gay men seen in clinical and pastoral settings suffer from the consequences of low self-esteem born of shame about their fundamental being. Often these clients or careseekers want to be "healed" of their homosexuality in hopes of finding a more positive sense of self in the heterosexual masculine ideal.

The experience of HIV disease coincides with the existing sense of shame in gay men and exacerbates that condition as they try to make sense of this new experience of perceiving themselves as "damaged goods." An HIV diagnosis is seen as proof-positive that there is something inherently wrong with one. Closely related to shame, and often confused with it, is guilt.

Guilt

Guilt is the feeling that one has done something wrong. Guilt may be characterized as moral when it is based on the reality of having done something wrong, or it may be characterized as neurotic when it is the transgression of some ideal not grounded in reality.[12] It is usually accompanied by a sense that one must pay for or suffer some consequence for one's misbehavior. In the case of gay men, misbehavior may be seen as engaging in sexual behavior that is inconsistent with one's personal values although acceptable to the value system of the subculture. For example, practices associated with the sexual freedom of gay liberation of the 1970s—bathhouses, public sex, multiple partners, casual and anonymous sex—all potentially contribute to a sense of guilt in those for whom more traditional values would characterize authenticity as it also does for many now living with HIV disease.[13] The reverse may also be true in terms of gay men feeling guilt for adhering to traditional values that are not consonant with their authentic needs. For these, guilt may manifest as the feeling that their more circumspect behavior is a betrayal of their gay identity and their gay brothers.

This latter phenomenon finds a special connection to the complex notion of survival guilt. Survival guilt is common for those gay men who have watched so many in their community die of AIDS. They come to believe that somehow HIV and AIDS is a part of what it means to *be* gay.[14] Many see their HIV disease as punishment for their misbehavior. In concert with a toxic sense of shame, guilt can add to the burden one bears in living with HIV disease, and can actually contribute to an immobilizing condition for some sufferers. Feelings of shame and guilt are linked with stigmatization and marginalization in the complex social phenomena of homophobia, heterosexism, and misogyny.

Homophobia, Heterosexism, and Misogyny[15]

Homophobia was originally defined by George Weinberg as an irrational fear on the part of heterosexuals of being in close proximity to people they believe to be homosexual.[16] Since Weinberg coined the term in 1972, it has taken on a much larger meaning and is often paired with the term heterosexism because the fear is more complex than originally delineated. Homophobia is now more commonly used to incorporate prejudice against anything having to do with homosexual being and behavior.

Homophobia and heterosexism are essentially opposite sides of the same coin. The disdain for homosexuality that is homophobia is based on a fear of difference. What is this difference? Are the feelings and expressions of a gay man fundamentally different from those of any other human being? Not really. The root of the difference is in the reification of heterosexuality, the insistence that because heterosexuality is the experience of the majority, it is the only acceptable sexual option for healthy human beings. Heterosexuality, as *one* of the options for sexual expression in God's created order, is lifted up as *the only* option, thereby becoming heterosexism. Heterosexism is a tyranny that denies to human beings appreciation and modeling of, as well as support for, other forms of sexual expression including homosexuality. Gay men are criticized and condemned for not living up to an ideal that is dissonant with their fundamental being and, at the same time, are frustrated or denied in their attempts to develop expressions that are consonant with that being.

Another important aspect of these reified social constructions of sexuality for gay men is the assumption that if one is not a heterosexual male—the paradigm of power in this culture—then he cannot be male, at least not fully. So part of the disdain and hatred of gay men is rooted in disdain for and hatred of women in this culture. Heterosexual masculinity becomes the ideal against which all other forms of human sexual expression are measured, and all other forms are found wanting. A culture in which a particular heterosexual ideal, characterized by a double binding, double standard of male domination and abuse of females, is paired with "traditional family values" leaves little room for any sexual and/or lifestyle variation that would bring attention to the absurdity of this double standard or challenge the dominance of this bizarre ideal.

An important aspect of homophobia, related to the discussion of stigma, shame, and guilt, is the tendency of many, if not all, gay men to internalize their experiences of homophobia, thereby blaming themselves for the exigencies of their condition, secretly or openly agreeing that the dominant sociocultural ideal of masculine heterosexuality is right, and, concluding, therefore, that they and their sense of reality are wrong.

170

PSYCHOSOCIAL STIGMATIZATION

Many psychologists as well as psychotherapists and pastoral caregivers have believed they could change a person's sexual orientation from homosexual to heterosexual if given enough time.[17] Like Freud,[18] they have tended to project their own—largely male and heterosexual—ways of being in the world outward onto patients, clients, and careseekers in expectation that this "like me" projection represents the ideal. By virtue of being in helping professions, they have tended not to condemn gay men outright but have either worked long and hard at, or despaired of, "fixing" careseekers' homosexuality. There is ample evidence that these attempts are unsuccessful and misguided. Much of the so-called change that has been seen is the result of patients, clients, and careseekers suppressing their same-sex feelings in the service of a social conformity that sometimes results in some relief from the pain of stigmatization. However, these attempts at change may just as easily lead to self-destructive behavior such as suicide. Little is written by these "masters of change" about the cost to individuals, families, and society of making such a "false self" adjustment.[19]

In addition to the psychological, there is also important literature on social deviance that is relevant here since there seems to be something of an obsession in this culture with what is and is not "normal." Normalcy is a complex and misunderstood concept. Some of this literature describes social norms in relatively value-free ways. Some of it tends to lift social norms to the level of the ideal, thereby saying, or at least implying, that what is normative is also what is natural, right, or good.[20] This latter is an abuse of the term "normal," which technically means what is statistically most prevalent, but too often has come to characterize the way a dominant group believes something *should* be. The judgments of society on those who do not conform to social norms, and of psychology on those who do not fit a particular psychological profile, are significant factors in the layering of suffering for gay men.

RELIGIOUS JUDGMENT

The Judaeo-Christian tradition has been particularly harsh in its judgment of homosexual persons and homosexual practices.[21] Presently, most Protestant denominations as well as the Roman Catholic Church have official pronouncements that homosexuality, or at least homosexual behavior, is sinful. As a result of these judgments, sexual minority persons experience outright banning from these bodies or, at least, are denied full membership in the sense of being denied such rites as ordination and the blessing of their relationships. Much of this judgment is a function of the heterosexism and homophobia that are ingrained in the culture, and is based on culture-bound interpretations of the Bible.

Some biblical scholars argue that Old Testament holiness codes, designed to protect the existence, as well as the racial purity, of the Children of Israel, are awkwardly applied to twentieth-century experience in ways that are not useful, meaningful, or accurate. These scholars believe that certain homosexual behaviors were seen as a threat to the social and cultural identity of those wandering monotheists. Similar arguments are raised about New Testament writers who wanted to distinguish themselves and their evolving religious identity from the pagan culture in which they were immersed.[22] From these ancient proscriptions of sexual behavior comes a belief system in which anyone appropriating a gay lifestyle is judged to be inferior and evil in the eyes of those who subscribe to the system.[23]

Currently in the United States these ancient texts are being transferred whole cloth to a defense of the "traditional family"—that is, a nuclear family with a mother, father, and 2.3 children. The "traditional family" is interpreted to be God's will for all human beings (with the possible exception of those who are celibate for religious reasons). Anyone found outside the "traditional family" model, whether by choice or circumstance, is considered less than ideal—unclean and impure. For example, there have been court judgments in many states forbidding, or at least interfering with, the rights of gay and lesbian parents to raise their own biological children. Related judgments preclude stable, nurturing homosexual couples and individuals from adoption and foster care thereby denying loving homes to needy children. There are constant, ongoing strategies, especially from the religious right, to talk about "*the* gay lifestyle*,*" in an attempt to characterize gay men in terms of myths and stereotypes—preoccupied with sex, promiscuous, preying on children, and determined to destroy the traditional nuclear family.

172

Some of this judgment must be seen as backlash to liberation movements of all kinds; though, in this culture in which heterosexism cuts across all party and cultural lines, gay liberation seems particularly vulnerable as sexual minority persons are attacked from liberal as well as conservative quarters.

The deification of the "traditional family" appears as a misguided effort to secure some misshapen ideal of happiness in a world experienced as being increasingly insecure and unhappy. The current obsession, especially of the religious right, with protecting "traditional family values," coupled with a long tradition of sex-negative interpretation of ancient texts that originally referred to sexual behavior in relation to particular religious practices, has helped to create a hostile and painful environment in which to identify oneself as a gay man. The particular suffering of gay men, as they have struggled to accept their orientation, to find identities that embrace that orientation, and then to live fully in the world, has been greatly aggravated by religious proclamations and practices that have judged them to be inferior human beings and perversions of God's creative intent. These proclamations and practices have shaped significantly contemporary culture as well as the experiences of gay men.

HIV DISEASE AND THE AIDS EPIDEMIC

In the early 1980s, a strange disease was first observed, in this country, that seemed to be spreading largely among gay and bisexual men. Initially, this disease was called GRIDS, or Gay Related Immune Deficiency Syndrome. Eventually, the cause of the disease was shown to be a blood-borne virus that attacks the human immune system and makes it vulnerable to opportunistic infections. Most of these infections are the result of the immune system's inability to fight off bacteria and other viruses, many of which are commonly present in the human body but have no deleterious effects as long as the immune system is healthy and keeps them at bay.

Although the virus can be transmitted from one person to another through any blood-to-blood contact, including blood transfusions, fetal contact, and sharing unclean instruments (notably needle sharing in intravenous drug use), the most common form of transmission is through sexual contact. The fact that the vast majority of cases worldwide have been heterosexually transmitted has been largely overlooked by the public in the United States. The majority of cases in the United States are among the gay and bisexual male population; the other significant population, in terms of numbers, are intravenous drug users.[24] Now, increasingly, those being infected in the United States in both of these categories are people of color on the poorer end of the socioeconomic scale.

Even though the label for the disease was changed from GRIDS to AIDS (Acquired Immune Deficiency Syndrome)—a recognition that the virus itself is quite neutral about whom it infects—it is still widely considered a "gay disease," something that gay men have brought on themselves. This is especially evident in the often-made distinction between those "innocent victims" of AIDS (infants, hemophiliacs, transfusion recipients) and those whose bad behavior caused their infection (sexually transmitted cases and intravenous drug users). Some actually see AIDS as God's judgment on gay men for their evil ways.[25]

As with the phenomenon of homophobia, many gay men have tended to internalize this "blame the victim" mentality, believing that they are being punished by God (or the universe) for their misbehavior and their mis-being. Wrestling with the disease not only taps into their guilt about risky sexual behavior but also their shame in being gay in the first place. The combination of stigmatization from the general culture and the self-acceptance of that stigmatization by many gay men has added significantly to the suffering of gay men living with HIV disease.

STRENGTHS OF GAY MEN

Although it is difficult to live a healthy life in a heterosexist and homophobic environment, there are persons who learn to embrace their sexuality and live with it in positive and creative ways. The contemporary United States is a sex-negative society, yet there are sexually healthy gay men living in it who rise above stigma, pain, and suffering to live full, rich lives.

One of the strengths of gay men comes directly from these experiences of pain. It is profound empathy, a deep and integrated

174

sensitivity to the feelings, wants, and needs of others. Sometimes this sensitivity may manifest as self-effacing or codependent behavior born of shame in one's own identity—for example, the "Best Little Boy in the World" syndrome, wherein one is exceedingly helpful and compliant in order to keep others from discovering the terrifying secret of one's homosexuality. More often, this sensitivity, when encouraged, has helped gay men to engage in healthy and fulfilling relationships, and to challenge the insensitivity of macho stereotypes in which self-interest is always placed ahead of relationships.

A second strength has been the heroic way in which gay men have risen up to care for one another in the AIDS epidemic.[26] There are countless stories, too many of them untold, of tender care and sacrificial giving in support of lovers, friends, and strangers wrestling with HIV disease and AIDS. In San Francisco, a model for professional and volunteer care, largely designed and directed by members of the gay, lesbian, and bisexual communities, has been widely envied throughout the world.[27] Part of what makes this model unique is the concentration of lesbian, gay, and bisexual people in the San Francisco Bay area, and the ways in which those people already had begun to affirm, develop, and celebrate sexual minority lifestyles before the epidemic.

A third strength comes from having suffered stigmatization and marginalization. William James refers to this as the blessing of the "twice-born," those who have experienced real distress in their lives and yet have managed to make meaning from that experience. Because of their experiences, these "twice-born" understand and embrace the richness of life that incorporates suffering.[28] Those who have suffered are often more sensitive to and compassionate with others who are suffering. Some gay men have, in John Fortunato's term, come to "embrace the exile."[29] They have learned to accept, celebrate, and love aspects of their marginalized experience, aspects that, while constraining them, have also led them to clearer understanding of their personal values and of the value of community life. In creating the communities of support and understanding vital to experiencing the fullness of being human, many have learned well to rely on their own resources and those of like-minded people. Where one might be blindly and mindlessly drawn into the heterosexist, misogynist, and homo-hating values of the dominant cul-

175

ture, the experience of being gay, and of accepting that state of being, gives many gay men a richer appreciation of life and its possibilities.

A fourth strength is the struggle of many gay men to live beyond the traditional masculine expectations of the culture. Part of the struggle in accepting gay identity has been to understand and accept the more feminine aspects of oneself. Because gay men have often been stereotyped as effeminate,[30] they have had to wrestle with what that stereotype means for them externally and internally. The result has been ongoing gender confusion for some, a kind of hypermasculinity for others, and for still others, a sensitive understanding and acceptance of the richness that comes to one's being when one embraces those aspects of oneself that have been labeled, and therefore condemned, as feminine. These characteristics include attention to relationships beyond their function or usefulness; sensitivity to emotions; and a passion for justice that sees men and women, in fact, all of God's creation, as being of incomparable value.

There is a growing literature for counseling lesbian, gay, and bisexual people[31] that takes as its starting point that homosexuality is within the range of naturally occurring sexual variation in human beings. This literature serves to affirm and support healthy sexual minority lifestyles, to build self-esteem, to encourage assertive behavior, and to ease the sociocultural burdens of being other than heterosexual. But what of pastoral care and counseling?

ISSUES OF CONCERN FOR PASTORAL CARE AND COUNSELING

Some of the concerns and needs of gay men that should be addressed by pastoral caregivers are: identity, development, socialization, emotions, relationships, and health, both physical and spiritual.

Identity

Identity here is related to the notion of a core sense of self and to ideas about persona and self. That is, one must receive from parenting figures enough nurture, feedback, and structure to have a kernel of who one is and who one might become. A man moves from undifferentiated potentiality to developing a core sense of self with

176

both ego strength and persona, to reflecting on the authenticity of that identity in the "second half of life."[32]

A major difficulty for gay men centers around claiming a sense of identity that is comfortable and authentic. Gay men are born with the same undifferentiated potentiality present in other humans, but, for whatever combination of reasons—nature and/or nurture—[33] they are faced with incorporating an attraction to members of their own gender into the process of becoming men. Expectations within the dominant cultural paradigm about being a man, at least in the United States in the late-twentieth century, offer little support for claiming and developing a gay male identity.

Many gay men know at an early age that they are different from other boys, and they trace their sexual identity to this point of recognition. Some seek to hide their growing awareness of difference and their attraction to other boys in a flurry of overachievement and compliant behavior. Others develop a kind of hypermasculinity to hide behind, and the world is particularly shocked when a sports hero or military man declares his gayness. Still others give up the idea of hiding and take on stereotyped effeminate behaviors and, as scapegoats, carry the ridicule the others so desperately avoid.

Conflicts arise around cultural, social, and religious beliefs about male superiority and dominance that imply the need for an inferior class of beings (traditionally women, though gay men may suffice) who must submit in order for men to be men. A potential ongoing struggle for gay men in relating to one another may be characterized by tension over who is dominant and who is submissive. The struggle to claim a gay identity becomes enmeshed in the misogynist expectations of culture and church.[34]

Development

Because personal and social support is lacking, gay men have few, if any, models for being gay. It is not uncommon for gay men to experience a kind of delayed adolescence in the sense that important developmental tasks ordinarily accomplished in adolescent dating and relationship experiments are not altogether successfully learned by gay men. Even though many gay men do date women in an effort to fit into the group and in response to peer pressure, these experiences do not carry the sexual charge of actually dating someone to whom the gay man is physically attracted. Sometimes years later, a gay man will find himself struggling with developmental tasks he did not accomplish as an adolescent that are necessary to the formation of solid, adult relationships. It is awkward, if not painful, for an adult male to attempt to revisit adolescent dating and relationship experiments at an advanced age. He often believes there is something wrong with him and goes to great lengths to cover up this developmental attenuation or to avoid the effort altogether.

Socialization

The experience of delayed adolescence has ramifications for the gay man's social interactions. Not only may he be somewhat awkward in forming relationships, he may have developed a life-long habit of believing that those relationships and other social expressions of his gayness are inferior and unacceptable. Often he has found his sexual as well as his social outlets in underworlds that the dominant culture judges as unacceptable and unclean. The real and perceived necessity of keeping one's identity and social reality a secret has profound implications for how one interacts with persons, groups, and institutions.

Emotions

Gay men experience the same range of emotions as other human beings, though there may be some unique aspects to their experience of emotions. Emotions such as shame, guilt, and rage may dominate the gay man's interior landscape, as they do that of other victims. One therapist who specializes in working with gay men refers to the "bellyful of tears"—a powerful mix of sadness and anger—that many gay men carry around. Some of this phenomenon is undoubtedly related to the "Best Little Boy in the World" syndrome in which a boy learns to hold his emotions tightly in check lest he draw undue attention to himself. Too often gay men bury their feelings so deeply they lose awareness of them and how those feelings shape their lives (much like their heterosexual male counterparts).

Shutting off some feelings means shutting off all feelings. It is impossible to numb the emotions that one experiences as painful and labels as negative without also numbing emotions of happiness, joy, and love as well.[35] Many gay men believe they are not entitled to such "positive" feelings anyway by virtue of their inferiority. Here, of course, self-esteem becomes an issue as well.

In the age of AIDS an additional burden of grief is added as gay men wrestle at an early age with phenomena of multiple loss. It is common in some urban settings for a gay man to have lost his entire circle of friends and acquaintances to AIDS. How does one replace one twenty-year friendship, let alone several? It cannot be done. Many men are left lost and alone with no one to share their grief at the very time they must face the daunting prospect of trying to rebuild their lives. The question of whether it is worth the effort is often asked—and too often answered in the negative.

Relationships

Gay men's relationships are too often characterized by an inability to share intimacy and by difficulty in sustaining interpersonal links over time. Lack of support and modeling are significant in shaping this problem as is the devastating experience of losing one's friends and partner(s) to AIDS. Internalized homophobia, fear of losing another partner, the acute pain of rejection for men who already feel inadequate, and the lack of social sanction and support all add to the difficulties in forming and maintaining meaningful relationships among gay men.

Health

For many gay men, struggling with issues of physical health also brings up issues of spiritual health. As gay men seek to make meaning of lives threatened with the possibility and the reality of death, they have found themselves alienated from traditional religious resources. Means of spiritual support and development have not been in place and readily accessible. While bodies disintegrated under the onslaught of disease, vital tools for making meaning were not available. This has added to the burden of being gay in the United States in the late-twentieth century.

Yet the reader must not take these statements of issues facing gay men as characteristic of all gay men or the inevitable result of the

179

"sin" or pathology of *being* gay. Many gay men have found their way through to health and wholeness in spite of the burdens of a dominating culture that has sought to demonize them. In many cases this movement has happened in spite of the church and the added weight of the church's condemnation.

Pastoral caregivers and counselors reading this chapter must be aware of the dilemmas *and* the strengths that gay men will bring as careseekers. Pastoral caregivers and counselors should understand that, as in most caregiving situations, they will gain as much as they give in caring for and with gay men. The task here is to humanize the processes of care by recognizing that any gay man, as much as the caregiver he seeks out, is made in the image and likeness of God. Without this as a starting point, a caregiving relationship should not be begun.

CASE STUDY[36]

Jerry is a thirty-seven-year-old gay white male living in San Francisco. Though he has a responsible job as a computer programmer, he has returned to school for a master's degree in counseling. Jerry is a healthy and reasonably attractive man who lives alone. He, with his younger brother and sister, was born and raised in a midwestern city. His parents and his sister, with her husband and child, still live there. His brother lives on the east coast with his wife and two children.

He comes for counseling because he is unhappy with his life. He had hoped the professional transition from computers to counseling would give him a sense of fulfillment, but now he finds himself stuck in producing his thesis, an exploration of the psychological effects of HIV disease on HIV-negative gay men. Though he was drawn to this topic through personal concerns, now professors and colleagues see the work as valuable, and he is worried he will never finish it.

Initially, his counselor Fred, the director of the Good Shepherd Counseling Center, thinks Jerry's being stuck is typical graduate student procrastination. He interprets it as Jerry's resistance to growing up and leaving school and encourages Jerry to keep working. He also explores with Jerry the reasons for his more general unhappiness.

What he discovers is Jerry's loneliness and insecurity about his identity. Jerry is not "out" to his family, though he assumes they suspect. No one has addressed the possibility of his being gay, though they have stopped asking him about dating and marriage. Part of the problem with completing his master's thesis is that his proud family will want to see it, but how will he explain its subject matter without coming out?

Growing up, Jerry sensed that he was different. He did not seem interested in typical boy things and was not good at sports. He tended to be friends with girls in his classes, though he felt a strange attraction to other boys. He was particularly fascinated with the masculinity of his father and some of his uncles and older cousins. Part of his attraction was a desire to be more like them, though he couldn't imagine how.

His own father thought him an anomaly. He didn't know what to do with this son who couldn't throw a ball and liked to play house. His mother appreciated his willingness to help around the house. Though both his parents were proud of his good work in school, they worried about his tendency to isolate himself in books as he grew older. He did not seem close to his peers or siblings. Little did they realize the shame he felt about being different and the ridicule, real and perceived, he experienced.

Even though he had known something about his sexual orientation for most of his life, he found it difficult to express this reality. He tried to date girls in high school and college, but felt insincere and lost when there was no spark between them. He prayed fervently to be healed of his homosexuality. In college he even sought out counseling in which the counselor raised the imponderable question of how he could be sure he was gay if he had never "been with a woman." Since he had never "been with a man" either, the counselor's challenge did not make much sense to him.

Ironically, the question encouraged him to think more about what he wanted from life. Finally, he summoned the courage to go to the gay bar in the town where he attended college. Initially, he was quite excited by the prospect of finding the man of his dreams, but he was put off by the bar's dark, noisy atmosphere and, as he did not drink or smoke, he felt very much out of place. He sat in a corner feeling ashamed and guilty. No one spoke to him, nor he to anyone, not that there was anything inviting about his anxious and confused countenance. He did observe others talking, laughing, dancing, and making out—which public display of his private fantasy both fascinated and repulsed him.

In his mind this experience confirmed what he had heard and read about homosexuals—they were shallow, sex-obsessed, and promiscuous, alienated from families and churches, and held none of the values he did. These beliefs created painful conflict in him because he still felt attracted to men and longed to be involved with one.

Jerry's conflict is compounded by having been raised in a conservative Protestant church in which he found a sense of belonging as a child and in which he was very involved as a youth. His family still is active in that church. At one time, Jerry had considered ministry. He rejected that idea as he came to grips with his gayness and realized that there would be no place for a gay minister in his denomination. The thought of living in the closet was too painful for him, though the idea of "coming out" was equally troubling. He knew he longed for a life partnership with another man and that it would be too difficult to hide that relationship while attempting to serve a congregation.

In response to these conflicts, he had lived a lonely, celibate existence until he came to San Francisco. Here, in "the gay Mecca," he hoped that life might be different. Perhaps he would find the partner of his dreams and settle down. But in some ways his situation worsened. While it was true that there was more public gay life than he had ever imagined, he found it difficult to participate. He had never dated other men and, in spite of the apparent opportunities, he did not know how to begin to make his desires known to another man. He was tongue-tied when faced with someone attractive. It was easier to escape into his school work, and he soon found himself in his familiar position of isolation.

Fred has come to see that not only is Jerry having difficulty finishing his thesis, he is struggling with fundamental concerns about identity and living life with integrity. In order to mask his sense of being different and his attraction to men, Jerry became an overachiever. People do not ask a lot of questions of a boy or young man who is obedient to parents, cooperative with peers, and doing well at school, church, and work. If Jerry was experiencing pain, no one knew it. He was just shy and quiet—no trouble to anyone except himself.

Fred encouraged Jerry to explore support groups at a gay/lesbian community center. There Jerry found a coming out group in which he has met several men, mostly younger, who are struggling with similar concerns. In the spring he plans to participate in the center's dating and relationships group for gay men. Fred has also been able to talk to Jerry about his fears about coming out to family and friends at home. Fred has talked about how coming out is more a process than an event. Though the act of telling about his sexual orientation may seem overwhelming in the moment, people's responses will evolve over time. Fred has given Jerry a list of congregations that welcome and affirm sexual minority persons and encouraged him to explore these. Jerry, amazed to find an open congregation of his own denomination, has been attending. He has met gay and lesbian folk there and been invited to social events. There is one man, a little older, whom Jerry would like to ask out. Fred and Jerry have scheduled a session to role play how that might be done. Finally, Fred has given Jerry a reading list of gay-affirming books that includes Don Clark's *The New Loving Someone Gay* and John Preston's collections, *Hometowns* and *Families* as well as books with gay-affirming approaches to the Bible and theology.

Jerry is still insecure about his gay identity. He is frightened of the consequences of being completely open about who he is. He knows about gay bashing and discrimination against sexual minority persons, and Fred does not minimize the costs of coming out. With trepidation, Jerry has begun to work on his thesis again and is thinking about what kind of life he would like to have when he finishes school. Everything that is troublesome in Jerry's life is not fixed. However, Jerry is on his way to leading a happier, healthier, and more productive life because Fred was there to hear his story, help him uncover his pain, accompany him in exploring his gay identity, and encourage him to accept what he could not change while changing what he could. For Jerry, it is liberating to understand that his gayness is a given and cannot be changed, thereby freeing him to change other aspects of his life to accommodate that reality in positive and affirming ways.

CHAPTER NINE

MEN AND WOMEN AT WORK: FOSTERING COLLEGIAL RELATIONSHIPS

Joretta L. Marshall

Collegial relationships in the workplace remain difficult to create and maintain as we approach the twenty-first century. There are those who yearn for the "good old days when men were men and women were women," seeking specific roles applicable for each gender. At the same time, there are women and men who promote "justice" by seeking equity in opportunities and resources, balances of power, and clear structures of accountability. Many persons experience the desire for equity while feeling confused about how the mandates for justice are to be adjudicated.

The notion of collegiality is important for pastoral care with men for two reasons. First, men and women face the struggle of relating to each other in work contexts where conflict, confusion, and tension are present. Pastoral caregivers can encourage parishioners, clients, churches, and communities to continue the task of building relationships even when it is demanding.

Second, the workplace symbolizes broader efforts to examine the meaning of sexuality, harassment, economic justice, mutual relationships, and family roles and responsibilities. Work settings embody the challenges for developing human relationships that are discussed in more conceptual ways by communities of faith and by other meaning-making centers in the culture. Pastoral caregivers participate in these dialogues by engaging men and women to articulate their concerns from the perspectives of their faith.

The work setting is often experienced by men and women as a place of crisis. In talking about "The Contemporary 'Crisis' of Masculinity," Michael Kimmel suggests two things important to the topic at hand. First, he notes that men are less likely to initiate change since they have largely benefited from the more rigid gender roles for women and men in the past.[1] Caregivers who work with men, in particular, can be instrumental in challenging them to intentionally change their problematic patterns of relating to women.

Second, Kimmel suggests that historical changes have created a crisis as men have struggled to respond to women and the feminist movement in new ways. He argues that men, by and large, choose three responses to the challenges of women: antifeminist ("which cast[s] women as the source of men's troubles and s[eeks] to reestablish a perceived erosion of male dominance"); promale ("re-assertion of traditional masculinity"); and profeminist ("men [who] openly embrace feminist ideas and ideals as the signposts pointing toward a radically different future").[2] Because pastoral caregivers work with men from all of these perspectives, it is important to offer thoughtful interpretations for the concerns brought to them. Collegiality can be helpful as one frame of interpretation, not only for men but for all persons.

The issue of collegiality has ramifications for relationships outside the workplace. As persons build collegial professional relationships, they participate in systemic changes that can eventuate in more liberating and justice-oriented ways of relating to one another in other arenas of society. Relationships are systemically interwoven in the fabric of life such that one relationship affects others. Work relationships have an impact on the way persons relate to partners, spouses, lovers, families, and friends.

The collegiality that is described in the following pages reflects Kimmel's profeminist perspective. This chapter encourages men and women to find intentional ways of creating relationships that are informed by the qualities of respect, honesty, compassion, a mutual sharing of resources and power, and a passion for justice. Profeminist men are challenged to build collegiality not only with women but also with antifeminist or promale men. Pastoral caregivers are invited to create atmospheres in the context of care and counseling that offer opportunities for men and women to share what they experience in the workplace, the feelings that arise in those settings, and the creation of strategies for fostering ongoing relationships.

This essay examines some of the characteristics inherent in collegial relationships from a pastoral theological perspective. It then turns to an examination of differences in the internalizations women and men face in terms of work and relationality. Finally, concrete implications for pastoral caregivers are provided through the use of two case studies.

A PASTORAL THEOLOGICAL PERSPECTIVE ON COLLEGIALITY

A primary goal of pastoral theology is to constructively examine those situations that require a reappropriation of tradition, faith, and theology. Circumstances such as those in the case studies that conclude this chapter invite pastoral caregivers to reflect theologically with persons at many different levels of care. Individual care and counseling must include attention to communal and structural issues, not only to personal interactions. The assumption with which this chapter is written is that pastoral caregivers intentionally work to build relationships that embody love, justice, and mutuality in all communities. In so doing, pastoral theologians engage in systemic, as well as individual, transformations.

The term *collegiality* is a rather elusive one. For some the word means relational equality, particularly in terms of power. Others come to think of collegiality as getting along with those with whom one works, being nice, friendly, or cordial. Precisely what is the definition of collegiality? Must persons always have access to equal power in order to operate as colleagues? Is it possible to be colleagues if one person chooses not to participate in fostering a relationship of equity? What happens when the principles of justice operate on behalf of some individuals and against others? These are a few of the questions to be considered as persons struggle to define what it means to be colleagues.

The definition of the verb *colleague* is "to bind together" or "to become allied with."[3] Collegiality occurs as persons appropriately invest in one another's interests and concerns, seeking for ways to foster alliances with one another. This does not imply that persons must always agree with one another or see things from the same

186

perspective. Nor does collegiality mean that persons must take on one another's concerns with the same kind of intensity or investment they have for their own concerns. Instead, to be bound with one another suggests that colleagues must have the other person's best interests at the forefront of their thinking as they make decisions, contemplate actions, or work toward a common goal. Colleagues intentionally work for the good of one another and the whole.

For purposes of this article, I will describe four tasks for colleagues: they seek just and mutual ways of relating; they respect the gender of others; they attend to systemic issues; and they embody honesty in their relationships. This essay offers directions for caring with those who experience the presence, or the absence, of collegiality in the workplace.

The first task of colleagues is to build relationships of justice and mutuality with one another. Justice is here defined as common access to resources and power in ways that lessen domination and control by particular individuals or systems. Colleagues do not always experience equality in terms of having the same titles, identical positions or job descriptions, or equal salary packages. Yet, persons from unequal positions can be colleagues when they seek to intentionally relate to one another as allies or as persons who work toward just ways of relating. Larry Graham suggests the following about just relationships:

> Rather than perpetuating the domination and subordination that seem so pervasive in our political and moral economy, relational justice seeks to correct power imbalances. . . . The caregiver promotes conditions in which power is accountable and flexible, rather than exclusive, hidden, or inaccessible.[4]

Colleagues become allies with one another as they seek the best opportunities for one another, taking sides with one another as appropriate to their common life.

This activity of becoming allies across gender lines challenges the patriarchal and hierarchical norms of a culture that has moved to rather covert and sophisticated forms of sexism, often difficult to discern clearly. For example, sexual harassment in the workplace is less obvious and seemingly less intentional than it once was. How-

187

ever, it remains just as destructive in attempts to build collegial relationships as women (and sometimes men) are treated in ways that are demeaning and costly to all. Women are not looking for a "kinder, gentler patriarchy" from men.[5] Instead, most women are asking of men a desire and a willingness to change the systems from the traditional patriarchal structures into something more mutual and justice-oriented.

Because women and men in the workplace have not experienced justice and mutuality in the realm of work, it is important to recognize that collegiality requires from those who have more power an increased attentiveness and awareness of their place in the system. Those individuals, systems, or communities with more power are obligated to consider the needs, desires, opportunities, resources, and realities of those with less power. Those with more power in the system must take the extra steps necessary to listen and learn from those who have less. Colleagues seek out one another's opinions and serve one another's interests in ways that mutually enhance the whole.

An illustration of this might be a situation in which those with greater power are salaried persons whose partners have jobs that allow for the flexibility necessary to care for the needs of their children. Hence, those in power have few daily demands made upon them in terms of child care. In this same organization, however, are persons who make less money, who work by the hour and are not salaried, and who do not have the luxury of having flexible work time or other family members who can care for the needs of their children. Those in the higher levels of the administration must find ways to listen carefully to the experiences of those with less. To be colleagues in this situation means that solutions to the problems of child care should rest not with those who have less power but with the company as a whole. The needs of the least powerful are taken seriously.

Collegiality presupposes that business cannot operate as usual, and that those who have more access to power are called into active participation in changing the structures of domination in which they are main participants. Persons closer to the sources of power must work harder to discern what those with less power are actually experiencing or attempting to say. This requires a willingness to value perspectives and experiences that may feel unfamiliar or contrary to traditional practice.

A second task for those who would be colleagues is to have mutual respect for what it means to live out of particular genders in this culture. In an attempt to define gender, Faye Ginsburg and Anna Lowenhaupt Tsing note that it refers to "the ways a society organizes people into male and female categories and the ways meanings are produced around those categories."[6] The authors go on to illustrate how the meaning of gender shifts and changes with the contexts in which people live. Women and men carry different understandings of what it means to be a specific gender.

Misconceptions of gender often result in stereotyping attitudes and behaviors, and at times, they can lead to attacks on the person-hood and character of those who do not clearly fit into more traditional understandings of gender. For example, men may be seen as the enemy or women as the problem in today's world. Or, in more extreme examples, men who appear to be nonheterosexual in our culture are traumatized by brutal violence, sometimes eventuating in death, because they do not "fit" into the stereotypical characterizations of men.

One way to devalue gender is to move too quickly toward an idealized androgynous, or nongendered, way of relating to one another. This concern appears in literature that seeks to develop the "feminine" in men and the "masculine" in women, or to eliminate any connection to issues and concerns of gender. These attempts to deal with the struggles of women and men are dangerous because they dismiss, deny, or disembody the engendered presence of individuals. There is no right way to be women or men. There are ways to develop relationships that recognize how gender participates in the shaping and delineating of human living.[7]

Respecting gender means separating being a male from the extension of male privilege. By male privilege I am referring to the attitudes (sometimes unconscious and other times conscious) that intentionally or unintentionally create more positive possibilities and opportunities for men than for women. Male privilege, for example, assumes that women who have children and who work outside the home should be identified as "working mothers" while men who work outside the home have no adjective attached to their work that indicates their role or place in the family. Similarly, male privilege assumes that women do not make good construction workers or that men are not naturally good at being secretaries. The experience of male privilege is present in our culture in ways that are insidious and pervasive. Those who respect gender pursue the elimination of male privilege.

Mutual respect as women and men implies a willingness to work together to avoid the stereotyping that traps either gender into particular ways of being or relating. Pastoral caregivers can work toward gender justice by refusing to blame or attack men for being created as men, or women for being women. What is important to confront are the destructive and unjust behaviors that oppress either gender.

A third task of becoming colleagues is to attend intentionally to the broader systems of which women and men are a part. Those who seek collegiality must reflect together upon the connections of race, class, gender, and orientation. The harsh realities of economics means that women continue to earn less than white men, single-headed households for women of color struggle more concretely with issues of poverty, and lesbians and gay men experience bias in lack of career opportunities or lack of benefit packages for same-sex partners. While some of the reports suggest that the disparity between genders, races, and orientations is lessening, inequity is still dramatically persistent and present.[8]

The complexity of race and class in the lives of women of color is witnessed to by Lillian Comas-Diaz and Beverly Greene:

> Women of color tend to be heavily concentrated in the lower-paying specialties, in the female-dominated professions, serving other people of color, poor and/or working-class people in the public sector.... African American women are more likely than White women to support a household on a single income, and ... work slightly more hours than White women.[9]

It remains impossible to separate racism, sexism, and heterosexism from economic factors that have affected, and that continue to affect negatively the lives of women of color. Those who would be colleagues must exhibit a genuine concern not only for those in the immediate relationship but for all those who experience the injustice of destructive systems of power. Those most vulnerable in our culture continue to be persons of color and, even more specifically, women of color.

In collegial relationships between persons of differing color, women and men need to honestly address the issues of race. For example, a working-class Latina head of household experiences herself in the workplace in a very different way than a middle-class white man. As a Latina from Mexico, for example, she may be conscious of the overt messages about her race present in the culture, as well as with internalized messages that arise from her cultural heritage about what it means to be a woman or a mother. She is probably acutely aware of the struggles of maintaining a household economically and emotionally.[10] To be a colleague of this Latina woman means to have more than a superficial interest in her story. Instead, a colleague would be committed to changing the structures that currently work against her.[11]

Collegiality requires accountability and solidarity with others beyond the personal realm of relationships. Movements toward justice compel those who have had the most communal power to give up some of that power, even at individual costs, when they recognize that it is experienced as an injustice against others. For example, solidarity with the poor means taking seriously the perspective of the poor in the culture and remaining attentive to exploitations in the political and social realms. For business managers and executives, solidarity means recognizing, honoring, valuing, and working toward greater equity with those who are in the "service" aspects of their organizations and who are often working for minimal or menial wages. Pastoral caregivers can work with those who are at the "top" of an organization to respond to the concerns of those who have less and to reflect intentionally on the connections of racism, sexism, classism, and heterosexism.

A fourth task in building collegiality is the embodiment of honesty, intentionality, and willingness to disagree with one another. Colleagues seek out ways to communicate that are open and forthright, accepting the inherent reality that disagreement is appropriate and necessary in the process. This degree of honesty and intentionality is not easy to create, for it demands a genuine validation of differences and an understanding of the risks people take in speaking their concerns. Collegiality should not be confused with everyone having the same, being the same, or thinking the same.

Environments that offer opportunities for openness in communication without retribution are rare. However, if persons are to become colleagues they must be allowed, and even encouraged, to voice their concerns without having to worry about jeopardizing their jobs or their relationships. The risks are very real for those who enter into this open communication process. For example, it is possible for one with less power to ignore the power inequity in a relationship, thereby rendering themselves vulnerable to the other in ways that may not be beneficial. The risks of building collegiality are often subtle and surprising. Pastoral caregivers can be particularly helpful as they assist others in thinking through the risks that may be involved in becoming colleagues, especially when there is a disparity in terms of power.

Collegiality should also not be confused with false intimacy or friendship. While on occasions persons who work together might become friends, it should not be presupposed that colleagues are always social friends or are emotionally connected to one another. Instead, collegial relationships are those that can be counted on in the context of work, where persons work together around mutual concerns and issues, where boundaries are clear, and where communities can sustain an openness that fosters ongoing mutual and justice-oriented ways of relating. Collegiality is not immediate access to friendship, but is a careful and intentional way of being in honest mutual relationships where power and justice are considered carefully and are adjudicated in ways that serve those with less power.

These four tasks for those who would be colleagues offer directions for thinking about what it means to be allies with one another in the workplace. Genuine differences in perspectives, particularly arising from understandings of gender, are often the result of internalizations that have become part of the cultural milieu for women and men.

GENDERED INTERNALIZATIONS OF WORK AND RELATIONALITY

Asymmetry describes the lack of balance between women and men in terms of the messages persons receive about work and relationality. Internalization refers to the processes by which persons take into their internal world the realities, expectations, and qualities of their external environments. While these processes are complex and cannot be explored in depth in this chapter, it should be noted that the experiences and the messages of families and of culture, become internalized in ways that guide and direct people in their thinking, belief systems, and actions.[12] An appreciation of these processes can be helpful for persons who seek to build collegial relationships for two reasons.

First, women and men are engendered in distinctive ways through the cultures of which they are a part. For example, white men in lower-class America have a different internal sense of their gender, race, and class than do Cuban-American middle-class women. Internal messages about who we are as individuals, as persons of particular races, and as women and men affect the manner in which we engage one another in the workplace and in the world in general.

Second, internalizations are important as women and men self-consciously seek to consider the impact of gender, race, class, and orientation in their collegial relationships. The more intentional persons are about the role of gender and race in their relationships, the greater the chance for a collegiality that moves beyond superficiality.

Two areas of internalizations relate specifically to the fostering of collegiality between women and men: understandings of work and of relationships. Intrapsychic processes attended to most clearly by those within the psychodynamic community, are not the only factors relevant to the creation of internalizations. Messages from cultural systems, from subcultures, from interpersonal relationships and experiences, from families of origin, and from socioeconomic status or sexual orientation also participate in creating self-understandings out of which persons operate. While it is not helpful to overgeneralize or be simplistic, it is possible to articulate some of the distinctive patterns that emerge for women and men through the process of engendering.[13]

The meaning of work, the first important area of internalization, is central to how persons foster collegial relationships. Women and men internalize different messages about "work," such as what constitutes valid work, what kind of work is (or should be) preferred, and what particular gender roles are related to specific aspects of work. For example, persons may internalize messages that "women's work" is work done in the home and "men's work" is related to work outside the home and in the public sphere. Although these traditional patriarchal generalizations are being challenged and reformed, they are still persistent in the wider culture, in media, and in messages of churches and communities of faith.

The traditional understandings of work for men are summed up by Philip Culbertson when he says:

> Men derive the proof of their masculine identity from their jobs, for the workplace is the arena where champions were made or broken, where one can prove whether he is tough enough to take it, clever enough to work his way to the top, or mature and reliable enough to be given responsibilities that will make him a model of success.[14]

While a monolithic understanding of men at work is impossible to capture, it is clear that for a vast majority of white men in North America, work has been a place where they have shaped and formed significant aspects of their identities.

Women, on the other hand, carry different internalizations of work. For many women "work" is something that happens in the public sphere, but also at home. Being a mother or housewife, however, does not share a status equal to that given to men's more public sphere of work.[15] While changes in the roles of women and men, economic necessities, less time needed for childbearing and rearing, and increased life spans have resulted in more women working outside the home, many women experience feelings of distress as they attempt to discern the "meaning" of public work in relation to internalized messages about "women's work" and its centrality to families and homes.

Illustrative of this are the internalizations many working women of color carry from their cultures about the importance of being present for their families while also working outside the home for economic survival. In this regard, Comas-Diaz and Greene note that women of color who have immigrated to the United States often "develop more dynamic, flexible, and adaptive gender roles."[16] At the same time, they experience the burden of token employment and an added anxiety that many men or white women may not experience.

As women continue to enter the workplace in greater numbers and as men become more concerned with child-rearing, there is hope that what constitutes meaningful work for women and men is changing. The harsh reality, however, is that men have not responded to the needs of home life in ways proportional to women moving into the public work arena. Hence, many women still feel the burden of having to work outside the home while being the primary caretakers of the house and family relationships. Francine Blau and Marianne Ferber refer to this as the "housework gap."[17]

These engendered internalizations create different realities in the workplace for women and men. Irene Stiver argues that, in part, while men experience work as a place to develop self-esteem and to enhance their personal lives, women often experience work as a place of conflicting values between their private and public worlds. She states, "The successful man is perceived as more masculine than the man who is less successful. Many women, on the other hand, experience considerable conflict between their sense of self at work and their sense of self in their personal lives."[18] Stiver notes, in particular, that women experience greater self-doubt and anxiety around such things as competition, success, and differentiation from their mothers whose primary place of employment was other than the home.

The impact of these differences between women and men in building collegiality arises particularly as persons deal with expectations of one another and with definitions about what makes for a good working environment. For some women, good working environments are those places where they are able to work without being seen as "token" examples of hiring. For some men in today's culture, child-care issues need to be taken seriously as they participate in attempts to dismantle the "housework gap" and become partners in raising children. Building collegial relationships between men and women means that there must be a willingness to talk honestly about different internal understandings of what it means to "work," as well as different experiences of gender and race biases that emerge in that work context.

A second area important to consider in the establishment of collegial relationships is that of relationality. The impact of social and psychodynamic constructions of gender are inherent in the cultures of which we are a part.[19] Patriarchal and cultural structures, combined with experiences from families of origin, often collude to create in women a greater sense of relationality through connection, while in men relationality is experienced through a sense of difference.

Nancy Chodorow, one of the first to draw out the implications of the asymmetrical pattern of engendering, argues that women are "mothered" into being in ways distinct from the experience of men. Chodorow claims, then, that women develop a stronger internal sense of relatedness because they are most like the ones who have "mothered" them in the culture. Since nurturing and caretaking is still largely women's work in our culture, girls learn a great deal from watching their mothers, from interacting with them, and from sensing how others treat them. Chodorow claims that boys, on the other hand, tend to establish their first sense of relationships around the experience of being different from their mothers, and in turn, men tend to relate through their sense of difference from others.[20]

Chodorow's claim, when combined with a culture that usually encourages boy-children to move toward independence and "career," and girl-children to move toward nurturing and caretaking activities, illuminates the complexities of relationships for women and men in the workplace.[21] What these asymmetrical patterns suggest is the need to attend to the manner in which women and men relate to one another. Authority, for example, may be established for women as something that is built within the context of relationships, while for many men authority may be established by differentiating or "taking charge" of things.

These differences in relationality are significant as women and men uncover places of disagreements. Many women have difficulty confronting men with their anger and disappointment. Jean Baker Miller suggests that women have a more difficult time confronting those in power because of three fears: that the women will be seen as selfish, that they might destroy a relationship that is present, or that they will be abandoned.[22] Those who would be colleagues are

196

admonished to honestly and forthrightly talk about how they experience and understand confrontation in the midst of relationships.

Finally, the stereotypical perception that women are best at "doing" relational things and men are best at "doing" business things is not helpful for fostering collegiality. Relationality does not belong to women, although most women are engendered to be relational in ways that appear more connected to others. Women are culturally engendered to care for, and take care of, others including colleagues at work.[23] Fostering collegiality should not be the task of women alone. Instead, men must take equal initiative to develop relationships that have clarity and honesty.

CONCRETE IMPLICATIONS FOR PASTORAL PRAXIS

Consider the implications of the above discussion in the following two cases. Each story illustrates issues that are present when women and men work together.

From Senior Pastor to Copastor

Jackson has been the senior pastor of Good Hope Church, a community of faith that is currently expanding in membership. The church recently decided, with the encouragement of Jackson, that they would expand their pastoral team by seeking a woman to join their staff as copastor. After the search process, Helen was invited to join the church staff in time for the fall programming. A formal installation of Helen as copastor included a public statement recognizing that there were now two pastors of the church who should be understood by church members as "colleagues" in ministry.

Helen eagerly began her ministry, clinging to the vision that had been articulated in the installation service. By January it was clear to Helen that, while the verbal messages from the church were that she was to be a copastor, in reality that meant she preached about once a month, participated in committees that were often seen as peripheral to the "real ministry" of the church, and made occasional hospital calls. It was not uncommon for her to be met at the hospital with a question about when the "pastor" was going to visit, implying that Jackson was still seen by many as the "unofficial" senior pastor. Although this made Helen uncomfortable, she did not want to confront Jackson with her perceptions for fear it would create hard feelings. Instead, she assumed that he noticed these things and would work hard to make her position in the church one of mutuality. Jackson, in the meantime, was comforted by the fact that he was now part of the growing number of men who were attempting to change the church by incorporating more women into the mainstream of pastoral leadership.

As the spring came to a close, Helen and Jackson met to plan for a worship event to be held the next fall. Once again, Jackson assumed he would be the "preacher" and she would do the "children's moment." Helen felt angry and confided in Jackson about her feelings of frustration and hurt. Jackson, assuming that everything had been going fine, was caught off guard as Helen presented some ideas she had about shifting the dynamics of power in the church. Helen suggested that in the fall she take on the major responsibility for preaching three times a month, visiting with prospective families, and working with the board of the church. In exchange, Jackson could teach an elementary church school class, work with the youth, and begin recruiting teachers for the educational program of the church.

During the conversation with Helen, Jackson experienced Helen's comments about him being seen as the "senior pastor" in the eyes of the congregation as confrontations to his credibility and intentions. He immediately defended his position by noting that his intentions were to create a pastoral team that changed some of the gender inequities of the past. However, his gifts and graces were in worship, and he had been hired as the primary preacher by the congregation before Helen came. Jackson found himself recounting the many ways that he had been forced to change in order to accommodate Helen's presence and to increase her power in the church and community. Helen countered by raising concerns not only about their respective roles in the church but also about the salary structures that offered Jackson considerably more than her in terms of compensation, even though they were close to one another in age and experience.

Jackson left the meeting feeling personally and professionally betrayed because he had tried to be a different kind of leader and it had not worked, according to Helen. He turned to one of his pastoral colleagues for support and counsel.

The pastoral caregiver whom Jackson approaches for consultation can reflect on a number of issues in assisting Jackson, Helen, and the church. First of all, Jackson is to be respected and affirmed for his efforts and intentions. He is honest in his desire to be profeminist and to work toward change. At the same time, caregivers must not summarily dismiss the concerns raised by Helen simply because Jackson intended to act in good conscience. The pastoral caregiver must be honest, confrontive, and supportive in assisting Jackson to name the covert dynamics present in his relationship with Helen and the church.

Second, it is important for Jackson to articulate and affirm his willingness to take more risks to change the system. Jackson's ability to remain steadfast to his commitments means that he must honestly reckon with any loss of power he may experience in the congregation. Jackson currently has more power than Helen, and he needs to remain accountable for challenging the church in its perceptions. The responsibility for teaching about oppression and injustice often falls to the persons with less power. This is the case in this particular scenario as Helen becomes the one to name the issues that are before them, calling their attention to Jackson. Jackson, however, has greater potential for creating change in the dynamics of power as he is the one with power.

Finally, it is important to note that Helen, Jackson, and the congregation are involved in this process together. Honest, forthright, and careful conversation between Helen and Jackson must occur. At the same time, deliberations need to be held at the more public levels of the church as all parties consider what it means that this church has "copastors." Pastoral care specialists will want to talk and work with Jackson and Helen to suggest ways to broaden the conversation within the community of faith of which they are a part.

Racism, Sexism, and the Workplace

Barry, a 53-year-old white male, is employed by a medium-sized agency in which he has worked for the last five years. Prior to this time he established himself in the profession in two other places, finally landing a good promotion in this company. He is one of several middle managers, working with a number of support persons, many of whom are female and who work as office administrators, managers, typists, and service personnel. At the midmanager level there are three men (all white) and one woman (African American). Together the four of them comprise a decision-making team for their branch of the agency. Those in the upper-management offices are all men and also all white. The absence of people of color is true at every level in the company, except among the service personnel who work in the blue-collar sphere of the company. This is a fact that few at the upper- or midmanagement levels have attended to in any open way.

Having invested much of his professional life in trying to "move up the ladder," Barry is hopeful that his next promotion will move him toward upper management. However, he has become aware of the fact that his African American female colleague, Suzanne, has been promoted more quickly than he ever was. Although she has had much less experience in this profession, she has had a great deal of experience in other management positions. As the time for his evaluation draws closer, he becomes more anxious when he realizes that he and Suzanne are up for the same position for advancement. The one who lands the job will become the supervisor of the other. Added to his anxiety is the fact that those in the upper management are becoming increasingly concerned about "diversifying" the leadership team. There has been little conversation about what "diversity" means in the company, and hence Barry is left feeling quite vulnerable in his position.

When the announcement is made that Suzanne has received the promotion that he had hoped for, Barry feels betrayed and angry. Barry asks his supervisor why he was not given the promotion and was told that since both he and Suzanne were equally qualified for the position, the decision was made to promote Suzanne. Prior to this experience, Barry and Suzanne were beginning to build a collegial relationship. Now, however, Barry finds himself avoiding Suzanne because he feels angry and hurt. He feels resentful of Suzanne and the company for what he experiences as their discrimination against him. At the same time, in a conversation with Suzanne, Barry learns that she feels as if she is being set up in the company and has been given the promotion as a "token" African American woman. She expresses to Barry her concern that they maintain a collegial relationship as they work through their feelings about this process.

Barry approaches his church school class with his concerns. The church school class, made up of women and men representing class structures of lower-middle class to upper-middle class, responds with mixed feelings. Some of his peers are obviously experiencing similar situations, and they begin to speak out about their feelings of injustice from affirmative action decisions. Others in the class offer a counterargument about the need to change the systemic injustices that have been perpetuated in the past. At the same time Suzanne is troubled by her feelings and approaches her pastoral caregiver for feedback on this situation.

The pastoral caregivers in this situation can reflect intentionally with Barry and Suzanne about the connections of racism, sexism, and economics without dismissing feelings either of them have. While Barry expresses his feelings of vulnerability in this situation, it is also true that Suzanne is experiencing her own anxieties. Women of color are often caught in many double binds, including becoming the token employee to represent not only particular races but also gender. It is important for a pastoral care specialist to work with both of these persons to address the chaos perpetuated by racism and sexism.

Perhaps one of the most important pieces for Barry and Suzanne to address is their willingness to continue to struggle with what it means to be colleagues. Is there a desire to talk honestly about what it means to share power? Is there enough mutual respect between Suzanne and Barry to openly discuss what it means for them to be from different cultural backgrounds? These conversations are imperative but difficult for most persons as they work on developing collegial relationships.

Finally, it is important to recognize that the company to which Suzanne and Barry belong is accountable for engaging honestly in ongoing conversation about what it means to hold "diversity" as an important value. On many levels this situation not only is about Barry having to give up his male privilege but also reflects the many changes that must occur if we are to work for a system of equity.

Conversations about justice must occur not only between Suzanne and Barry but by all within the organization.

For Jackson and Helen, Barry and Suzanne, the feelings of pain are real and complex. Pastoral caregivers should be careful not to collude with injustices by refusing to name them when they are present or by refusing to engage the entire community in responding to these concerns. The integrity of pastoral care is present as all persons are invited to create a more just and holy place in which to live and work.

CONCLUSION

Fostering collegial relationships between women and men in the workplace is important if we are to continue to create an environment of justice for all persons. What is required from women and men is a willingness to honestly and openly struggle with one another, engage disagreement with integrity, and work to respect one another. Men who are sensitive and who feel compelled by the need for changes in the society will seek to build collegial relationships, even when those are difficult and full of potential conflicts.

The role of the pastoral caregiver to participate in ongoing conversations about justice and equity cannot be underestimated. As persons of faith we are mandated not only to care for those who feel the pain and hurt of injustice but to actively work to change the systems that perpetuate those injustices.

CHAPTER TEN

MEN AND GRIEF: THE HIDDEN SEA OF TEARS WITHOUT OUTLET

Herbert Anderson

The central character in Pat Conroy's novel *Beach Music* is Jack McCall. Jack's wife, Shyla, committed suicide when their only child, Leah, was two years old. After Shyla's funeral, Jack reflects:

> A sadness took over me that seemed permanent, and I lost myself in the details and technicalities connected to death in the South. Great sorrow still needs to be fed, and I dealt with my disconsolate emptiness by feeding everyone who gathered around me to offer their support. . . . I alternated between cooking and weeping, and I prayed for the repose of the soul of my sad, hurt wife. I suffered, I grieved, I broke down, and I cooked fabulous meals for those who came to comfort me.[1]

Some years later, when his own mother was dying, Jack thought again about the tears Shyla deserved that never came. "In the days after her death I waited for them to come in floods, but none appeared. Her death dried me out and I found more desert in my spirit than rain forest. My lack of tears worried, then frightened me."[2]

In order to arrive at a theory that would explain his own stoicism in response to Shyla's death, Jack McCall began to study other men. He was comforted to discover he was not alone.

> "I could feel the tears within me, undiscovered and untouched in their inland sea. Those tears had been with me always. I thought that at birth, American men are allotted just as many tears as American women. But because we are forbidden to shed them, we die long before women do, with our hearts exploding or our blood pressure

rising or our livers eaten away by alcohol because that lake of grief inside us has no outlet."[3]

Jack's inability to grieve is similar to the way he loves. In a conversation with his mother when she is near death, he concludes that the only way he can love is in secret. "There's a deep, sourceless river I can tap into when no one else is near. But because it lies hidden and undiscovered, I can't lead expeditions to it. So I love strangely and obliquely. My love becomes a kind of guesswork. It brings no refreshment nor eases any pain."[4] This hidden river where love resides is like the inland sea of tears: it has no outlet.

Jack McCall's story helps to identify three questions that need to be examined in this chapter about men and grief. First, how do men grieve? Men have grief. That is not the issue. But because their grief is hidden and because the ways men grieve are not always recognized, it is often wrongly assumed that a grieving man is an oxymoron. Therefore, understanding how men grieve is a critical issue for ministry. Second, for what do men grieve? The loss of a spouse or lover creates a "disconsolate emptiness" not easily assuaged. In addition to the loss of a loved person, there are three other losses particularly troublesome for men: the loss of a father, loss in the workplace, and the loss of dreams. Third, how do we care for men who have experienced loss in ways that will enhance their freedom to grieve? Our response to men who grieve should be modulated by an awareness of their ways of grieving.

It should be said at the outset that it is both necessary and impossible to generalize about the human response to loss. Every person's reaction to a significant loss is unique because of the particularity of the relationship to the lost person or object and because of the uniqueness of individual personality.

Every conversation with a grieving person begins with honoring the particularity of grief. However, in order to break the isolating effect of grief's uniqueness, we also need to discover a common language for sharing the pains of loss. The loneliness of grief is transformed into sadness that can be shared through an experience of empathic mutuality. If we can find a language for expressing grief, it is possible to create communities of sorrow.

HOW MEN GRIEVE

The Hiddenness of Male Grief

My grandfather emigrated from Sweden in the 1890s. When he had saved enough money, he returned to Sweden for Emelia, his wife to be. They married in 1900 and homesteaded on the prairies of North Dakota. Emelia died in 1905 shortly after their third child was born, leaving my grandfather with three children under the age of four. He did not marry again. I remember my grandfather as a gentle, sad man who lived for fifty-seven years after the death of his beloved Emelia. He seldom spoke of her. Nor did he speak of his sadness. My grandfather was a simple man who lived silently and privately with grief and sorrow.

In a sense, the story of my grandfather is every man's story. From childhood, men are encouraged to control their grief. "Big boys don't cry," they are told. The mark of being a man is to suffer in silence: showing pain is a sign of vulnerability or weakness. While this stereotype has been modified significantly, it is still difficult for men to share their grief with others. As a result, the pain of sadness is compounded by loneliness and isolation. Because it is frequently hidden for a long time, men's grief is often old. The following story illustrates how grief that is hidden for a long time isolates and creates its own kind of loneliness.

> My father died with I was two years old. My mother has told me over and over again that he was a good and God-fearing man who had loved me very much. After forty-three years, I am still depressed and angry at my father for leaving me. Not surprising, I don't let my wife or children or mother or stepfather know how utterly lonely I am. (Melvin)

Because men grieve secretly, their pain is often increased by isolation. My grandfather seldom spoke of his wife or his grief. His sadness and his loneliness were interchangeable. Melvin's loneliness is particularly poignant because his grief was hidden for so long. Men are often doubly disenfranchised when they experience loss. They should not feel the pain *and* if they do, they should not express it. Or if they do grieve, it takes a form that others do not recognize as mourning and they are easily ignored. When Jack's wife died, in Conroy's novel *Beach Music,* he lost himself in the oils and condiments of his well-stocked kitchen cooking for those who came to help him mourn. Jack's way of grieving was not self-evident to his friends or family. As a result, *men like Jack are isolated by their grief or the form of their grieving or both.* This is the first and most familiar theme that informs our reflections on men and grief.

Grief as the Male Mode of Feeling

According to Robert Bly, grief is the door to male feeling. If that is true, the hiddenness of male grief is all the more problematic. Men may not know what they are grieving about, or the grief may be impersonal, but it is always present. "The grief in men has been increasing steadily since the start of the Industrial Revolution and the grief has reached a depth now that cannot be ignored." [5] For Bly, the process of becoming a man includes a downward movement, a time of ashes, a descent into grief. The way of initiation into manhood is an experience of separation, loss, and hence grief.

The practice of initiation rites in traditional cultures is a dramatic experience of separation. The men *take* the boys from the women and ritually transport them to the male world. In western cultures, the process of separation from the mothering one is less dramatic, less ritualized, and less clear. The formation of male identity, therefore, includes a separation that is experienced as the loss of the maternal bond. It is not a loss for which boys are free to grieve, however. In traditional rites of initiation, the boys are expected to leave the safety of mother's world and enter father's risky realm with determination and courage. In order to make the separation to manhood, sadness and fear are numbed. *Unacknowledged grief is therefore at the core of male identity from the beginning.*

> A man's effort to move to the father's house takes a long time; it's difficult, and each man has to do it for himself. For Hamlet (in Shakespeare's play by the same name) it meant giving up the immortality or the safe life promised to the faithful mother's son, and accepting risk of death always imminent in the father's realm.[6]

This journey to manhood takes time. It is best taken in the company of older men. When young men are required to make the transitions alone, male identity is doubly wounded. They must discover what it means to be a man without clear models or supportive fathers to show the way and then welcome them when they leave behind the maternal world. When the fathers are themselves wounded because of workaholism, abusiveness, addiction, or general weakness, sons may try in vain to save their fathers in order to find them again.

When men must make the journey alone, the denial of emotions must be comprehensive in order to endure. Later in life, these boys have become men who are told that they don't talk enough about their feelings or don't know what they feel. It is not true that men do not have grief. Rather, grief is hidden from view in part because the formation of male identity requires it. The absence of fathers doubles this grief. Becoming a man cannot be done alone. Finding our fathers later in life is a gift for men, but making the journey to manhood without the help of older men has already established male patterns of hiding or suppressing grief that create the kind of loneliness expressed by Melvin.

The Denial of Finitude

Being finite creatures is common to both women and men. Each of us is similarly bounded by birth and death. And, in the broadest sense, the denial of human finitude is true for both women and men. *One of the reasons men are reluctant to grieve is because grieving is an implicit recognition of the limitations of being human.* For men, for whom linear, long-range thinking is a norm, the denial of limits is a common experience. Men would like to be faster than a speeding bullet, more powerful than a locomotive, able to leap tall buildings in a single bound.

As a young teenager, I wanted to be Superman. In my imagination, I would transport myself beyond the confines of a small Iowa farm where I lived. I would be the man (or boy-hero) who would save some young and beautiful girl, or I would get to serve the betterment of humankind by defeating evil, or I would gain fame without fortune by fulfilling ordinary human needs. When I was sixteen years old, I learned the painful truth that we cannot deny the laws of gravity. (Peter)

Not every young man longs to be Superman, but many men fear vulnerability. Men are willing to spend large sums of money to eliminate all windows of vulnerability in life. They are inclined to disdain or at least ignore whatever is small, weak, and needy. Even pictures of God are shaped by this denial of finitude. God's power and strength are preferable to mercy and gentleness. The idea that God suffers with us does not fit easily with the male desire to maximize power and minimize vulnerability. German theologian Dorothee Soelle has described the tension between the masculine desire for invulnerability and Christian theology in this way:

> It is a male fantasy to be the strongest and at the same time to be invulnerable. . . . They want to wall up all the windows. No light is to peek in; nothing must ever touch them. Transcendence is dangerous because it makes us vulnerable. . . . [Therefore] the masculine myth of the invulnerable hero is opposed to the unarmed carpenter's son from Galilee: there is nothing here to harmonize.[7]

Each of these dimensions of male experience is a source for the unique ways in which men respond to loss. Men are neither ignorant of nor resistant to the griefs of loss. They have simply been taught to respond differently, sometimes because the cultural stereotypes demanded that men hide pain, sometimes because the separation on the way to manhood must be endured with courage, and sometimes because the male way of being does not provide regular reminders of finitude. From this perspective, the male reluctance to mourn is an understandable lacuna.

Strategies That Magnify the Inability of Men to Mourn

Even when the grief is hidden, the human need for solace is not eliminated. Men want to connect with those they love when they hurt or communicate their pain in order to be comforted, but they do not want to be exposed. As a result, men have developed a number of strategies for use at home and at work that seek to effect contradictory goals: connecting with others and hiding the self from further exposure. In his book *Wrestling with Love,* Harvard psychologist Samuel Osherson has identified a number of these self-defeating strategies.[8]

(1) *Men assume a hypermasculine pose when threatened with diminishment.* When the loss men experience produces a fear of being made smaller, the temptation is to swagger and strut so as not to appear diminished. The connective impulse in such seemingly isolating behavior is that without puffing oneself up, one might be overlooked or regarded as pathetic. Unfortunately, when people around "feel diminished by our attempts to assert our fragile manhood, we become more isolated."[9] If manliness is equated with poise and composure in the face of tragedy, grief must be kept hidden so that male invincibility retains its veneer.

(2) *When men feel out of control in relationships, they insist on autonomy as a way of regaining control.* Insisting on autonomy, when interdependence is the appropriate response, is a way of protecting oneself against further loss. The denial of dependence aims to avoid further hurt, and in the process, achieves the very hurt one seeks to avoid. In general, men are encouraged to deal with loss by (a) taking charge, (b) helping others bear up, or (c) accepting the loss or the death as a challenge. Men do not create this sense of responsibility alone. "Families expect strength and security in the male figure in times of stress. This, in turn, invokes a sense of responsibility to become that invincible image, however exaggerated, leading to a cultural process that disallows an outlet for grief."[10]

(3) *Disdain and ridicule is a way of finding fault with others in order to avoid vulnerability.* By criticizing others for the unacceptable feelings we know in ourselves, we are able to defend ourselves against exposure *and* be loved at the same time. When a man harbors shameful feelings about himself, he often masters those feelings by taking the one-up position. Virtue is also an effective protection against vulnerability.

(4) *Men often use a fix-it mode in the face of significant loss in order to stay connected without being emotionally involved.* Taking independent action to solve problems helps men "manage fears of being embarrassed or shamed, overwhelmed by feelings of anger, sorrow, or neediness."[11] Men need to do something to take away the pain in

others or in themselves. Jack McCall cooked for those who came to help him mourn, first when his wife committed suicide and then again when his mother died of cancer. By having answers or filing a lawsuit or mobilizing a search party or giving orders in a confusing situation, men want to help in order to escape the painful feelings of powerlessness and vulnerability.

Samuel Osherson tells a poignant story of someone who came late for a men's retreat. He looked forlorn and upset when he arrived. Midway through the second day, the man admitted it was hard for him to be there because his brother, the troubled one in the family, had committed suicide the week before. His grief and shame and anger were, Osherson reports, palpable but "he kept his feelings buried deep behind his manly facade of being the brother who takes care of others, without regard to himself."[12] Looking out for the needs of others or trying to fix things that are broken are trusted patterns of responding to loss that are difficult for men to give up.

(5) *Becoming abstract or intellectual is a way for men to avoid being overwhelmed with emotions.* When men become abstract and pretend to be wise, they want people to honor them without ever being vulnerable. "But along the way we fail to learn or forget how to talk about vulnerability, sorrow, shame, how to heal wounds that continue to ache, how to draw others close and not just drive them away, how to be more responsive to those we love."[13] In order to avoid acknowledging neediness, men flinch from the connections they want when loss occurs. When they do, they reinforce the common myth that grown men have little to offer one another in times of emotional need. If the hidden river where love resides has no outlet, then neither does the inland sea of grief. For that reason, learning to love and learning to grieve are reciprocal.

Because each of these strategies for avoiding the work of grieving is learned, they can be unlearned as well. Men will be free to modify these strategies when they are able to reject the cultural myths about masculinity that undergird them. The cultural myth supporting the idea men should not be vulnerable probably has the most power to determine male response to loss. If it is not masculine to be vulnerable, then men will spend time and energy and sometimes considerable money to eliminate vulnerability, that is, their susceptibility to being wounded. For this reason, accepting vulnerability as part of being human is a necessary prelude to men grieving.

Two things are important about these counterproductive strategies: they deny the grief, that is sure; but they also seek to maintain connections with people in clumsy ways when loss occurs. In our care of men in grief, we would do well to acknowledge the denial but emphasize the covert need for connection. This longing to be connected means that, for men, friendship is more than a desirable option. It is necessary for survival. In a little book on *Friendship*, Martin Marty made this observation. "We have friends, or we are friends, in order that we do not get killed."[14] Nowhere is that statement more applicable than in grief. Encouraging men to mourn presupposes friends with whom to mourn. Fostering friendships is part of learning to grieve.

WHAT MEN GRIEVE FOR

The reality of loss is not gender specific. When a child loses a pet or a son or daughter leaves home or when a person is fired or a friend moves away or when a marriage ends in divorce or a parent dies, the loss is real for women and for men. The meaning of the loss varies widely, however. The meaning of the loss depends on the value ascribed to what has been lost or the significance of the relationship with the lost person or object. For those who prize possessions highly, for example, the loss of things like cars or tractors or precious china is the occasion for grief.

Although Jack McCall, in Conroy's novel *Beach Music,* speaks for many men when he describes his love as hidden and not easily expressed except by action, the loss of a spouse or other loved person creates in men a malignant ache and a terrible loneliness that is not healed either by bravado or frantic activity. This section begins with a brief consideration of the death of a spouse and the grief of men. Although the focus is on death in marriage, the loss of a lover will have similar dimensions. In addition to the death of a spouse, there are three other areas of loss troublesome for men today: the absence of father and the loss of blessing, loss in the workplace, and the loss of dreams. These three areas of loss have been chosen in part because they are difficult to share. As a result, they are often hidden even from men themselves.

The Loss of a Spouse

A man's response to the death of a spouse has been described eloquently by C. S. Lewis in *A Grief Observed*. After living most of his life as a single person, Lewis had married Joy Davidman. Joy died of cancer not long after they married. This book contains four notebooks that Lewis wrote as part of his grieving. His reflections begin with rage at God as a "cosmic sadist" and conclude with a recognition that we live with the mystery of God as the "great iconoclast." In the end, he admits that we cannot understand the mysteries of life and death. We can only know the pains of absence.

> Her absence is like the sky, spread over everything. But no, that is not quite accurate. There is one place where her absence comes locally home to me, and it is a place I can't avoid. I mean my own body. It had such a different importance while it was the body of Joy's lover. Now it's like an empty house. . . . I know that the thing I want is exactly the thing I can never get. The old life, the jokes, the drinks, the arguments, the love-making, the tiny, heartbreaking commonplace. . . . And that, just that, is what I cry out for, with mad midnight endearments and entreaties spoken into the empty air.[15]

Although the imagery that Lewis uses to describe his own grief is emotionally charged and highly evocative, he writes in notebooks rather than ranting with friends. In that sense, Lewis responds to the death of his spouse in a way consistent with general studies about men and grief. The literature on grief regularly reports that men in Western societies try to control the overt expression of emotion. "Sex-determined role expectations for men tend to emphasize the importance of appearing competent, independent, under control and unemotional."[16] The expression of grief is suppressed even though the loss is felt deeply.

Although it is generally accepted that men and women grieve differently, these differences are more striking among younger or middle-aged women and men. The differences lessen with advancing age. "There would appear to be very little difference in the

212

reactions of very elderly men and women, i.e., 75 years or over, concerning the expression of emotion following the loss of their partner."[17] A sense of loneliness and loss of companionship penetrates the grief of the elderly. One finding, however, that consistently seems to distinguish men from women at any age "is that widowers are at greater risk for adverse health outcome than widows."[18] This outcome decreases significantly if a man marries again after the death of a spouse.

Absent Fathers and the Loss of Blessing

The story of absent fathers is told in many ways. There was a time when the prototype of the absent father was the corporate executive or busy professional who left for work before the children were awake and returned from work after they had gone to bed. The marriage was intact but mother was a single parent.

Sons who knew their fathers at a distance. More recently, the picture of absent fathers has shifted to deadbeat dads, men who do not pay child support or who have otherwise abandoned responsibility for their children. The visiting father, as David Blankenhorn has described him, perpetuates the pattern of distance. He cannot establish an enduring parental bond with a child.[19] What has happened to fathers is a complex problem for modern industrial societies and their families. The restoration of the "Good Family Man" is a noble ideal that can only be achieved both through recommitment to fathering *and* a fundamental reordering of the free-market society.

There are sons who have never known their biological father. In some instances, the biological father is not known. In other situations, the birth father is pictured by the child's mother as someone the son would not want to know. In such circumstances, the grief for the absent father is magnified by idealizations. This pattern of idealizing is particularly common when a father dies when the son is very young. Children who are separated from their fathers through divorce may even idealize the man who abandons them. When a boy loses a parent, he creates a myth of that parent in order to endure the grief. The grief is particularly painful when the fatherless family is an exception in society. However, when nobody's father comes to the piano recital or the sports banquet, the negative impact on the child may still be significant but the grief is diminished.

Wounded fathers may be physically present but emotionally inaccessible. There is another kind of absence. Children learn quickly that in order to survive, they must learn how to take care of their fathers or their mothers. The child becomes the parent. When the child becomes the man, he often goes in search of a father who was too wounded to parent. In fact, he is in search of a blessing.

Because we do not always get what we need from our fathers, there is a persistent longing for blessing and an unmet hope that someday we will find our fathers waiting to give us the gift we need. The tragedy is that men do not always believe that they have gifts to give one another.

Until men can acknowledge their own grief, it will be much harder for them to respond to their wives, children, bosses, and friends in ordinary ways. Samuel Osherson describes this dilemma in the following way. "Fathers and sons flinch from one another because we get overwhelmed by sorrow, hope, anger, and embarrassment at our need for each other, because of the common myth that grown men have little to offer each other, and because of the ease with which men and their fathers get separated emotionally from each other in the family."[20] The inability to mourn losses in one part of life affects the whole.

> My wife and I celebrated our twenty-fifth wedding anniversary by taking our children and their significant others at that time to a performance of *Les Miserables* in the elegant Chicago Theater. We had seats in the fourth row. At the conclusion of the musical when the father, Jean Valjean, sings a blessing to his daughter Cosette and her lover Mario, I began to sob uncontrollably. It did not take me long to connect my tears with hearing my father's voice for the first time in four years on our wedding tape at breakfast that morning. *I was crying for my father. But even more, I was crying for a blessing I had never received.* It is the deepest hole in my life. (Herbert)

The absence of fathers has many consequences. From the perspective of loss and grief, however, there is one constant theme in each of the forms of father-absence described above: it is unlikely that children will receive from their fathers a blessing for the journey toward adulthood. There is nothing more important that we can do for our children than to bless them. A blessing acknowledges the uniqueness of each child as a separate individual, worthy of respect. It sets them free to pursue their dreams and actualize their talents in order to make them available for the world. A blessing conveys the wish for success and happiness. It is a prayer for God's protective and sustaining presence on the way to an uncertain future.

When Fathers Die Too Soon. Carol Staudacher, in her book *Men and Grief,* makes the following bold statement. "For many young male survivors, hope of any kind is hard to come by. The promise of enjoying life without feeling isolated or full of despair is small."[21] The basis for her claim is that boys who experience significant loss have already learned to stifle emotions and maintain silence. Anger is deflected, sadness is hidden, and guilt for being the survivor is repressed. As a result, the grief is locked in the past in ways that limit thinking about the future in hopeful ways.

> I was eight when my father died. He had never been sick. When my mother told us he had died, my six-year-old brother started crying. I told him to shut up. I only allowed myself to cry when I was alone. Everyone told me I had to be strong because I was the "man of the house." I remember waiting in the driveway for weeks and weeks, hoping he would come back. Even now, thirty years after his death, I often get unpredictably sad driving home from work. (Richard)

Richard's story demonstrates how easy it is for boys to learn not to grieve. Adults who want to protect children from the pain of loss contribute to the denial by hiding their grief or withholding information. The effect on children is opposite of what is intended. They become more confused in their grief, more confirmed in their guilt, more isolated in their sadness. Richard had to be strong because he was prematurely expected to assume the duties of adult manhood. When a child loses the parent of their same gender, it is much too common for relatives and friends or the surviving parent to promote the child to a replacement role in the family, depriving the child of age-appropriate behavior.

> I was inducted into the status of pallbearer at age eleven. My sister died of scarlet fever and my closest childhood friend died of polio-

myelitis. These, and other serious deprivations imposed on my early life, were culminated by the accidental death of my father when I was thirteen. I was a pallbearer again. The "things of a child" were prematurely put aside to embrace the need to survive. I was a man before I finished being a boy. (Ron)

There are many losses in childhood that provide the occasion for teaching boys a different response to grief. Sometimes, as in Ron's story, the only lesson is how to survive when loss is overwhelming. Other times, honoring a child's grief when the gerbil dies or a bike is stolen begins the process of teaching boys (and girls) how to mourn. When a child loses a parent, adults need to promote full participation in the mourning process, find occasions for conversation about the one who has died, encourage age-appropriate expectations of children, and provide physical comfort and stability when the emotions are in chaos. Making a commitment to a grieving child must be taken very seriously by caring adults. For children who lose a parent, as for anyone in grief, the past can only become the past when the grief has been dealt with. When the grief is sequestered in the past, hope and the future are hidden as well.

When Middle-aged Sons Lose Their Fathers. The death of parents often has a significant impact on middle-aged sons and daughters. Some adult sons or daughters feel abandoned when a parent dies. They are like orphans. Some are frustrated or guilty because they had postponed dealing with unfinished business with a parent until it was too late. Carl Jung's mother is presumed to have said about his father's death that "he died in time for you." Sometimes the death of a father or a mother is the occasion for daughters and sons to claim the autonomy they could not exercise as long as the parent was alive. In those instances, the death of a parent is a prelude to freedom. The process of grieving is complicated, however, when a middle-aged daughter or son must stand on the casket of a parent in order to claim personal authority. Guilt is added to the sadness of grief when that occurs.

Especially when the last parent dies, that death is a reminder to adult daughters and sons that they are next in succession to die. The buffer is gone. Both of my parents died before I turned fifty. Since I am the oldest of twenty cousins, I have taken some comfort in the fact that my mother had four living siblings. One of them, my uncle Harold, died while I was writing this chapter. He was ninety-three. We all work out some little trick to keep death at a distance. But the death of a parent is an unmistakable sign that finitude is unavoidable and death is a little nearer.

For men who have been working hard to avoid finiteness, the death of a parent is often a double loss. They lose a parent but they also lose a buffer between themselves and death. There are often other losses at the same time that add to the complexity of grief for middle-aged sons when a parent dies. Sometimes a parent's death occurs when adult daughters and sons are being launched or a company is downsizing or when people begin to have health problems that are also a sign of aging. The middle years are tainted with loss. Options are fewer. The horizon is cluttered. Men may even withdraw from life itself and from the relationships that sustain human living in order to avoid the awareness of finiteness.[22]

Loss in the Workplace

When a plant is closed or a business fails or a company downsizes or a worker becomes redundant because the product line is discontinued or a corporate executive is given a "golden parachute" at fifty-two, the reality of loss is inescapable and pervasive. The grief that follows job loss or downsizing is often very intense, filled with a mixture of shock and rage and shame. Losing a job means more than the loss of financial security. It is the loss of the role of an employed person, the loss of belonging to a company or group of people who enjoyed working together, the end of a future to hope for.

> I lost the job as manager of a small business that I had put much effort into and had held for two years. There was no advance warning. To this day, I do not understand what happened. I came to work one day and my desk was locked. I felt only that I had been railroaded out by someone. No one would talk to me. It was a shock that I was treated unfairly by people I thought were my friends. I not only lost the job; I lost some of my trust in people. After ten years, it still hurts when I think about it. My father never lost a job in forty-five years of working. (Mark)

I began my job in the company with energy and high expectations. My impressions of my new boss were very positive. Within a month after I began working, I realized how distant, demanding, and controlling he was as a manager and boss. Moreover, I found out that I did not have the authority I thought I would have. And my co-workers were competitive and distant. Within a year, I was asked to willingly accept a demotion. I still work there because I am afraid I have no other options but I feel trapped and smothered by an over-controlling manager. Most of all, I have lost the dream that led me to the job in the first place. I have struggled with discouragement and anger and depression ever since. (Kenneth)

Both of these stories describe the grief that men experience in the workplace around the loss of a job or the status of a job. In Mark's story, the pain of the work loss was compounded by the anger at what seemed to be unjust treatment and the shame in comparison to father's perfect work record. Work-related grief is complicated. It is difficult enough for a man to tell his family and friends that he is out of work. Moreover, there are other dimensions related to the job loss itself that are difficult to talk about: shame at being out of work, anger at the way it happened, sadness about losing a dream in Kenneth's story, or isolation out of fear because no one wants to hear about what may happen to them next. The grief is intensified when it is not shared and the grieving is prolonged when the sadness must be hidden.

The workplace may not be the context in which men express their sadness. Nonetheless, men need companions from their place of work *who understand what they are going through* and who will listen to their story and hold their grief. For some men, the pain of despair over losses in the workplace is so intense and the fear of losing everything so profound that they dare not let go of the grief because it is all they have. Everything becomes flat and meaningless and gray in color. Kenneth's depression is one expression of his grief. Caring for men who experience loss in the workplace must avoid two unhelpful responses: (1) we should not take away the grief prematurely because we are tired of the sadness or because we want to fix the grief; (2) we should not encourage persons to nurse the anger related to the loss in ways that prevent them from moving toward the future in hope.

218

I am a Vietnam veteran with a master's degree that does not seem to count for much anymore. Almost every position I apply for is swallowed up by women and minorities. I used to have a family, two kids, a dog, two cars, insurance, self-respect, and a little piece of land by a lake. Now I have a new wife who earns more than I do, lots of debt, and occasional work. I should be grateful but I'm not. I fought to protect my country but I cannot provide for my family. It is hard for me to know who I am. (Jeffrey)

Jeffrey is overwhelmed by losses that are mostly hidden from view. The grief men like Jeffrey feel today because of the inability to get jobs or unexpected job loss or not getting the expected promotion is exaggerated by the loss of preferred status in this society. In one sense, this loss of assumed privilege is common to men of all races. In other respects, as Ellis Cose has observed, race is relevant. African American men are not "as exercised as white men about the decline of male power and privilege, since most don't believe they had very much of either to begin with."[23] However, if a person always expected to be at the head of the line or at least in the line, the perceived loss of privileged status is a painful internal transaction. Affirmative action has been a necessary exaggeration in recent times to rectify a legacy of injustice that gave preference to white males in a variety of situations. As a result, some men have not gotten jobs or promotions that might have been theirs a few decades ago. Few would disagree with Cose "that being a male, at least a white male, in American society has historically come with certain privileges."[24] Even for those who agree that it is necessary for white males to lose their preferred status in order to correct centuries of injustice against women and minority persons, the loss of preferred status is still a source of grief for men. This is true even for those who are committed to correcting centuries of injustice. From the perspective of those who are powerless, the white man's lament seems trivial. Suffering, however, is usually in the eyes of the beholder. We need to be able to care for men who mourn the loss of privilege that should have been taken from them long ago.

The Loss of Dreams

The loss of a dream is the most difficult grief to express. It is embarrassing because men don't want people to know what they have dreamed about being or having. When men tell people their dreams or hopes, they run the risk of ridicule or at least some kind of well-meaning reality testing. "Whatever possessed you to think you could _____ (fill in the dream)." Men sometimes keep expectations of marriage hidden, often to the detriment of the relationship, because they fear the rejection of what they hope for or dream about. Sometimes their dreams border on the grandiose and they are reluctant to tell because they fear people will laugh. When men become aware that their dreams will not be realized, they experience intrapsychic or internal loss that is difficult to mourn because, in order to talk about the loss, they have to talk about the dream.[25]

In a useful little book *Loss of Dreams: A Special Kind of Grief,* Ted Bowman has developed this idea of intrapsychic loss. "A loss of dreams relates to images or pictures of our personal world that we create and to which we attach strong emotional investment . . . the way things are supposed to be."[26] Fathers have dreams for their children that children reject or that are shattered by a son or daughter's knee injury. Men have dreams of lifetime job security. They dream of career advancement in their profession. Young men and women in rural America are less likely to farm the land their family has owned for a hundred years. The story of the death of a dream is often repeated and frequently unknown.

> I had been the secretary for Kevin Smith (and several others as well) who worked as salesmen for a seed company in Iowa. Kevin worked hard, was dependable with his customers, and dreamed that someday he would be a regional manager in the company. When Kevin was in his early forties, it became increasingly clear to him that one had to have a master's degree in business administration in order to become a regional manager. He did not have such a degree and could not get one. I think so much of his identity was tied up in that dream, that he could not bear to live without it. He committed suicide at age forty-four and no one but me knew why. (Nancy)

The grief is hidden because the dreams and consequent loss are secret. So it was with Kevin and so it is with many men. It is important that pastors and therapists and friends attend to the loss of dreams because the horizon is more narrow and less open for some men today. The cynicism and apathy that one hears from young people is born out of the realization that they have fewer options than their parents had. They are still free to dream, but there is less certainty that the dreams will be realized. And so they stop dreaming. The loss of "what might have been" generates grief sometimes as intense as the loss of a valued possession. We need to teach men and women how to mourn the loss of secret dreams so that they will be free to hope again.

The freedom to dream and hope for a new future also depends on a realistic assessment of loss, especially when that loss occurs internally. For men in middle years and beyond, there is a growing realization of a momentous gap between what one wishes to become and what one has become. It is increasingly unlikely that this gap between dreams and reality will be closed. There may also be a distance between the self as it is and one's self-perception. These discontinuities of the inner landscape are often the occasion for melancholy or sadness muted only by the intense desire to retain the appearance of personal continuity.

HELPING MEN TO GRIEVE

One of the ways of helping men to grieve is to develop new ways of thinking about being human and being men. The cultural stereotypes that limit the range of emotional expression for men will only be modified as men try new ways of responding to loss. The principle psychological barrier to grieving for men is the inability to acknowledge vulnerability. As a result, men do not know how to develop strategies for coping with loss that acknowledge their need for others when they have been emotionally wounded. The inability to understand human creatureliness as finite and dependent is a major theological barrier to grieving. Men need to discover a different view of being human in order to be more open to the gift of grieving.

Finding Common Ground for Grieving

Beyond changing the way they think about being human, men need to recognize the patterns of responding to loss that limit their freedom to grieve. Some of those patterns of traditional male behavior are essential to conducting a workable, effective life. As such, they are difficult to change. Men in grief readily agree that it is both frightening and freeing to relinquish the constricting aspects of traditional male behavior. In order to make the changes necessary to be free to grieve, men need to agree on two fundamental ideas: (1) grieving is a part of living because loss is an inescapable dimension of life; (2) The reason for grieving is not to weaken life but to strengthen it.

Helping men deal with loss begins by finding common ground in which they are free to grieve in their own way and at their own pace in the company of accepting friends. Generally, an all-male group provides a comfortable common ground for responding to loss. Therese A. Rando, in *Treatment of Complicated Grieving*, observes that it is fruitless for caregivers to strive to make men grieve like women. Better, rather, to translate what is required in grief and mourning into terms acceptable to men. Old male patterns of dealing with intense feelings do not fade quickly. Some men need freedom to grieve silently for a long time even though they might not want to be alone in that silence.

> This is not to disparage appropriate attempts to make the male mourner more comfortable with those aspects of mourning that may be prohibited by male social conditioning but that are necessary for healthy accommodation of the loss. However, these attempts should not become ends in themselves or obscure the more important goal of assisting the individual in mourning the loss of his loved one.[27]

It is a mistake, Rando insists, to equate crying with mourning. "Although the shedding of tears is an extraordinarily effective release of sadness, it is not the sole one. People can deal with their sadness and hurt in other ways besides crying."[28] Moreover, sadness is not the only issue in grief. Anger, shame, fear, loneliness, emptiness, bewilderment are all aspects of grief for which crying may not be the best release. All-male grief groups that are well-facilitated will seek for comfortable common ground so that participants "are more likely to (1) discuss issues regarding the fear of loss of control, (2) discuss sexual concerns, and (3) release feelings in an environment that allows tears among men."[29] Finding this common ground is one way of diminishing the need for the counterproductive strategies identified earlier that inhibit men from beginning the work of grieving.

Making Friends to Grieve With

Encouraging people to grieve presupposes that there are people who will listen to the story of loss and hear the pains of grief. One of the major impediments to grieving for anyone is the absence of empathic companions. This is a particular dilemma for men because they seldom form relationships that include emotional sharing. Traditionally, men have built relationships around doing something together. When men who have suffered loss are asked what they want from a friendship with another man, "the qualities they most frequently named were acceptance, honesty, and understanding."[30]

> My daughter was sixteen when she committed suicide. I could not go to work. I was hurt and angry and ashamed and confused. I do not know how I would have survived her death without two friends who listened to me rage and cry without judging or trying to take away my pain. Sometimes, they just sat with me when I needed to be silent. I have thought many times since how fortunate I am to have two friends. Too many men I know would have been alone with their grief. (Henry)

Besides being a listening presence, Carol Staudacher has identified several things that friends can do for men in grief. (1) Acknowledge the death. Ignoring the death ignores the person. (2) Express interest in the well-being of a friend in grief. (3) Be trustworthy with confidences. Sometimes a man's grief involves his deepest, most private feelings. (4) Accept tears. (5) Share silence. Even when the silence is an avoidance of the grieving work that must be done, friends will honor each man's own timetable. (6) Perform small acts of compassion. Ideally, we will have friends to turn to when grief comes. Sometimes, we make friends with those who honor us with their faithful, listening presence. Either way, men cannot endure grief without friends.

Finding Models of Men Who Grieve

Many men have grown up never knowing men who model ways of grieving. Sons learn from their fathers how to swallow their sadness and be brave. The story of my grandfather at the beginning of this essay is repeated over and over again. Men today who need to grieve have received a long legacy of denial and silence and hidden pain. This legacy of silence is also evident within the Christian tradition. The lament psalms of David have not been an ordinary part of the resources that churches make available for those who mourn. Nor have we understood the story of David the king as a story about a man of valor and violence who was also a man of grief. If kings lament, so can ordinary mortal men.

The story of David begins in grief. Samuel is grieving the loss of Saul who was no longer king over Israel because he had disobeyed the command of God. From the time he is anointed to be the next king until the death of his son Absalom, the story of David is filled with power and passion but also with loss and grief. When it was reported that Saul and his son Jonathan died in battle, David tore his clothes and the men who were with him did the same. "They mourned and wept, and fasted until evening for Saul and for his son Jonathan, and for the army of the LORD and for the house of Israel, because they had fallen by the sword" (2 Samuel 1:12). David's lamentation for Saul and Jonathan acknowledges their death but also affirms the gifts they gave in life. "Saul and Jonathan, beloved and lovely! In life and in death they were not divided; they were swifter than eagles, they were stronger than lions" (2 Samuel 1:23).

David's life is filled with loss and sorrow. When his first child with Bathsheba dies as Nathan had predicted, David did not mourn, saying that his mourning was pointless because it would not bring back his son (2 Samuel 12:20-23). When Absalom died, however, David was overwhelmed with grief. Even though his son had sought to take the kingship from him, David went to his chamber and wept for Absalom. "O my son Absalom, my son, my son Absalom! Would I had died instead of you. O Absalom, my son, my son!" (2 Samuel 18:33). David's response is common. When a parent loses a child, there is not only a part of oneself that is cut off, there is a loss of connection to the future. It is a very particular grief.

David was a great king of Israel. He was also a man of sorrows. We need to realize more fully the legacy of lament that has come to us from David. He was a man of power who wept. He was a seemingly invincible warrior who nonetheless was vulnerable to grief. Sometimes his actions were the occasion for his loss. Even so, David's life is testimony to the possibility of linking strength and vulnerability. The psalms of lament ascribed to David are a gift for anyone who has experienced loss. They provide a language for our grieving. It is particularly important for men to discover this resource from the heart of a strong king who wept.

Teaching Our Sons to Lament

We live in an age in which it is common to come under the sway of apathy. There is so much pain and suffering on the one side and so much powerlessness on the other that it is easy to conclude, as young people often do, that nothing matters. There are two alternatives in response to the anguish of our time. We may choose to shut out the suffering of the world, become apathetic, and die before we are dead. Or we may embrace suffering and live. We are not powerless in the face of suffering. We can lament. For that reason, learning how to grieve in our time is for the sake of life. Unless we learn to lament, we are consigned to cynicism and apathy.

Fathers have many things to learn and to teach their sons about being human and being men. None is more important than that we teach our sons to lament. The picture Jeremiah creates of the land of Judah is painfully contemporary of urban life today. "Death has come up into our windows, it has entered our palaces, to cut off the children from the streets and the young men from the squares" (9:21). In response to the close presence of violence, Jeremiah urges the mourning women to raise a dirge and teach it to their daughters. Men today, I submit, have a similar responsibility. For the sake of life in its fullest, men must learn to lament and teach their sons to lament.

> Hear, O women [and men], the word of the LORD,
>   and let your ears receive the word of his mouth;
> teach to your daughters [and sons] a dirge,
>   and each to her [his] neighbor a lament. (Jeremiah 9:20)

CONCLUSION

The freedom to grieve is only one aspect of many changes men are experiencing in our time. Men who have been socialized to hide feelings allow themselves to be vulnerable in order to mourn. Men who have been taught to devalue their inner world discover "the hidden river of tears" that includes sadness and loneliness and fear. Men who learned that independence is the masculine way begin to trust others enough to be cared for as they mourn.

Philip Culbertson, in a book on *Counseling Men,* describes the male dilemma this way. "Patriarchal masculinity denigrates and trivializes the world of inner experience, feeling, and intuition. This inner world is deemed weak, making men too vulnerable."[31] In order for men to find healing from their grief, they will need to find an outlet for their inner river of sadness and faithful friends who will affirm the complex set of emotions that follows when we lose what we love. The ultimate gift of grief, as Jack McCall discovered at the end of *Beach Music,* is that learning to mourn is a prelude to loving others more deeply. Love and grief flow from the same river.

CONCLUSION

Christie Cozad Neuger and
James Newton Poling

The purpose of this book has been to build theory and practices for the work of pastoral care and counseling with men of diverse backgrounds and experiences in a variety of contexts. Although some might say that the literature in theology, psychology, and pastoral care has always been about male experience, only very recently has it examined the experiences of men as a specific gender rather than as representative of all humanity. Consequently, there has been very little in pastoral care and counseling theory that has explored how we might best help men in our congregations in this time of transition and high stress.

The fact that this is a high stress time in the lives of men in general is documented in much of the current men's literature. Stresses come from a variety of sources—economic, employment, family, and so on—but they are occurring in a time when traditional coping resources for men are being called into question. As Ronald Levant and William Pollack suggest, there are some deep questions today about what it means to be male, and men are experiencing significant pressure to change their priorities and their normative strategies without much clarity about how they should go about making those changes.

> These new pressures—to commit to relationships, to communicate one's innermost feelings, to nurture children, to share in housework, to integrate sexuality with love, and to curb aggression and violence— have shaken traditional masculine ideology to such an extent that the resulting masculinity crisis has left men feeling bewildered and confused, and the pride associated with being a man is lower than at any time in the recent past.[1]

Yet, things *are* changing in the culture as gender roles are successfully challenged and changed and as women and men move into arenas previously denied to them. Men, or at least some men, are also beginning to recognize that the gender roles they have been taught as both normative and inescapable, have numerous problems associated with them. We have long recognized that men, on average, die sooner than do women, and there has been considerable research documenting that some of the stressors that contribute to mortality are related to male gender roles and behaviors. Richard Eisler, in reviewing the studies on men and health risks, discusses the various health problems that men seem to experience as a result of gender role socialization. He names cardiovascular disease as one primary area of current research and then goes on to say:

> What is not debated is the fact that men are nearly three times as likely to die in motor vehicle accidents and three times as likely as women to actually commit suicide. Higher death rates in men by homicide, suicide, and accidents have been attributed by some to the paucity of acceptable masculine alternatives for aggressive behaviors in coping with stress. Additionally, data compiled by Waldron and Johnson showed that men's death rate from lung cancer is nearly six times that of women and twice as high from cirrhosis of the liver, suggesting that masculine coping styles that incorporate higher rates of smoking and drinking are added health risk factors for men.[2]

Beyond the studies in male health risk there have also been the various studies that demonstrate men's sense of isolation, their preoccupation with prestige and success, and their spiritual emptiness. Several of the pastors interviewed for this project claimed a general uneasiness felt by many of the men in their congregations. Many of those men felt discontentment at the values they were supposed to hold and pursue as men but didn't know what new values might be found that they could, as men, find meaningful. Stephen Boyd suggests that men today are restless for several reasons but that "the most prevalent are: (1) guilt about our role in the mistreatment of others, (2) resentment about being overburdened and enervated, (3) anger at being unfairly blamed for things that are not our responsibility, and (4) deep feelings of isolation."[3] Boyd concludes his exploration of this restlessness by saying, "There is a

228

deep desire for more meaningful and compassionate relationships, work and play. . . . This longing is a profoundly religious or spiritual issue."[4]

And, yet, there is considerable evidence, particularly as found by our authors here, that men do not come to pastoral care and counseling in large numbers, despite these difficult and changing times and the root spiritual issues at stake. There seem to be several reasons why men don't seek pastoral care and counseling in large numbers. One of the main agreements, found in much of the literature on the psychology of men, is that men are deeply trained and socialized to avoid anything that seems female or feminine. Seeking out help, especially help that is strongly associated with both emotions and with religion, denies some of the basic norms of Western masculinity. This fear of the female/feminine is remarked upon by several of the authors in this volume. It seems to cross lines of sexual orientation, race, class, and pastoral context. The fear of being other than masculine (thus feminine in a dualistic culture) drives much of male behavior.

Consequently, there is a real question facing men (and women) today: Are there values and traits that men can claim that still respect, and even hold unique, the experience of being male, which are neither patriarchal and destructive nor harmful for men themselves? Our culture has been built on a dualistic system (explored in chapter 1) that claims what isn't of the male must be of the female. It also claims that since maleness and femaleness are complementary, or two halves of the same whole, then what is male cannot be female and vice versa. The mandate for men not to be "like women" is much stronger than the mandate in contemporary culture for women not to be "like men." The fundamental problem, of course, is the binary, dualistic system that keeps these two false and rigid distinctions of masculine and feminine in place *and* the reality that anything womanlike is systematically devalued. It is only recently that studies in male psychology have focused on gender socialization and its impact. As Levant and Pollack note:

Men's studies over the past 15 years have begun to examine masculinity, not as a normative referent, but as a complex and problematic construct. In so doing, they have provided a framework for a psycho-

229

logical approach to men and masculinity that questions traditional norms for the male role . . . and that views certain male problems . . . as unfortunate but predictable results of the male socialization process.[5]

One of these important studies was done in the early 1980s. At that time, Joseph Pleck developed a new paradigm for masculinity that he called "gender role strain." This was set up in contradiction to the prior paradigm for masculinity, which suggested that gender role identity was a developmental process that, if successfully achieved, resulted in well-adjusted males. Pleck discovered that gender roles as understood in this culture were contradictory, inconsistent, and, to a certain extent, dangerous for both women and men; and trying to either attain those gender identities *or* failing to attain those identities resulted in strain and often dysfunction.[6] In reviewing the studies in gender role conflict over the fifteen years since Pleck's proposal, O'Neil, Good, and Holmes found the foundational problem in gender role socialization for men was this fear of femininity and that it had significant consequences in six patterns of gender role conflict. Those six patterns include: (1) restrictive emotionality; (2) socialized control, power, and competition; (3) homophobia; (4) restrictive sexual and affectionate behavior; (5) obsession with achievement and success; and (6) health care problems. Beyond causing these individual problems, the authors conclude that "these six patterns of gender role conflict interact with personal and institutional aspects of sexism. In other words, how men are socialized produces sexist attitudes and behaviors that explains much of the personal and institutional sexism in society."[7]

The shift to understanding men's psychology in the context of this gender role conflict or gender role strain has provided significant resources for trying to help men cope with the kinds of problems they face in this culture while understanding the important interconnections between individual problems, cultural changes, and gender socialization. Without a good understanding of these interconnections, pastoral care and counseling with men will be unable to serve a transformative function and will, at best, only help men to temporarily adjust to their stressful surroundings.

This book has attempted to explore the pastoral needs of men in a variety of contexts but with a fundamental agreement about the interlocking issues named above. When one understands the connections between gender construction and socialization; cultural power arrangements based on sex, race, class, sexual orientation, and physical ableness; and the kinds of stresses men (women and families) are experiencing in their lives, then appropriate, relevant, and transformational pastoral care and counseling can be developed.

This is not a monolithic construction. The very awareness that socialization, power/control dynamics, and idiosyncratic circumstances must all be considered helps to create a matrix within which we can analyze and assess the appropriate approach for the needs of particular populations of men and of particular men. This is especially important when looking at issues of class, race, and sexual orientation. As Judy Orr says so powerfully in her chapter on working-class men,

> The main axis of power within culture aligns authority with masculinity. A second axis of power denies authority to *some* men. Hence, gender as well as race and class are formative constructions of a hierarchy among men resulting in hegemonic masculinity (white, heterosexual, professional class), marginalized/traditional masculinities (winner and respectable working class), and subordinated masculinities (. . . racial minorities and gay men). (p. 75)

Issues of masculinity are deeply culture bound and are defined by the power arrangements of various groups of men within the culture. A social constructionist point of view, which is held to a certain extent at least by each of our authors, says that the meaning and definitions of masculinity vary across race, ethnicity, class, sexual orientation, and even over time for any given culture. This means that when the dominant male culture defines and normalizes masculinity through its various cultural media, it also begins to define certain males as either unable or unwilling to meet those definitions and therefore as deviant and of less value.

Lazur and Majors explore the ways in which various cultural particularities across race and ethnicity shape the meanings of masculinity for groups of men. They speak persuasively of the double bind in which men of differing colors and ethnicities from the dominant find themselves.

For a man of color, defining his own gender role involves integration of the dominant society's restrictions. Measuring himself against the standard that dictates the male gender role for the dominant culture yet denies equal access to the opportunities that sustain that standard evokes in the man of color frustrations, unexpressed emotions, and a drive for survival. . . . If he acts according to his culture, those in the dominant culture view him as "different," bar his access to resources, and may even engage in acts of violence against him. If he acts according to the prescriptions of the dominant culture, he ascribes to a system that, in effect, negates him, and he is considered by his own people to have "sold out." Whatever his choice, a man of color is constantly faced with the challenge of dealing with the consequences of how he acts. This pressure creates in him additional stress and conflict in fulfilling the male gender role.[8]

Gay men face similar conflicts. Many would say, as Rick Mixon does in chapter 8, that "if one is not a heterosexual male [and we might add, a heterosexual male that displays the dominant cultural norms of masculinity] . . . then he cannot be male, at least not fully. So part of the disdain and hatred of gay men is rooted in disdain for and hatred of women in this culture." And, as Orr points out in chapter 3, working-class men cannot afford to deviate from certain stereotyped culturally masculine behaviors because they are emasculated by their lack of prestige and success as measured by dominant masculinity norms. African American men, as described by both Matthews and Wimberly, are persistently denied access to masculinity status and thus need to develop new masculinity norms that grant both identity and prestige. These complexities about gender role strain, which emerges from both attempting to meet *and* failing to meet dominant cultural masculinity norms, need to be fully explored and understood as we build methods of pastoral care that will help diverse populations of men.

Despite the emphasis on diversity in this book on the care of men, there are certain themes that surface in all or most of the chapters that are helpful to examine as we engage in this theory-building process. All of the authors, to one degree or another, understand gender roles to be socialized over the life cycle of men and women and to exist because of cultural values about men and women more than or over against biological definitions. The authors vary in their conceptualizing of the dynamics undergirding gender role stereo-typing. Some authors focus more on an analysis of the socialization process and consequent internalizing of gender roles and values. Others focus more on the analysis of power dynamics in a patriarchal culture where women, and things womanlike, are devalued and disdained. In the midst of these different emphases, though, each author is profoundly affected by an analysis of culture and the impact of cultural engendering on the health and well-being of men, women, children, families, institutions, and creation. The conclu-sion they reach is that pastoral care must have a strong educational component about these dynamics and a strong countercultural message when helping men (and women) to create new and health-ier self-definitions.

Closely related to this theme is a commitment shared by most of the authors to the relationship between caring for the individual and caring for the community. There is general recognition that helping men to change also means helping to change the culture. If men learn to challenge dominant norms of masculinity and the associated higher value of things designated masculine (stoicism, aggression, isolation, rationality, control, maleness, whiteness, heterosexuality, and so on) then those norms and values will change.

Several authors of men's studies literature suggest that there are signs of those changes around us. In various reports of contemporary male college students, researchers are finding that these men are not endorsing many of the traditional norms of masculinity (which are named as avoiding all things feminine, restricting emotional life, seeking high status and success above all else, nonrelational and objectifying attitudes about sexuality, and fear and hatred of homo-sexuality). The most stubborn masculine norms in these studies tend to be self-reliance and aggressiveness. The author reviewing these studies reports these changes but also cautions the reader, "I need to also point out that for many working class and lower class men, the traditional norms may not be changing." In these contexts he suggests that one of the most resistant masculinity norms is the fear of all things that are "feminine."[9]

The clear recognition is that norms for masculinity will only change when (1) it is safe for men and men's self-esteem for the changes to happen and (2) there is a high level of consensus that these norms are harmful for all, including for men.

And, finally, a third theme that emerges in these chapters is a common method of identifying root causes, primarily sociocultural in nature, of the problems men face and then developing strategies for pastoral care and counseling that maintain that tension between the "personal and the political." No author is content to help men learn to live with the stresses that gender (and race, class, and orientation) conflicts cause. There is no isolated intrapsychic focus in these chapters. The pastoral care and counseling strategies that emerge here make justice an overarching category of care alongside support, affirmation, and confrontation. Phil Culbertson suggests that there are three major tasks for the pastoral counselor of men. First, he or she must "listen behind the lies." Culbertson says that men are prone to telling partial truths because they are so deeply socialized to present themselves to be more than they are. This is a vulnerable and precarious position that creates a great deal of stress (as well as damage to others) and Culbertson urges the pastoral caregiver of men to get behind the lies. When the pastoral caregiver and care receiver are both able to generate new perspectives that represent a fuller set of truths than the original story did, then shame also tends to be revealed. Culbertson suggests that the pastoral caregiver affirm the one who feels shame and help him to face that shame (based in falling short of being the ideal man) directly. The third strategy is to offer support to the man as he tells and broadens the narratives of his life and enlarges the options for his ongoing story.[10] And the story is, at its heart, a religious story—a narrative of meaning.

The theology expressed in these chapters includes liberation, resistance, and transformationist perspectives. All of them carry a deep belief in God's persistent invitation to a fullness of life for men and for all of creation. All of them believe that we are called, as pastoral caregivers, to participate in God's intentions for justice and compassion. Pastoral theology, then, as it relates to the care of men and the reconstruction of healthy gender roles, conveys the notion of a God who loves deeply and asks much.

Each of the authors in this book carries a vision for new ways of being male and female in all of the diverse contexts that men and women find themselves. The common hope is that there will be a new cooperation and a new collaboration across lines that have tended to divide and destroy and that we will be able to seek diversity, welcome differing perspectives, and work against stereotypes and derisions that name some people as less than others.

The work in exploring the specificities and implications of gender socialization in a patriarchal, racist, homophobic, and classist culture is still at its beginning. As several of the authors point out, the church and its ministry of pastoral care and counseling faces huge challenges when it considers its work of care with men. Not only have men traditionally not come to ministers for help in times of need, but the church itself has deeply colluded with the very structures we have named to be at the heart of the destructiveness in men's lives. On the other hand, the abiding messages of resistance to evil, commitment to justice, the power of grace, and the persistence of God's lure toward the fullness of life are the very resources needed to do this work. We are on this journey together as people who give and need care with one another. And, as theologian Nelle Morton has powerfully said, it is the journey that is our home.

NOTES

INTRODUCTION

1. Alice Walker defines a womanist as "a black feminist or feminist of color." See *In Search of Our Mother's Gardens: Womanist Prose* (New York: Harcourt Brace Jovanovich, 1983), xi. For further discussion see Emilie Townes, editor, *A Troubling in My Soul: Womanist Perspectives on Evil and Suffering* (Maryknoll, N.Y.: Orbis, 1993).

2. For discussion of the changing global economic scene, see John B. Cobb, Jr., *Sustaining the Common Good: A Christian Perspective on the Global Economy* (Cleveland: Pilgrim Press, 1994), and Herman E. Daly and John B. Cobb, Jr., *For the Common Good: Redirecting the Economy Toward Community, The Environment, and a Sustainable Future* (Boston: Beacon Press, 1989).

3. Henry Louis Gates, Jr., "Thirteen Ways of Looking at a Black Man," *The New Yorker* (October 23, 1996): 56-65.

4. Edward Gilbreath, "Great Awakening," *Christianity Today* 39 (February 6, 1996): 22; Laurie Goodstein, "Men Pack RFK on Promise of Religious Renewal," *The Washington Post* (May 28, 1995): A6; Evelyn Kirkley, "Is It Manly to Be Christian? The Debate in Victorian and Modern America," in Stephen Boyd, Mark Muesse, and Merle Longwood, editors, *Redeeming Men: Perspectives on Religion and Masculinity* (Louisville: Westminster John Knox, 1996).

5. James Nelson, *Body Theology* (Louisville: Westminster, 1992), 76-79.

6. Three such organizations are Men's Rights, Inc., Box 163180, Sacramento, CA., 95816; Equal Rights for Fathers, Inc., Box 90042, San Jose, CA 98109-3042; and National Congress of Men, 223 15th St., SE, Washington, DC 20003. *Network* is the newsletter of the National Congress of Men.

7. See two journals: *Wingspan: Journal of the Male Spirit* (Manchester, Mass.), and *Inroads: Men, Creativity and Soul* (Minneapolis). See the following books: Robert Bly, *Iron John: A Book About Men* (Chicago: University of Chicago Press, 1990); Robert Moore and Douglas Gillette, *King, Warrior, Magician, Lover* (San Francisco: Harper San Francisco, 1990); Sam Keen, *Fire in the Belly: On Being a Man* (New York: Bantam Books, 1991). For an interesting response, see Glen A. Mazis, *The Trickster, Magician and Grieving Man: Reconnecting Men with Earth* (Santa Fe: Bear and Company Publishing, 1993).

8. NOMAS, 54 Mint Street, Suite 300, San Francisco, CA 94103-9671.

9. See the following journals: *Brother* (Los Angeles), *Changing Men* (Madison, Wis.), and *Changing Men* (Harriman, Tenn.). See the following books: John Stoltenberg, *Refusing to Be a Man: Essays on Sex and Justice* (New York: Penguin Books, 1989); John Stoltenberg, *The End of Manhood: A Book for Men of Conscience* (New York: Penguin Books, 1993); Franklin Abbott, *New Men, New Minds: Breaking Male Tradition* (Freedom, Calif.: Crossing Press, 1987); Franklin Abbott, editor, *Men and Intimacy: Personal Accounts Exploring the Dilemmas of Modern Male Sexuality* (Freedom, Calif.: Crossing Press, 1990). Michael Kimmel and Michael A. Messner, editors, *Men's Lives* (New York: Macmillan Publishing Co., Second Edition, 1992), summarizes some of the debate within University Men's Studies programs.

10. For a variety of responses from feminist and womanist perspectives, see Kay Leigh Hagan, editor, *Women Respond to the Men's Movement: A Feminist Collection* (San Francisco: Harper San Francisco, 1992).

11. For a summary of what some of the Protestant denominations are doing, see Cecil Murphey, *Mantalk: Resources for Exploring Male Issues* (Louisville: Presbyterian Publishing House, 1991).

12. Among the first theologians to respond to the crisis of men's identity from a Christian perspective were James E. Dittes, *The Male Predicament: On Being a Man Today* (San Francisco: Harper and Row, 1985); James B. Nelson, *The Intimate Connection: Male Sexuality, Masculine Spirituality* (Philadelphia: Westminster, 1988) and *Body Theology* (Louisville: Westminster, 1992); and Philip L. Culbertson, *New Adam: The Future of Male Spirituality* (Minneapolis: Fortress, 1992) and *Counseling Men* (Minneapolis: Fortress, 1994).

13. See chapter 2 in which Christie Neuger discusses the results of her interviews with twenty pastors about men's issues and programs.

14. Maxine Glaz and Jeanne Moessner, editors, *Women in Travail and Transition: A New Pastoral Care* (Minneapolis: Fortress, 1991).

1. GENDER AND THEOLOGY

1. Kenneth Gergen, "Social Constructionism and Psychotherapy," an unpublished lecture from the Family Therapy Networker Conference, Baltimore, 1992.

2. Ibid.

3. Bonnie Miller-McLemore, "Epistemology or Bust: Where Are We Really Headed?" *Journal of Pastoral Theology* 2 (Summer, 1992): 61.

4. Gerda Lerner, *The Creation of Patriarchy* (New York: Oxford University Press, 1986), 5.

5. Lerner, 4.

6. Rebecca Chopp, *Saving Work: Feminist Practices of Theological Education* (Louisville: Westminster/John Knox Press, 1995), 56.

7. Rosemary Radford Ruether, "Patriarchy and the Men's Movement," in *Women Respond to the Men's Movement*, ed. Kay Leigh Hagan (San Francisco: HarperCollins, 1992), 17.

8. Lerner, 220.

9. Elizabeth Dodson Gray, *Patriarchy as a Conceptual Trap* (Wellesley, Mass.: Roundtable Press, 1982), 17. Gray suggests that a conceptual trap is "a way of thinking that is like a room which—once inside—you cannot imagine a world outside."

10. Nelle Morton, *The Journey Is Home* (Boston: Beacon Press, 1985), 52.

11. Mary Daly, *Beyond God the Father* (Boston: Beacon Press, 1973), 19.

12. Rebecca Chopp and Mark Taylor, *Reconstructing Christian Theology* (Minneapolis: Fortress Press, 1994), 5.

13. "A Report of the World Council of Churches," *Ecumenical Review*, 33, no. 1 (January 1981): 77.

14. Brian Wren, *What Language Shall I Borrow? God-Talk in Worship: A Male Response to Feminist Theology* (New York: Crossroad, 1989), 4.

15. Sallie McFague, *Metaphorical Theology: Models of God in Religious Language* (Philadelphia: Fortress Press, 1982), 145.

16. Philip Sheldrake, "Spirituality and Sexism," in *Who Needs Feminism? Men Respond to Sexism in the Church*, ed. Richard Holloway (London: SPCK, 1991), 91.

17. Wren, 162.

18. Marjorie Suchocki, "God, Sexism and Transformation," in Chopp and Taylor, 39-46.

19. Rosemary Radford Ruether, "The Liberation of Christology from Patriarchy," in *Feminist Theology: A Reader*, ed. Ann Loades (Louisville: Westminster/John Knox Press, 1990), 138.

20. Jacquelyn Grant, *White Women's Christ and Black Women's Jesus* (Atlanta: Scholars Press, 1989), 216.

21. Susan Brooks Thistlethwaite, *Sex, Race, and God: Christian Feminism in Black and White* (New York: Crossroad, 1989), 114.

22. Christine Smith, "Preaching as an Art of Resistance," in *The Arts of Ministry: Feminist-Womanist Approaches*, ed. Christie Cozad Neuger (Louisville: Westminster Press, 1996), 43.

23. Annie Imbens and Ineke Jonker, *Christianity and Incest* (Minneapolis: Fortress Press, 1992), 212.

24. James Newton Poling, *The Abuse of Power: A Theological Problem* (Nashville: Abingdon Press, 1991), 169.

25. Poling, 168-81.

26. Rita Nakashima Brock, *Journeys by Heart: A Christology of Erotic Power* (New York: Crossroad, 1988), 56.

27. See, for example, the edited volume *Christianity, Patriarchy, and Abuse,* Joanne Carlson Brown and Carole R. Bohn, editors (New York: Pilgrim Press, 1989) for several articles on the relationship between Christian doctrine and the abuse of women and children.

28. Valerie Saiving, "The Human Situation: A Feminine View," in *Womanspirit Rising,* ed. Carol Christ and Judith Plaskow (San Francisco: Harper Row, 1979), 26.

29. Christine M. Smith, "Sin and Evil in Feminist Thought," *Theology Today,* no. 2 (July, 1993): 210-211.

30. Chopp and Taylor, *Reconstructing Christian Theology,* 4.

31. Ibid., 5.

32. Ibid., 8.

33. Ibid., 11.

34. John B. Cobb, Jr., "The Religions," *Christian Theology: An Introduction to Its Traditions and Tasks,* 2nd ed., edited by Peter C. Hodgson and Robert H. King (Minneapolis: Fortress, 1985), 373, quoted in Chopp and Taylor, 11.

35. Chopp and Taylor, 20.

36. Ibid., 21.

37. Ibid., 22.

2. MEN'S ISSUES IN THE LOCAL CHURCH: WHAT CLERGYMEN HAVE TO SAY

1. Ages of pastors ranged from 30 to 68. Church size ranged from 150 to 800 and were found in inner city, suburban and rural locations. All pastors were married, heterosexual men who tended to range theologically from "middle of the road" to liberal. Congregations ranged from primarily working class to primarily professional, upper middle class but most had a broad spectrum of membership. Most of the congregations were predominantly white, although there were two interview contexts where the congregations were heavily African American. Only one congregation had a significant number of out gay members. Seventeen of the pastors were European American, two were African American, and one was Caribbean American. As I requested names for potential interviewees from a variety of sources my only requirement was that they be "reflective" about issues of gender and pastoral care. I wish to thank the 20 clergymen who gave their time and their careful reflections to this interview process.

2. Phil Culbertson, *Counseling Men* (Minneapolis: Augsburg/Fortress, 1994), 9.

3. Two pastors also talked about a high percentage of crisis requests for food, gasoline, or a place to stay. However, these crisis needs did not generally lead to discussions about other, more subtle, pastoral care concerns.

4. Richard Meth, "The Road to Masculinity," in *Men in Therapy,* ed. Richard Meth and Robert Pasick (New York: Guilford Press, 1990), 6. Meth suggests that one of the most central components of men's gender training is a deep fear of femininity and feminine values that includes sharing feelings with another person.

5. Robert Pasick, "Raised to Work, " in *Men in Therapy,* ed. Richard Meth and Robert Pasick (New York: Guilford Press, 1990), 36.

3. HARD WORK, HARD LOVIN', HARD TIMES, HARDLY WORTH IT: CARE OF WORKING-CLASS MEN

1. This chapter was greatly enhanced by the author's conversations with several pastors of working-class men, including Lucille Barb, Pat Buss, Fred Droege, John Gingrich, Dennis Matthews, Judy Voss, Karyn Wiseman, and Larry Yeo.

2. Marie Haug, "Social Class Measurement: A Methodological Critique," in *Issues in Social Inequality*, ed. Gerald W. Thielbar and Saul D. Feldman (Boston: Little, Brown, 1972), 429.

3. The U.S. Bureau of the Census used the 1917 Alba Edwards hierarchical scale of "head" and "hand" occupations. "Head" workers were ranked by training and prestige and "hand" workers by level of skill. See U.S. Bureau of the Census, *Methodology and Scores of Socioeconomic Status*, Working Paper no. 15 (Washington: GPO, 1963).

4. Gerhard Lenski, *Power and Privilege: A Theory of Social Stratification* (New York: McGraw-Hill, 1966), 74.

5. See Rosemary Crompton, "The Classical Inheritance," in *Class*, ed. Patrick Joyce (Oxford: Oxford University Press, 1995), 48; and John Pease, William Form, and Joan Huber Rytina, "Ideological Currents in American Stratification Literature," *American Sociologist* 5:2 (1970): 131.

6. Erik Olin Wright, "American Class Structure," *American Sociological Review* 47 (1982): 709-26.

7. Albert Szymanski, *Class Structure: A Critical Perspective* (New York: Praeger Publishers, 1983), 230.

8. J. R. Snarey and George E. Vaillant, "How Lower- and Working-Class Youth Become Middle Class Adults: The Association Between Ego Defense Mechanisms and Upward Social Mobility," *Child Development* 56 (1985): 899-910.

9. Richard Parker, *The Myth of the Middle Class: Notes on Affluence and Equality* (New York: Harper & Row, 1972), 136. David Halle, *America's Working Man: Work, Home, and Politics Among Blue Collar Property Owners* (Chicago: University of Chicago Press, 1984), 323, notes that many blue-collar men do not want to be supervisors because they do not want the extra worry and responsibility.

10. John C. Goyder and James E. Curtis, "A Three-Generational Approach to Trends in Occupational Mobility," *American Journal of Sociology* 81:1 (1975): 129.

11. Strong forces at work for one's class to perpetuate itself are described in Melvin L. Kohn, *Class and Conformity: A Study in Values* (Chicago: University of Chicago Press, 1977) and in Paul Willis, *Learning to Labor: How Working Class Kids Get Working Class Jobs* (New York: Columbia University Press, 1977, repr. 1981).

12. Michael Lewis, *The Culture of Inequality* (New York: New American Library, 1978), 15.

13. John C. Raines and Donna C. Day-Lower, *Modern Work and Human Meaning* (Philadelphia: Westminster, 1986), 34.

14. Lillian Rubin, *Families on the Fault Line* (New York: Harper Collins, 1994), 26. Also Barbara Ehrenreich, *Fear of Falling: The Inner Life of the Middle Class* (New York: Harper, 1985), 8, notes that during the 1950s the lower strata had so dropped from view that in the early 1960s the poor were "discovered" and in the late 1960s the working class was "discovered."

15. William Form, *Divided We Stand: Working Class Stratification in America* (Urbana: University of Illinois Press, 1985), 255.

16. Tex Sample, *Blue-Collar Ministry: Facing Economic and Social Realities of Working People* (Valley Forge, Pa.: Judson Press, 1984). Ben Hamper, *Rivethead: Tales From the Assembly Line* (New York: Warner Books, 1986), saw three groups of blue-collar kids in the Catholic school he attended, not unlike the Respectables, Survivors, and Hard-Living categories in Sample's work: "the obedient eggheads, the robots of mediocrity, and the who-gives-a-shit underachievers," 10.

17. Lynne Segal, *Slow Motion: Changing Masculinities, Changing Men* (New Brunswick, N.J.: Rutgers University Press, 1990), 110.

18. Kohn, *Class and Conformity: A Study in Values*.

19. Tex Sample, *Hard-Living People and Mainstream Christians* (Nashville: Abingdon Press, 1993).

20. Ehrenreich, *Fear of Falling*, 120. See also pp. 7, 27, 107, 117, for references to other stereotypes.

21. Robert W. Connell, *Gender and Power: Society, the Person, and Sexual Politics* (Stanford: Stanford University Press, 1987), 23-36, critiques and finds wanting theories influenced by Marxist analysis (masculinity shaped by capitalism and patriarchy), by liberal sex-role theory (masculinity shaped by social expectation and position), and by categorical theories (masculinity shaped by enduring structures such as domination or by biology).

22. Mary Ann Clawson, *Constructing Brotherhood: Class, Gender, and Fraternalism* (Princeton: Princeton University Press, 1989), 245.

23. Sallie Westwood, "Racism, Black Masculinity, and the Politics of Space," in *Men, Masculinities, and Social Theory*, ed. Jeff Hearn and David Morgan (London: Unwin Hyman, 1990), 57.

24. Connell, 110.

25. Ibid., 269.

26. Sigmund Freud, "New Introductory Lectures on Psychoanalysis," Lecture 33, "Femininity," *Standard Edition*, 22:112-35.

27. Michel Foucault, *Discipline and Punishment* (Harmondsworth: Allen Lane, 1977), cited in *Dislocating Masculinity: Comparative Ethnographies*, ed. Andrea Cornwall and Nancy Lindisfarne (Routledge, 1993), 37.

28. Clawson, 4. The 19th- and early 20th-century growth of fraternal organizations was the precursor to labor union brotherhoods.

29. Stan Gray, "Sharing the Shop Floor," in *Beyond Patriarchy: Essays by Men on Pleasure, Power, and Change*, ed. Michael Kaufman (New York: Oxford, 1987), 225. For a first-person account of a General Motors "shop-rat" see Ben Hamper's *Rivethead*. See also Anthony Easthope, *What a Man's Gotta Do: The Masculine Myth in Popular Culture* (Boston: Unwin Hyman, 1986), 19. Pierre Bourdieu in *Language and Symbolic Power* (Cambridge: Harvard University Press, 1991), 87-88, helpfully discusses the domestication of language and the body as one moves up the socioeconomic ladder. Such domestication proscribes and censors gross remarks, coarse jokes, outspokenness, and excessive appetites and feelings. This dominant style denies the social and sexual identity of many working-class men.

30. Segal, 264.

31. Michael Messner, "Masculinities and Athletic Careers," in *Race, Class, and Gender: An Anthology*, ed. Margaret L. Andersen and Patricia Hill Collins (Belmont, Calif.: Wadsworth, 1992), 157.

32. John Crowley, "Howells, Stoddard, and Male Homosocial Attachment in Victorian America," in *The Making of Masculinities: The New Men's Studies* (Boston: Allen and Unwin, 1987), 301-24.

33. See Lillian Rubin, *Intimate Strangers* (New York: Harper & Row, 1984).

34. See Steve Trimm, *Walking Wounded: Men's Lives During and Since the Vietnam War*, Frontiers in Psychotherapy Series, ed. Edward Tick (Norwood, N.J.: Ablex Publishing, 1993).

35. Messner, 156; his study of 30 former male athletes also found that 15 of the 16 Black and Hispanic men were from poor and working-class families, while 9 of 14 white men were from middle-class families.

36. Messner, 147.

37. Richard Gillett, "Church Role Vital for Justice in New Workplaces," *The Witness* 69:2 (1986): 12-15.

38. Marvin E. Ceynar, *Healing the Heartland: Nonviolent Social Change and the American Rural Crisis of the 1980s and 1990s* (Columbus, Ga.: Brentwood Communications, 1989), 13.

39. Janet Fitchen, *Endangered Spaces, Enduring Places: Change, Identity, and Survival in Rural America* (Boulder: Westview Press, 1991), 2-4.

40. Paul David Wellstone, *How the Rural Poor Got Power: Narrative of a Grass-Roots Organizer* (Amherst: University of Massachusetts Press, 1978), vii.

41. Judith Stacey, *Brave New Families: Stories of Domestic Upheaval in Late Twentieth Century America* (New York: Basic Books, 1990), 256.

42. Rubin, *Families on the Fault-Line,* 8. See also Elijah Anderson, *Streetwise: Race, Class, and Change in an Urban Community* (Chicago: University of Chicago Press, 1990), 29, for fuller discussion of the strong association of ethnic identity with particular neighborhoods, which were often close to the workplace. Newcomers meant conflict over jobs, housing, and community.

43. David R. Roediger, *The Wages of Whiteness: Race and the Making of the American Working Class* (London: Verso, 1991), 7. See also David Roediger, *Towards the Abolition of Whiteness: Essays on Race, Politics, and Working Class History* (London: Verso, 1994).

44. Derald W. Sue, *Counseling the Culturally Different* (New York: Wiley & Sons, 1981). See also Paul Pedersen et al., *Counseling Across Cultures,* rev. ed. (Honolulu: University Press of Hawaii, 1981).

45. Salvador Minuchin et al., *Families of the Slums: An Exploration of Their Structure and Treatment* (New York: Basic, 1967).

46. David W. Augsburger, *Pastoral Counseling Across Cultures* (Philadelphia: Westminster, 1986) and Charles Kemp, *Pastoral Care with the Poor* (Nashville: Abingdon Press, 1972).

47. See John E. Mayer and Noel Timms, *The Client Speaks: Working Class Impressions of Casework* (London: Routledge & Kegan Paul, 1970), 39-48; Albert K. Cohen and Harold M. Hodges, Jr. "Characteristics of Lower Blue-Collar Class," *Social Problems* 10 (Spring, 1963): 323; and Herbert J. Gans, *The Urban Villagers* (New York: Free Press, 1962), 236-37. Mirra Komarovsky, *Blue Collar Marriage* (New York: Random House, 1962) states that working-class families are much closer to relatives than to friends.

48. Frank X. Acosta, Joe Yamamoto, and Leonard Evans, *Effective Psychotherapy for Low-Income and Minority Patients* (New York: Plenum Press, 1982), 38.

49. August B. Hollingshead and Frederick C. Redlich, *Social Class and Mental Illness* (New York: Wiley, 1958), suggested that Upper Class = 3.4%, Upper Middle Class = 9.0%, Middle Class = 21.4%, Lower Middle (Working) Class = 48.5%, and Lower Class (Poor) = 17.7%.

50. Eric Bromley, "Social Class Issues in Psychotherapy," *Psychology and Psychotherapy: Current Trends and Issues,* ed. David Pilgrim (London: Routledge & Kegan Paul, 1983), 204-27.

51. Larry Graham, "From Relational Humanness to Relational Justice: Reconceiving Pastoral Care and Counseling," *Pastoral Care and Social Conflict,* ed. Pamela D. Couture and Rodney J. Hunter (Nashville: Abingdon Press, 1995), 220-34.

52. See also Larry Martens, "Care in the Congregation," *Church and Society* 81:3 (1991): 73-80, for an understanding of communal care by the household of faith.

53. Roy Steinhoff Smith, "The Politics of Pastoral Care: An Alternative Politics of Care," *Pastoral Care and Social Conflict,* ed. Pamela D. Couture and Rodney J. Hunter (Nashville: Abingdon Press, 1995), 148.

54. Presenting problems of over 3/4 of the English working-class clients studied in the late 1960s included 34% marital discord, 23% economic difficulties, 13% parent-child relationship, and 7% single-parent family, in Mayer and Timms, 24.

55. See also Michael Lerner, "Pain at Work and Pain in Families," *Tikkun* 6 (1991): 15-20, 93-94. See also Halle, 145.

56. Lerner, "Pain at Work," 17-18.

57. Carl Ridley and Mari S. Wilhelm, "Adaptation to Unemployment: Effects of a Mine Closure on Husbands and Wives," *Lifestyles: Family and Economic Issues* 9:2 (Summer, 1988): 145-60. The observation that underemployment—loss of 20% of income from the previous five years—is psychologically more stressful than an absolute level of poverty is made by Anisa M. Zvonkovic, "Underemployment: Individual and Marital Adjustment to Income Loss," *Lifestyles: Family and Economic Issues* 9:2 (Summer, 1988): 161-78.

58. Hamper, 55.

59. Pertti Alasuutari, "Alcoholism in Its Cultural Context: the Case of Blue Collar Men," *Contemporary Drug Problems* 13 (Winter, 1986): 641-86, notes that the pattern of blue-collar drinking is alternating heavy drinking and dry times, while the pattern of white-collar drinking is regular ingestion, 674.

60. Jeff Hearn, *The Gender of Oppression: Men, Masculinity, and the Critique of Marxism* (Brighton: Wheatsheaf, 1987), 19. This is especially true among those not previously unemployed.

61. Taggart Frost and Dennis Clayson, "Measurement of Self-Esteem, Stress-Related Life Events, Locus of Control Among Unemployed and Employed Blue Collar Workers," *Journal of Applied Social Psychology* 21 (Sept. 1, 1991): 1402-17.

62. Paul C. Rosenblatt, *Farming Is in Our Blood: Farm Families in Economic Crisis* (Ames: Iowa State University Press, 1990), 123.

63. Joan Blundell, "Report to Select Committee on Children, Youth, and Family," paper presented to a Consultation and Education group at Northwest Iowa Mental Health Center (n.d.).

64. Halle, 55-64.

65. Ibid., xii.

66. Stacey, 267. Interestingly, labor's 8-hour day was fought for in order to gain some control over one's time and to provide some opportunities for educational growth and for time with one's family, according to Roediger, *The Wages of Whiteness*, 176.

67. Halle, 64, notes that alcoholism *is* more frequent in men than women, in those under 50 than over 50, in cities and suburbs than rural areas, among Catholics than Protestants.

68. See chapter 8 for a fuller discussion of male violence and the pastoral and ethical issues involved.

69. Segal, 242. She also says that nonmarital rape/violence *is* related to economics; when gainful employment and economic success are blocked, frustrated masculinity is expressed against women, 245.

70. Ellison, 102, 107.

71. Cornelia Butler Flora et al., *Rural Communities: Legacy and Change* (Boulder: Westview Press, 1992), 85.

72. Clawson, 170.

73. Trimm, 78.

74. Michael Lerner, "Work: A Politics of Meaning Approach to Policy," *Tikkun* 8 (1993): 23.

75. Fitchen, 129.

76. David Halle notes a pervasive disrespect for religious representatives among working-class men due to financial greed, sexual misbehavior, excessive drinking, and arrogance of priests, pastors, et al., 254.

77. A. David Bos, *A Practical Guide to Community Ministry* (Louisville: Westminster John Knox, 1993), 2, 11, 75. A helpful resource from a community services perspective is Gale L. Zahniser and William L. Ashley, *Helping the Dislocated Worker: Planning Community Services* (Columbus, Ohio: National Center for Research in Vocational Education at Ohio State University, 1984).

78. Ceynar, 49-50.

79. Tex Sample, *Ministry in an Oral Culture: Living With Will Rogers, Uncle Remus, and Minnie Pearl* (Louisville: Westminster John Knox, 1994), 71.

80. Rosenblatt, 159. See also David W. Stamps, "Vocational Pastoral Care: Attuned to the Work World," *Christian Ministry* 18 (January, 1987): 22-23.

81. Lerner, "Work: A Politics of Meaning Approach," 25.

82. Jeremy Brecher and Tim Costello, *Building Bridges: The Emerging Grass Roots Coalition of Labor and Community* (New York: Monthly Review Press, 1990).

83. Joan Blundall, "Peer Listening Program: Empowering Community Members as Helpers," unpublished paper (n.d.).

84. Alan Parry and Robert E. Doan, *Story Re-Visions: Narrative Therapy in the Postmodern World* (New York: Guilford, 1994), 27-28. See also Michael White and David Epston, *Narrative Means to Therapeutic Ends* (New York: W. W. Norton, 1990) for a compelling discussion of erudite (dominant) knowledge/narrative and indigenous (resistant) knowledge/narrative.

85. Everett L. Worthington, "Treatment of Families During Life Transitions: Matching Treatment to Family Response," *Family Process* 26:2 (1987): 303.

86. Salvador Minuchin, "Conflict-Resolution Family Therapy," *Changing Families,* ed. Jay Haley (New York: Grune and Stratton, 1971), 149. Solution-focused family therapy is also elaborated in David B. Waters and Edith Lawrence, *Competence, Courage, and Change: An Approach to Family Therapy* (New York: W. W. Norton, 1993).

87. Seymour L. Halleck, "Family Therapy and Social Change," *Social Casework* 57:8 (1976): 483-93.

88. Acosta et al., 12-14.

89. Ibid., 4. See also Mayer and Timms, 78.

90. See Michael F. Hoyt, editor, *Constructive Therapies* (New York: Guilford Press, 1994).

91. Halle, 180-83.

92. Sample, *Ministry in an Oral Culture,* 38.

93. Richard Voss, "Pastoral Social Ministry in the Ecosystem of the Poor: Breaking Through the Illusions," *Journal of Pastoral Care* 47 (Summer, 1993): 100-108.

94. Acosta et al., 6.

95. John Lovatt, "Jesus in the Workplace: Toward a Better Theology of Work," *The Modern Churchman* 34:2 (1992): 10-16.

96. Paul Marshall, "Work and Rest," *The Reformed Journal* 38 (June, 1988): 9-14.

4. LOVE AND WORK AMONG AFRICAN AMERICAN MEN

1. Recent work in pastoral theology by James Poling, Archie Smith, Jr., and Don Browning has emphasized the need to engage in ministry that is practical. Much of their work is based on the descriptive and revised correlational theologies of James Gustafson and David Tracy. The view espoused here utilizes these scholars' contributions toward the development of a truly practical theological ethic of pastoral care.

2. Donald H. Matthews, *The Spiritual: A Narrative Interpretation of African American Religion and Culture* (New York and London: Oxford University Press, 1996).

3. William J. Wilson, "Poverty and Family Structure: The Widening Gap between Evidence and Public Policy Issues" (with Kathryn Neckerman), in *The Truly Disadvantaged* (Chicago and London: The University of Chicago Press, 1987).

4. Mark Testa, Nan M. Astone et al., "Employment and Marriage," in *The Ghetto Underclass,* ed. William Julius Wilson (Newbury Park: Sage, 1993), 98-99.

5. Andrew Hacker, *Two Nations: Black and White, Separate, Hostile, Unequal* (New York: Scribner and Sons, 1992), 74-75.

6. Robert T. Michael, John Gagnon et al., *Sex in America: A Definitive Survey* (Boston: Little, Brown and Co., 1994), 236-39.

7. Cornel West, *Race Matters* (Boston: Beacon Press, 1992).

8. Donald H. Matthews, "Proposal for an Afrocentric Curriculum," *Journal of the American Academy of Religion* LXXI/3 (1994): 885-92.

9. Alex Haley, *The Autobiography of Malcolm X* (New York: Ballantine Books, 1964), 201.

5. THE MEN'S MOVEMENT AND PASTORAL CARE OF AFRICAN AMERICAN MEN

1. The narrative model on which this chapter is based can be found in Edward P. Wimberly, "Pastoral Counseling with African American Men," *The Urban League Review* 16 (1993): 77-84.

2. For a definition of masculine values see Nathan Hare and Julia Hare, *Bringing the Black Boy to Manhood: The Passage* (San Francisco: Black Think Tank, 1985), 20.

3. Romney M. Moseley, *Becoming a Self Before God* (Nashville: Abingdon Press, 1991).

4. Ibid., 70.

5. Erik Erikson describes the cultural role in meaning-making in *Childhood and Society* (New York: W. W. Norton, 1963), 261.

6. Erikson, 241.

7. Ibid., 242.

8. See Edward P. Wimberly, "Pastoral Counseling with African American Men," *The Urban League Review* 16 (1993): 78-79.

9. Ibid., 78.

10. Ibid.

11. For a discussion of masculine reactions of African American males, see Dionne J. Jones, "African American Males: A Critical Link in the African American Family," *The Urban League Review* 16 (1993): 3-7. See also Victor De La Cancela, "Coolin: The Psychosocial Communications of African and Latino Men," *The Urban League Review* 16 (1993): 33-44.

12. Cancela, "Coolin," 33.

13. Ibid., 14.

14. Ibid., 35.

15. Ibid.

16. Wimberly, "Pastoral Counseling with African American Men," 78.

17. Cancela, "Coolin," 41.

18. Ibid., 41-42.

19. Wayne R. Davis, "An Examination into the Process of Grief As Experienced by African American Males," (Ph.D. diss., Southern Baptist Theological Seminary, 1994), 41-45.

20. Robert Staples, *Black Masculinity: The Black Man's Role in American Society* (San Francisco: The Black Scholar Press, 1982), 1-2.

21. Cancela, "Coolin," 33-44.

22. Clarence Walker, *Biblical Counseling with African Americans* (Grand Rapids: Zondervan, 1992), 26-27.

23. Jawanza Kunjufu's works include *Countering the Conspiracy to Destroy Black Boys,* vols. I, II, and III (Chicago: African American Images, 1985); *The Black Peer Group* (Chicago: African American Images, 1988); and *Hip-Hop Vs. MAAT: A Psycho/Social Analysis of Values* (Chicago: African American Images, 1993). Another author in this school of thought who draws on Kunjufu's work is Mychal Wynn, *Empowering African-American Males to Succeed* (South Pasadena, Calif.: Rising Sun Publications, 1992).

24. Kunjufu, *Countering the Conspiracy,* vol. III, 71.

25. Kunjufu, 22.

26. Nathan Hare and Julia Hare, *Bringing the Black Boy to Manhood: The Passage* (San Francisco: The Black Think Tank, 1985), 21.

27. Hare and Hare, 16.

28. Na'im Akbar, *Visions for Black Men* (Nashville: Winston-Derek, 1991), 43-62.

29. This definition represents a modification of the definition found in Wimberly, "Pastoral Counseling with African American Men," 77.

30. Ibid.

31. The resource for the sources of African American manhood in culture is Wimberly, "Pastoral Counseling with African American Men," 79-84.

32. Charles S. Finch III, *Echoes of the Old Darkland: Theme from the African Eden* (Atlanta: Khenti, Inc., 1991), xiii.

33. Walter Allen, "The Search for Applicable Theories of Black Family Life," *Journal of Marriage and the Family* (1978): 117-129; Diane Lewis, "The Black Family Socialization and Sex Roles," *Phylon* 36 (1975): 221-37; Bernadette Gray-Little, "Marital Quality and Power Processes Among Black Couples," *Journal of Marriage and the Family* (1982): 633-46; and Ledand Axelson, "The Working Wife: Differences in Perception Among Negro and White Males," *Journal of Marriage and the Family* 32 (1980): 457-464.

34. Edward P. Wimberly, *African American Pastoral Care* (Nashville: Abingdon Press, 1991).

35. Edward P. Wimberly, "Spiritual Formation in Theological Education," in *Clergy Assessment and Career Development,* ed. Richard A. Hunt et al. (Nashville: Abingdon Press, 1990), 27-31.

36. Wimberly, "Pastoral Care with African American Men," 81-82.

37. See William Oliver, *The Violent Social World of Black Men* (New York: Lexington Books, 1994), 19.

38. Oliver, 11. For more information on masculinity, see Richard Majors and Janet Mancini Billson, *Cool Pose: The Dilemmas of Black Manhood in America* (New York: Lexington Books, 1992).

39. Oliver, 23.

40. Ibid., 25.

41. For the trend describing the cultural connectedness of African American women, see Katie G. Cannon, *Black Womanist Ethics* (Atlanta: Scholars Press, 1988), 87-88.

42. Janice Hale, *Black Children: Their Roots, Culture, and Learning Styles* (Provo, Utah: Brigham Young University Press, 1982), 69.

6. THE SHAMAN SAYS. . . WOMANIST REFLECTION ON PASTORAL CARE OF AFRICAN AMERICAN MEN

1. For a complete description of "womanist," see Alice Walker's now legendary definition in Alice Walker, *In Search of Our Mothers' Gardens: Womanist Prose* (New York: Harcourt, Brace, Jovanovich, 1983), in. In brief, it refers to "a black feminist . . . committed to the survival and wholeness of an entire people, male and female."

2. See George E. Curry, "After the Million Man March: Farrakhan Seeks to Redefine Black Leadership," *Emerge* (February, 1996): 41, in which Curry notes in a somewhat euphoric account that "After the march, leaders of local organizations and churches reported that African Americans were signing up as volunteers in record numbers. And that spirit is still evidenced around the country."

3. Edward P. Wimberly, *Pastoral Care in the Black Church* (Nashville: Abingdon, 1979), 23.

4. A particularly telling example of the disapproval of prominent African American women of the Million Man March is that of the comment made by Anita Hill and bell hooks, as reported by Henry Louis Gates: "When Anita Hill heard that O. J. Simpson was going to be part of the Million Man March on Washington, she felt it was entirely in keeping with the occasion . . . [an event in which] matters of gender had been "bracketed" . . . by a march from which women were excluded. . . . bell hooks argues, 'both O. J.'s case and the Million Man March confirm that, while white men are trying to be sensitive and pretending they're the new man, black men are saying that patriarchy must be upheld at all costs, even if women must die'." See Henry Louis Gates, Jr., "Thirteen Ways of Looking at a Black Man," *The New Yorker* (October 23, 1995): 60.

5. See for example, Haki R. Madhubuti, *Black Men: Obsolete, Single, Dangerous? The Afrikan American Family in Transition* (Chicago: Third World Press, 1990). Richard Majors and Janet Mancini Billson, *Cool Pose: The Dilemmas of Black Manhood in America* (New York: Lexington Books, 1992).

6. Edward P. Wimberly, *African American Pastoral Care* (Nashville: Abingdon Press, 1991), 26.

7. Black men at the Million Man March were enjoined to adopt a code of behavior by repeating after Louis Farrakhan this promise: "I, (say your name), pledge that from this day forward I will never raise my hand with a knife or a gun to beat, cut, or shoot any member of my family or any human being, except in self-defense. I, (say your name), pledge from this day forward I will never abuse my wife by striking her, disrespecting her. For she is the mother of my children and the producer of my future. "(say your name) will never use the 'B' [bitch] word to describe any female, but particularly my own black sister. I (say your name. . . . ") See George E. Curry, "The Million Man March: Farrakhan Seeks to Redefine Black Leadership," *Emerge* (February, 1996): 37.

8. See Toinette M. Eugene, "Swing Low, Sweet Chariot! A Womanist Ethical Response to Sexual Violence and Abuse," in *Violence Against Women and Children: A Christian Theological Source Book*, ed. Carol J. Adams and Marie M. Fortune (New York: Continuum, 1995), 185-200.

9. See Horace L. Griffin, "Giving New Birth: Lesbians, Gays, and "The Family": A Pastoral Care Perspective," in *The Journal of Pastoral Theology* (1993): 89-98. Griffin declares "as a gay African American pastoral theologian, my primary concern has to do with a social justice for all types of families . . . including African American single-headed households and lesbian and gay parents. Jesus' concept of 'family,' which allows for a broader understanding of family and

involves the participation of the church community, should be used as our starting point for organizing family structures," 96.

10. See Mary Burnham, et al., "Scapegoating the Black Family: Black Women Speak," in *The Nation* (July 24/31, 1989); C. Franklin, "Black Male-Black Female Conflict: Individually Caused and Culturally Nurtured," *Journal of Black Studies* 15 (1984): 139-54; J. Kunjufu, *Countering the Conspiracy to Destroy Black Boys* (Chicago: University of Chicago Press, 1983); R. Majors and J. Billson, *Cool Pose: The Dilemmas of Black Manhood in America* (New York: Lexington Books, 1992) for scholarly and theoretical positions about the role of African American women in relationship to African American men and boys.

11. Sojourner Truth as quoted in Bert James Lowenberg and Ruth Bogin, editors, *Black Women in Nineteenth Century American Life: Their Words, Their Thoughts, Their Feelings* (University Park and London: The Pennsylvania State University Press, 1976), 236.

12. Toinette M. Eugene, "Moral Values and Black Womanists," in *The Journal of Religious Thought* 44:2 (1988): 28.

13. Alice Walker, *In Search of Our Mother's Gardens* (New York: Harcourt Brace Jovanovich, 1983), 5.

14. Michael Harner, "What Is a Shaman?" in *Shaman's Path: Healing, Personal Growth, and Empowerment,* ed. Gary Doore (Boston: Shambala, 1988), 11.

15. Saunders Redding, *The Lonesome Road,* 81.

16. Martin Luther King, Jr., "The Drum Major Instinct," in *A Testament of Hope: The Essential Writings of Martin Luther King, Jr.,* ed. James Washington (San Francisco: Harper & Row, 1986), 265-67.

17. King, 267.

18. Paule Marshall, *Daughters* (New York: Athenaeum, 1991).

19. Marshall, 13.

20. This criterion of "truth-in-action" is attributed to Sojourner Truth by my colleague Susan Brooks Thistlethwaite in *Sex, Race, and God: Christian Feminism in Black and White* (New York: Crossroad, 1989), 24. Thistlethwaite's extended commentary on this notion is one of the most "useful" and instructive that I have encountered.

21. See the chapter on "Remoralization" in Cheryl J. Sanders, *Empowerment Ethics for a Liberated People* (Minneapolis: Fortress Press, 1995).

22. Sanders, 112-13.

23. See Edward Wimberly's sage pastoral commentary on the use of a narrative approach for pastoral care in the black community in chapters on "A Narrative Approach to Premarriage, Marriage, and Family Counseling," "Personal Resources for Developing a Narrative Approach," and "Indigenous Pastoral Care Facing the Twentieth Century," *African American Pastoral Care,* and his chapter in this book, pp. 128-55.

24. Sojourner Truth, "Ain't I a Woman," in *Feminism: The Essential Historical Writings,* ed. Miriam Schneir (New York: Vintage, 1972), 96-98.

7. MALE VIOLENCE AGAINST WOMEN AND CHILDREN

1. For a more complete discussion of many of the issues in this chapter, see James Poling, *The Abuse of Power: A Theological Problem* (Nashville: Abingdon Press, 1991) and James Poling, *Deliver Us From Evil: Resisting Racial and Gender Oppression* (Minneapolis: Fortress, 1996).

2. Carole Warshaw and Anne L. Ganley, *Improving the Health Care Response to Domestic Violence: A Resource Manual for Health Care Providers* (San Francisco: The Family Violence Prevention Fund, 1995), 16.

3. Mary P. Koss, Lisa A. Goodman, Angela Browne, Louise F. Fitzgerald, Gwendolyn Puryear Keita, Nancy Filipe Russo, *Male Violence Against Women at Home, At Work, and in the Community* (Washington, D.C.: American Psychological Association, 1994), xvi.

4. Warshaw and Ganley, 16-24. See also John Archer, editor, *Male Violence* (London: Routledge, 1994), 2, 7. and R. Emerson Dobash and Russell P. Dobash, *Women, Violence and Social Change* (London: Routledge, 1992).

5. Charlotte Krause, *The Technique of Feminist Psychoanalytic Psychotherapy* (Northvale, N.J.: Jason Aronson, 1993), 213.

6. Koss et al., 44.

7. Archer, 6.

8. Ibid., 4.

9. Ibid., 3.

10. Ibid., 4.

11. Prozan, 212.

12. Koss et al., 70.

13. Warshaw and Ganley, 25.

14. Ibid., 26.

15. Koss et al., 51.

16. Warshaw and Ganley, 26-27. See also Robert L. Hampton, editor, *Violence in the Black Family: Correlates and Consequences* (Lexington, Mass.: Lexington Books, 1987), 21-22. Evelyn C. White, editor, *The Black Women's Health Book: Speaking for Ourselves* (Seattle: Seal Press, 1994). Pearl Cleague, *Mad At Miles: A Blackwoman's Guide to Truth* (Southfield, Mich.: The Cleague Group, 1989). Evelyn C. White, *Chain, Chain, Change: For Black Women Dealing with Physical and Emotional Abuse* (Seattle: Seal Press, 1985).

17. Mary P. Ross, *Journal of Interpersonal Violence* 8, no. 2 (June 1993): 198-222.

18. Dante Cicchetti and Vicki Carlson, editors, *Child Maltreatment: Theory and Research on the Causes and Consequences of Child Abuse and Neglect* (Cambridge: Cambridge University Press, 1989), 48.

19. Cicchetti and Carlson, 98-99.

20. Richard J. Gelles and Murray A. Straus, *Intimate Violence* (New York: Simon and Schuster, 1988), 104.

21. Prozan, 213.

22. Archer, Part IV, "Explanations and Theoretical Perspectives," 233-389. See also A. Bandura, *Aggression: A Social Learning Analysis* (Englewood Cliffs, N.J.: Prentice-Hall, 1973).

23. Gelles and Straus, 17.

24. For further discussion of evangelical Christianity on issues of gender, see Andy Smith, "Born Again, Free From Sin? Sexual Violence in Evangelical Communities," in *Violence Against Women and Children: A Christian Theological Sourcebook*, ed. Carol J. Adams and Marie M. Fortune (New York: Continuum, 1995), 339-50. See also Susan D. Rose, *Keeping Them Out of the Hands of Satan: Evangelical Schooling in America* (New York: Routledge, 1988).

25. For a good summary of this debate within the liberal churches, see Tracy Trothen, "Prophetic or Followers? The United Church of Canada, Gender, Sexuality, and Violence Against Women," in Adams and Fortune, 287-313.

26. For a fuller discussion of the feminist alternative to conservative and liberal theologies, see Carol Adams, "Toward a Feminist Theology of Religion and the State," in Adams and Fortune, 15-35. See also Catherine MacKinnon, *Feminism Unmodified: Discourses on Life and Law* (Cambridge: Harvard University Press, 1987), and Catherine MacKinnon, *Toward a Feminist Theory of State* (Cambridge: Harvard University Press, 1989).

27. For further discussion of these issues, see Marie Fortune and James Poling, "Calling to Accountability: The Church's Response to Abusers," in Adams and Fortune, 451-63.

28. For further perspective on the assessment, referral, and care of men who are violent, I suggest the following: Carol J. Adams, *Woman-Battering* (Minneapolis: Fortress, 1940); Carolyn Holderread Heggen, *Sexual Abuse in Christian Homes and Churches* (Scottdale, Pa.: Herald Press, 1993); Judith Lewis Herman, *Trauma and Recovery* (New York: Basic Books, 1992); Carrie Doehring, *Taking Care: Monitoring Power Dynamics and Relational Boundaries in Pastoral Care and Counseling* (Nashville: Abingdon Press, 1995).

29. See the strong emphasis on issues of safety in Adams, *Woman-Battering*, 69-86, and Judith Herman, 155-74.

30. Marie Fortune, *Violence in the Family* (Cleveland: Pilgrim, 1991), 227. See also Carol Adams's chapter on "Accountability" in *Woman-Battering*, 87-102.

31. "Many people do not know the origin of the expression 'the rule of thumb,' which dates to medieval times when English law declared that a man could not beat his wife with a stick wider than his thumb" (Prozan, 211).

32. For a detailed curriculum on issues of denial and deception, see the materials of the Domestic Abuse Intervention Project, Minnesota Program Development, 206 West Fourth Street, Duluth, MN 55806.

33. Fortune and Poling in Adams and Fortune, 460. Marie Fortune, *Violence in the Family: A Workshop Curriculum for Clergy and Other Helpers* (Cleveland: Pilgrim Press, 1991), 230-31.

34. Don Browning, *The Ethical Context of Pastoral Care* (Philadelphia: Westminster, 1976); James N. Poling "Ethics in Pastoral Care and Counseling," *Handbook of Basic Types of Pastoral Care and Counseling,* ed. Howard Stone and William Clements (Nashville: Abingdon Press, 1991), 56-69.

35. Herman, 135.

36. Robert Langs, *The Bipersonal Field* (New York: Aronson, 1976).

37. For a fuller discussion, see Carol Adams, *Woman-Battering,* 56-58. Gus Kaufman, "The Mysterious Disappearance of Battered Women in Family Therapists' Offices: Male Privilege Colluding with Male Violence," *Journal of Marital and Family Therapy* 18, no. 3 (July 1992): 233-44.

38. "Child Sexual Abuse: A Rich Context for Thinking about God, Community, and Ministry." *Journal of Pastoral Care* XLII, no. 1 (Spring, 1988): 58-61. "Issues in the Psychotherapy of Child Molesters," *Journal of Pastoral Care* XLIII, no. 1 (Spring, 1989): 25-32.

39. For further discussion of religious issues, see Adams and Fortune, *Violence Against Women and Children: A Theological Sourcebook,* ed. Joanne Carlson Brown and Carole R. Bohn *Christianity, Patriarchy and Abuse: A Feminist Critique* (New York: Pilgrim Press, 1989); Emilie M. Townes, editor, *A Troubling in My Soul: Womanist Perspectives on Evil and Suffering* (Maryknoll, N.Y.: Orbis, 1993). Elisabeth Schüssler Fiorenza and Mary Shawn Copeland, *Violence Against Women* (Maryknoll, N.Y.: Orbis, 1994).

40. See discussions in Carolyn Heggen, 121-34 and Marie Fortune, *Sexual Violence: The Unmentionable Sin: An Ethical and Pastoral Perspective* (New York: Pilgrim Press, 1983), 211-15.

41. Marie Fortune, "Forgiveness: The Last Step," in Adams and Fortune, 204.

42. Ibid., 204-5.

43. Ibid., 201-6. See Frederick W. Keene, "Structures of Forgiveness in the New Testament," in Adams and Fortune, 121-34.

44. Annie Imbens and Ineke Jonker, *Christianity and Incest* (Minneapolis: Fortress, 1992), 15.

45. Fortune, "Forgiveness: The Last Step," in Adams and Fortune, 203.

46. The image of mending the relational web is nicely developed by Christine Smith, *Weaving the Sermon: Preaching in a Feminist Perspective* (Louisville: Westminster, 1989).

47. I am indebted for these ideas to Karen Doudt, author of chapter 3 in *The Abuse of Power: A Theological Problem.*

48. Marie Fortune, *Sexual Violence: The Unmentionable Sin: An Ethical and Pastoral Perspective* (New York: Pilgrim Press, 1983).

49. See Poling, *The Abuse of Power,* and "Sexuality: A Crisis for the Church," in *Pastoral Care in a Society in Conflict,* ed. Pamela Couture and Rodney Hunter (Nashville: Abingdon Press, 1995).

50. See James Poling, *Deliver Us from Evil.*

51. Hazel Carby, *Reconstructing Womanhood* (New York: Oxford University Press, 1987), 23.

52. See Kelly Brown Douglas, *The Black Christ* (Maryknoll, N.Y.: Orbis, 1994); Jacquelyn Grant, *White Women's Christ and Black Women's Jesus* (Atlanta: Scholar's Press, 1989); Maryanne Stevens, editor, *Reconstructing the Christ Symbol: Essays in Feminist Christology* (New York: Paulist, 1993).

8. PASTORAL CARE OF GAY MEN

1. In this chapter references to lifestyle are based on the assumption that there are different ways individuals live out sexual orientation. Therefore, it is appropriate to speak of gay lifestyles. There is no one way of living out a gay male orientation. For example, see Alan Bell